PRAISE FOR *The A*

"Funny, provocative, and vast
—GERALD ASHER

"Osborne is supple and erudite on the page [and] where he really tri-
umphs is in getting some true Big Kahunas to speak with the sort of
candor they rarely offer the wine media . . . [*The Accidental Connoisseur* has] head-turning insights and offhandedly learned observations."   —MATTHEW DEBORD, *The Nation*

"Lawrence Osborne's *The Accidental Connoisseur* is shrewd, apt,
acerbic, and often quite crazy. We are carried along equally by the
honed criticism and the fine writing."   —JIM HARRISON

"Great wine writing is extraordinarily rare. Ovid, A. J. Liebling,
Marcus Aurelius—that about does it (depending where you stand on
Rabelais). Enough only for one of those famous thin books like *The
Battlefield Victories of Charles de Gaulle* or *The Joy of Irish Sex* . . .
Osborne is a new voice in the wine world, smart, generous, perceptive,
funny, sensible, free of cant and arrogance and self-interest. It's about
time. *Great Wine Writing* just got a good deal thicker."
—TONY HENDRA, *The New York Times Book Review*

"Witty, sometimes withering, learned and often loopy musings on
the world of fine wine . . . It is [his] tireless, thirsty enthusiasm that
makes Osborne such a good guide . . . The book is, as one imagines
the author to be, an excellent drinking companion."
—ADAM SACHS, *Newsday*

"A rollicking ride through the wine regions of California, Germany,
France and Italy . . . *The Accidental Connoisseur* is wildly enter-
taining and refreshingly candid in its approach. It raises wine writing to a new level, both in its intense questioning of the status quo
and its free-wheeling sense of fun."
—CHRISTOPHER WATERS, *The Standard*
(St. Catharines, Ontario)

Also by Lawrence Osborne

Ania Malina

Paris Dreambook

The Poisoned Embrace

American Normal

The Accidental Connoisseur

The Accidental Connoisseur

An Irreverent Journey Through the Wine World

Lawrence Osborne

North Point Press

A division of Farrar, Straus and Giroux

New York

North Point Press
A division of Farrar, Straus and Giroux
19 Union Square West, New York 10003

The Library of Congress has cataloged the hardcover edition as follows:
Osborne, Lawrence, 1958–
    The accidental connoisseur : an irreverent journey through the wine
world / Lawrence Osborne.—1st ed.
        p.   cm.
    ISBN 0-86547-633-0 (hardcover : alk. paper)
    1. Wine and wine making.   I. Title.

TP548.O655 2004
641.2'2—dc21   2003013577

Paperback ISBN-13: 978-0-86547-712-4
Paperback ISBN-10: 0-86547-712-4

Designed by Jonathan D. Lippincott

www.fsgbooks.com

5   7   9   10   8   6

Contents

The Accidental Connoisseur

Introduction: A Matter of Taste

❧

Man's tongue, on the other hand, by the delicacy of its surfaces and of the various membranes which surround it, proves clearly enough the sublimity of the operations for which it is destined.
—Jean Anthelme Brillat-Savarin

I grew up in Britain in the 1970s, before wine became fashionable. Drinking it has therefore never been second nature to me. Like most Catholic children, my first memory of wine is on the altar, and it was always a game to see how much of the sacrament you could gulp down when it was your turn to taste Our Lord's hemoglobin. It was sour, its dim taste mixed up with sickly sensations: the greasy fingers of our priests, cheap pewter goblets, and chewy, bready, polystyrenelike wafers.

I now think this sacred wine was a cheaper Sainsbury's Beaujolais, an economical option in the 1970s retailing for about three dollars a bottle, because with its taste of sour raspberries came also a ghostly scent of ripe bananas, which I have ever after associated with Our Lord's unfortunate decomposition on the Cross.

To many in Britain, wine was exotic, especially in the puritanical small commuter town of Haywards Heath where I grew up just south of London. In those days the dominant British chain wine store was Unwin's, and the Haywards Heath Unwin's was a place to buy crates of Smirnoff and dark blue bottles of Liebfraumilch, but almost nothing else, aside from those three-dollar bottles of Beaujolais. All drinks came under the Arabic word *alcohol*, essentially reducing them to the level of a chemical sin, and none of them could be bought on Sunday.

The wine store with its windows stuffed with loopy bottles of Mateus rosé in straw flasks was a place of vague iniquity, a place where immigrant Iberian bricklayers perhaps slaked their addictions in secret. In our house, wine was never drunk. Sunday lunch came with sherry and reconstituted fruit drinks, but never a wine. Even the *word* "wine" struck a strained note in many English gatherings.

This alienation left an inevitable mark. For me, as for most English speakers, wine became a consumer interest, but not an instinctual one. I have always been haunted by the same question: Do I really know what I'm drinking and why? For that matter, how do I know that my own tastes are authentic? Wine is a dangerous game. Wherefore a sinister little hunch always creeps into my mind as I am drinking it: *I do not trust my own taste.*

Few things make us more insecure about taste than wine. Some seventy-five thousand different wines made in the world today sustain a $50 billion industry, but there are only a handful of real wine experts to help us sort them out. The language of their expertise may convince us on the page, but only adds to our confusion when we actually taste wine. Their encyclopedias tell us what we're supposed to taste, but never how each of us can appropriate the experience for ourselves. Taste is what defines our personality, but it's as solid as a soap bubble.

What, then, *is* taste? We secretly pride ourselves on our taste. Yet nothing is more terrifying to contemplate. And no taste is more awkward to contemplate than taste in wine. Wine is the ultimate exercise in this mysterious skill, this nuanced zone of pleasure. Nothing requires more taste than wine. For the greatest wines will provoke the most complex physiological reactions of any foodstuff.

Wine is now one of the dominant consumer fetishes of the Western world, with its own hyperventilating journalistic industry. One is bombarded with wine talk on all sides. Aimé Guibert, the noted French wine maker, has said: "For millennia wine was the center of Western civilization. It has always been a mystery. Today it has been transformed into a commodity."

Wine guides, those irrefutable encyclopedias of taste, are ubiquitous. From Robert Parker's *Wine Enthusiast* and *Wine Buyer's Guide*, to Frank Schoonmaker's 1964 *Encyclopedia of Wine*, to the works of the nineteenth-century connoisseur George Saintsbury and the twentieth-century one Gerald Asher, to Alexis Lichine's classic *Encyclopedia of Wines and Spirits* and the *Larousse Encyclopedia of Wine*. So many encyclopedias, so little time!

But there is the rub. Taste is not learned out of books; it is not given from one person to another. Therein lies its profundity. At school, fatuous masters would say of poems they didn't like, using the old Latin saw, *De gustibus non disputandum est*—there's no accounting for taste. And so there isn't. Taste is like a perverse coral: it grows slowly and inexorably into unpredictable shapes, precisely because it's an offshoot of living itself. Acquiring taste, then, is not a result of study; it's a talent for living life.

A distrust of our own taste is what defines us as what could be called accidental drinkers. And the more I have tried to make my little steps toward accidental connoisseurship, the more I have made a fool of myself.

I once happened to be sitting alone in the restaurant called Le Verger des Papes just underneath the ruined castle of Châteauneuf-du-Pape in the southern Rhône, in the heart of a world-famous wine country. The place was deserted except for a thin professorial type at the neighboring table eating a salad. The waiter came and asked me what I wanted to drink. I scanned the list and didn't recognize a single thing, an extraordinary feat since the list contained just about every popularly known Châteauneuf-du-Pape there is. My eye caught the name Beaucastel: the most expensive item on the list. I ordered it.

Halfway through the Beaucastel, which cost twice as much as the whole meal, I thought I should engage in some small wine talk with the waiter. We bantered about Beaucastel. Neither of us knew anything about it, but the waiter offered some opinions which he had probably read in the newspaper.

"Don't you find," he said, "that there's a funny taste of chicken coops in Rhône wines? Especially Beaucastel."

"Chicken coops?" Was he pulling my leg?

"Even the great wines, you know, have a whiff of chicken coops. It's well known."

I offered him a glass of the Beaucastel. I tasted it again, now frantically looking for traces of sublimated chicken coops. The waiter winked at me: was he suggesting I'd been had?

"Taste it?" he said. "A bit poopy, eh?"

"Well," I said, "maybe I *can* taste chicken coops."

I couldn't taste anything of the sort. But we swirled and sipped and agreed that the chicken-coop element gave the wine its complexity.

At this moment, the man next to us suddenly came to life, sat up erect, and said, "*Brettanomyces!*" He drawled this extraordinary word, suspending his fork in midair and sending us a wan smile.

"Excuse me?"

"*Brettanomyces.*" I saw that his nose was quite red and that he was possibly even drunker than I. "*Brett,*" he went on. "It's a yeast. That chicken-coop taste comes from a yeast called *brett. Brett* is everywhere in Rhône wines. Especially Beaucastel."

"It's very good," I said stupidly.

He and the waiter laughed.

"I can see, monsieur," the tipsy professor said, "that you are a man of taste. Men of taste, monsieur, are few and far between." The irony seeped delicately through his sentences and he wiped his mustache with a napkin as I poured him a glass as well. "Well," he said, "here's to chicken coops!"

The word "taste" comes from the Old French *taster*, "to feel," whose medieval English equivalent was *tasten*. The French word itself descended from the Latin *taxare*, "to evaluate, handle."

Ultimately, all these words derive from the Latin *tangere*, "to touch." In the sense of "aesthetic judgment," however, "taste" only arrived in English in 1674, and the term "tasteful" dates only from 1756. Our conventional notion of "taste" is essentially an eighteenth-century invention.

The eighteenth century was obsessed with taste. It became the greatest of all bourgeois fads, and dozens of treatises on taste duly appeared, almost none of them readable. The most famous of them all was Dr. Jean Anthelme Brillat-Savarin's *Physiology of Taste*, published in Paris in 1826. Many regard it as the gastronomic Bible; others think it's as overrated as Casanova's memoirs. But does it tell us anything about taste?

The doctor begins by admitting that it's a tough subject. "It is not easy," he concedes glumly, "to determine precisely what parts make up the organ of taste. It is more complicated than it seems."

Taste, he theorizes, is divided into three classes (eighteenth-century theorists nearly always divide everything into threes):

In physical man it is the apparatus by which he distinguishes various flavours. In moral man it is the sensation which stimulates that organ in the center of his feeling which is influenced by any savorous body. Lastly, in its own material significance, taste is the property possessed by any given substance which can influence the organ and give birth to sensation.

It was clear to Brillat-Savarin that the tongue was the central muscle of taste. But he also observed that people deprived of that subtle organ could still taste, in a manner. In Amsterdam, he had met an errand runner whose tongue had been cut out by Algerian slave dealers. Communicating by means of little written notes, the doctor and the lingual amputee carried on a lively discussion about taste. The errand boy could still taste things, though swallowing was a torture. Even so, the doctor concludes that all tongues are not created equal. And even though, as he says, "the space between something called good and something reputed to be excellent is not very great," some tongues are endowed with more taste buds than others.

Overall, Brillat-Savarin says, the human tongue is the glory of creation. It proves the "supremacy of man." Faced with the phrenologist Dr. Gall's contention that some animals might have better tongues than we have, Brillat-Savarin erupts: "This doctrine is shocking to hear and smacks of heresy."

He points out that the human tongue is capable of amazing feats. Roman gourmands could tell if a fish had been caught between the city bridges or lower down the Tiber; French palates could easily detect the special flavor of the leg a pheasant leans on when it rests. And wine appreciation was a case unto itself. All this, Brillat-Savarin concludes, proves that "man must be proclaimed *the great gourmand of Nature.*" The human tongue, moreover, has no equivalent in the animal world.

But do wine tasters have tongues even more masterly than those of the human species in general? Robert Parker, the all-powerful American critic, has hinted that such is the case with *his* tongue. He has argued in the same vein as Brillat-Savarin that some tongues— such as his own—have more papillae than others.

However, the human tongue doesn't vary from individual to individual; its anatomical structures are constant. No biologist could tell you how the tongue of Robert Parker differs from, say, the fearsome organ of Joey Buttafuoco. Taste, it seems, is biologically universal.

Anatomically, a taste bud consists of about twenty long, slender cells, with a tiny hair projecting from each cell to the surface of the tongue through a pore. Taste cells contain nerve filaments that convey impulses to the taste center in the brain. For all the subtleties which human taste is capable of, these buds themselves can only taste four elementary things: sweetness, sourness, saltiness, and bitterness. Curiously, only the buds most sensitive to salty flavor are scattered evenly over the tongue. Sweet-sensitive taste buds are concentrated on the tip of the tongue, sour flavors are detected at the sides of the tongue, and bitter flavors at the back.

There is now a whole branch of scientific research known as taste hedonics. For a while, this seemed to be a promising avenue of inquiry, especially as scientists are fascinated as to why animals like sweet things. Is my tongue like that of a cow? An anteater? Do I lick fruit like a chimpanzee? Yet in the end, such questions are quixotic. To discover my own tastes in wine, I would have to discard both books and science, and go into the world of wine and drink. For despite its biological universality, taste has no subjective truth that can be measured, no essence—as Susan Sontag once remarked, it "has no system and no proofs." It can only be developed by action, which is to say by pleasure itself.

A Road to Sassoferrato

All of life is a dispute over taste and tasting. —Nietzsche

The mansion of Antonio Terni sits among his family's craggy mulberry trees a few miles inland from the resort of Sirolo. A narrow track sweeps up through rows of Montepulciano vines, past the barns of the *fattoria* and smoothed cypresses to the old silkworm farm shrouded by walls and trees that give the house the atmosphere of a minister's villa or a high-class retreat for recovering alcoholics. Seas of vines prevent any interference from the outside world and make Le Terrazze seem farther from the Adriatic than it actually is. But it was raining and a storm battered Ancona, obscuring the weird sugarloaf mountain which gives Terni's wine its ancient Greek name: Conero.

As I rang the bell a huge German shepherd appeared on the far side of the electronically controlled gates. It watched me fumble with the buzzer and for a moment I wondered if I was really at the right house after all. Terni's famous wine estate is so locally renowned that all one has to do is follow the Le Terrazze signs from the road. Even in Sirolo there are signs for Le Terrazze everywhere, for it is perhaps the most noted domain in the Marches, a jewel in the crown of modern Italian wines whose bottles regularly score well in the Italian comestibles magazine *Gambero Rosso.*

As the yellow eyes of Terni's shepherd glared through the gate, his master's voice came over the speaker: *Entra!* The gates began to open. A loping, gangling figure suddenly appeared in worn corduroys and genteel elbow patches, dragging the beast away to a high-security cage on the other side of the gravel courtyard and then offering an aristocratic hand by way of assurance. He wore a gaudy Bob Dylan T-shirt under his corduroy blazer—Terni is rather known for his wild pop-culture enthusiasms.

"Lost?" he said.

"A little."

He shook a little water from his hair and shivered. "Let me lock up the Baskerville hound here and we'll drink inside." Terni has a subtle, carefully cloaked stutter.

The palatial house has been owned by the Ternis since 1884. They are a Jewish family and had been forced to leave the property in 1938. They had gone to make wine in Argentina during the war and only returned after Mussolini had been safely meat-hooked. Born on the Argentine pampas, Antonio had inherited a vast estate once devoted to silk and walnuts. He had once been a nuclear engineer: one of the multitude of young postwar engineers who had been seduced by Bob Dylan and presumably turned off from a technological career when he returned to the land in 1980. Sugar beets, sunflowers, and grain, however, had not appealed to him either. You can't put your own label on a sugar beet.

Terni's salon is a temple to esoteric pursuits. On the coffee table stood high piles of books containing the word "Zen." *Il Vero Zen,* by Taisen Deshimaru; Philip Toshio Sudo's *Zen guitar; La Zen del Juggling, La Via dello Zen,* and so on. On one pile lay a triangular green plectrum evidently paired with the Stratocaster guitar standing in a corner. A music stand bore the opened score of "This Wheel's on Fire," which the wine master had clearly been practicing. There were also family heirlooms and a delicate scent of the past: the ghostly figure of a painted hussar, family silver, Chinese vases, elaborate armoires, and a huge portrait on one wall of a dour sixteenth-century noblewoman in a ruff. I had come to talk to Terni about his wine—about wine in general—but it now seemed probable that our conversation would take off in different directions, especially since one of his best-known wines was named Visions of Johanna after the Bob Dylan song. Terni, in fact, is obsessed with Bob Dylan. For half the year he trails around the globe following his idol and forgetting completely the rigorous demands of enology. He is not one of those men who thinks that there is nothing in life but doing what you do well. Perhaps it was only natural, then, that he should make a Bob Dylan wine.

"A B-Bob Dylan wine?"

Terni reappeared with his arms full of bottles, though not with a bottle of the rare and expensive Visions of Johanna, which is almost impossible to find, even in Terni's own cellar. Only three hundred cases of it were ever made and in only one year, 1997.

"Does Bob Dylan like wine?" I asked.

"No idea. But what's wrong with a Bob Dylan wine? Oh, I *like* that idea. If *only* I could make a Bob Dylan wine."

Perhaps, I thought, you *have* made a Bob Dylan wine. One of the bottles had a bright psychedelic label bearing fractal curves and the ominous name Chaos. A wine called Chaos? The others, however, were more soberly conventional: Conero Rosso, a Chardonnay called Le Cave, and Sassi Neri, Terni's flagship Montepulciano.

Terni has a gleeful, mad-scientist aura. He hates wine snobs and wine bores; in fact, he seems to hate almost everything about the wine business except wine itself. I explained to him my current preoccupation with questions of taste.

"Taste . . ." He pawed his chin and looked at me. "Tilting at windmills, eh?"

Terni could see that I was eyeing the Chaos label in alarm, so he decided to explain it all to me. It was a little joke. Being a nuclear engineer, he is up on chaos theory, and wine, according to him, has quite a bit of chaos theory in it.

Every natural phenomenon, he began, is unpredictable, variable, and therefore indescribable. Somewhat like the weather. Wine contains two thousand different elements which are combined and recombined every time someone makes a bottle.

"I could name fifteen of them off the top of my head. A good wine maker could name about twenty-five."

"So that's why taste is so complicated?"

"How do I know? But most likely, yes. Taste is chaotic too."

Any of these two thousand elements can interfere with any of the others, leading to wine's potentially chaotic unpredictability. Turquoise, rose, and violet shapes collided and merged on the Chaos label. Did these suggest in some way a mixture of Montepulciano, Syrah, and Merlot designed for the American market? Whatever the fractal shapes mean, Terni finds it amusing that the same adjectives keep popping up in the world's hundreds of wine guides. "Red fruit," for example.

"Red fruit?"

Terni's eyes opened wide as he began to twist the corkscrew into the first bottle of Chaos. For a moment I thought he was going to throttle it into submission.

"Guess what? Grapes are a *red fruit*, so every wine tastes a bit like red fruit. And then what about tobacco?" His gray beard suddenly turned into a manic grin. "Don't you love the term 'tobacco'? Ah, wine writers!"

He held up the neck of the opened bottle and made me sniff it.

"Smell any red fruit or t-tobacco?"

"Both," I said.

"That's because I decided to make a wine they'd like."

Chaos tumbled into my glass. I still wanted to know if this was a Bob Dylan wine. It was plummy, smooth, plushly clean.

Terni makes two distinct styles of wines. One is "international" (the Chaos), and the other is a "terroir wine." It seemed likely that sooner or later a quest for the meaning of taste would have to grapple with these two opposing principles. The wine world never ceased talking about them. Could Terni define them for me?

"Terroir?" he groaned. "It's sort of like the word 'community.' We believe in terroir, but we're getting sick of the word itself."

Enologist Alain Carbonneau of Montpellier's Institut Supérieur de la Vigne et du Vin gives us a definition:

> The word "terroir" has a special power over both wine professionals and the general wine-drinking public. As such, it requires a precise definition. Examination of a French dictionary will yield the following: *Terroir* (from *terre* or land): Land as considered from an agricultural standpoint. Territory used by a village or rural community for growing crops. *Goût de terroir*: the aromas and tastes specific to wines of a given area. The etymology of the word terroir is not all that clear, since its origins in popular language are complex and in all likelihood rather recent . . . Terroir depends on the ecological, geological and pedological characteristics of the site. We can thus define "terroir" as the interaction of climate, grape variety and the soil.

Terroir is a wine's certificate of authenticity, its link to the deepest sense of place.

We drank the Chaos as rain began misting over the windows. I dared to offer a comment on the wine: it wasn't, I said meekly, very Zen. It was rather like a Chevrolet sedan. It was smooth as long as you were driving in a straight line—but it was a nice ride. Perhaps it was like fake Zen.

All of this provoked an exasperated but sweet expression.

"Oh, wine isn't a mystical experience as far as I'm concerned."

His eyes narrowed. "But in a way, you're right about Chaos here. It's a smooth ride, a nice drink."

"Not very chaotic."

He laughed. "No, not very chaotic."

Was it a charming slice of the not very chaotic International Style?

"I'm not sure I would say that!"

I asked him what the International Style *was*.

"I suppose," he said, "it's the opposite of terroir. It's like airport architecture: a sort of nowhereness. But airports can be pleasurable."

"Is that a bad thing?"

"That depends. Maybe we should have airports that look like country cottages. But with wine, it's tricky. Is a wine good if it doesn't express terroir? Almost everyone today would say no. But at the same time not that many people are making true terroir wines. It's a tiny minority. So why is that?"

"So," I persisted, "a man of taste must learn how to detect terroir in any given wine."

"Some would say so. They'd say taste *is* terroir."

"What would you say?"

"I'd say terroir is a complicated notion."

The day before, I had trawled through an old bookstore in Ancona and asked the owner if he had any books on wine. He came out with a tiny thing called *Sopra il detto del Galileo* by one Count Lorenzo Magalotti. Count Magalotti (1637–1712) was a Florentine aristocrat and aesthete who became intrigued by Galileo's assertion that "wine is a compound of light and humor." In trying to explain this cryptic observation, Magalotti came up with some pretty cryptic observations of his own. One of them was that what sparkled in wine was "powdered light."

"Light and humor?" Terni smiled. A delicious conceit. "But of course," he added, "what Galileo means by *umore* is moisture. That is, the characteristic moisture of a given land."

"Terroir?"

And of course, I thought, there was the medieval notion of humor as a disposition of mind, a temperament. What a shame that that useful sense has disappeared from our language. One could talk of the *humor* of a wine.

Magalotti also theorized that light poured into grapes and shattered inside them to form a kind of powder. These powders were released when fermentation occurred, eventually making themselves felt "upon the tongue and palate by the charming prickle of their many corners and twists."

It was a beautiful explanation. And probably not much more mystical than many explanations of terroir.

"I'd say," Terni observed, "that what we're drinking here is not a terroir wine. But it's still good. It's just doing something else."

The wine seemed to me tasty, but without a definable character. I drank half the glass and looked up at a painting on the facing wall, a kind of composite portrait of famous figures, among whom I instantly recognized Henry VIII, Che Guevara, and Errol Flynn, not to mention Merlin. I was suddenly curious to try his other wine, the wine with the terroir. What would its *humor* taste like?

Meanwhile, Terni took another stab at the vexing issue of internationalism.

"It's easy to sneer at it. But look at music. Do we all sit around listening to Italian folk music in order to be authentic? God no. We listen to Bob Dylan. *I* globetrot in order to follow Dylan around. Dylan is both American and universal at the same time."

He served two wines called Sassi Neri and the Conero Rosso—the terroir wines. Immediately, I sensed that they exposed the other half of his character, the mysterious half.

The Terni family has deep roots in the Conero, deeper perhaps than a mere century of interrupted habitation would suggest. Antonio's father was something of an amateur archaeologist and a fervent local archivist. He wrote four exquisite monographs on the ancient *pievi* or primitive churches that dot the strange mountain and the coves in the area. He also wrote about Greek artifacts found on the Ancona coast, such as hauls of drinking cups. Thus, while one of Terni *fils*'s keen eyes is on the fluctuations of the International Style, another is on the looming cliffs just beyond the mists, the unique earth which gives Conero Rosso its gritty individual warp, its *umore*.

"I don't mean to sound cynical," he said as he tipped the Conero sideways for a moment and eyed the tint. "But I do hate all this pseudo-intellectual mental masturbation about wine. I make two wines: one for Americans and one for myself. They're both fine."

Gambero Rosso's 2002 *Vini d'Italia*, which rates all Italian wines by assigning them a number of symbolic glasses from zero to three, gives the '97 Chaos a score of three glasses, its rare top accolade. "*Il Chaos*," it notes, "*è di colore cupo e impenetrabile*," before listing its flavors of tar, cocoa, vanilla, and the inevitable red fruit, in this case blackberry.

The Conero Rosso gets only one glass in *Gambero Rosso*, but it had an earthy scent, a keen feel on the tongue. It tasted of stones. Can wine taste of stones? I asked him.

"Well, that's funny. Because my most terroir wine is called Black Stones, Sassi Neri. Our land is full of stones."

Sassi Neri is named after the huge pebbles which fall into the sea near Sirolo. At first these are as white and glossy as dinosaur eggs; with time, however, mussels swarm over them and they become black, so much so that the beach is known as Spiaggia di Sassi Neri.

As he opened it, the wine had a whiff of salt. The sea invades everything around Conero, laying its iodine on the Montepulciano grapes of the region. Terni's father, too, was obsessed with Monte Conero, believing that places have spirits and that Conero had a spirit that suffused its wines. A fanciful notion, but then again, I had supposedly just tasted stones in some grape juice, had I not?

So, I said, getting back to our previous ruminations on terroir, was there really a war between the International Style and terroir?

"Isn't that the whole dilemma of the modern world right now?"

"Some would say it's all down to the influence of America. America as the enemy of terroir."

Terni frowned. "I will only say that Americans like *too much* in the glass. There's always *too much* going on. Other than that, if we're living on Planet America, that's not necessarily the fault of Americans."

Terni then cracked open a bottle of a wine which he still makes in Argentina, a Malbec called Vina Hormigas from Altos Los Hormigas. Surprisingly, it seemed to represent yet another side of Terni himself—but which side? For just as there was a technological and a money-lusting side to him, there was also a nuclear engineer side, a Zen side, a Bob Dylan side, and now a South American nostalgia side. "Ah, Argentina!" was all he said, gazing through the window. But as we drank it, I had an inexplicable intuition that it was not very Argentine. It tasted like the Chaos—pleasant but nondescript.

What I was beginning to think, in my inebriated state, was that wine was a bit Jekyll and Hyde. For some reason I thought that Terni would understand this. Wine was profound, contemplative; and then again it could just as easily be commercial, crass, and soulless. What I really wanted to ask him was whether he thought wine was becoming more and more debased the more it became a commodity defined by mass tastes. But instead, leaping out of this stream of murky thought like a desperate trout, I asked him if he knew a good hotel in Sirolo.

"There is no better hotel in Sirolo," he cried immediately, "than the Locanda Rossa!"

After leaving Terni, I drove down the long aristocratic road to the Numana highway, through the sluggish rain, past burned-out silk factories to the riffy-raffy seaside strip of Numana. I was so tipsy that I missed the turnoff for Sirolo and ended up in the strange no-man's-land of Lido di Riscoli. The sea was sullen, the nautical-theme restaurants completely deserted. It was difficult not to think of Fellini's raffish Rimini a few miles up the coast, the winter waste-land depicted in *Amarcord*.

Despite the nearby presence of renowned estates like Le Terrazze and Conte Leopardi, wine tourism has not yet beaten a path to Sirolo's becalmed little bay filled with mussel-black rocks and rotting boats. In fact, Conero is a little-known oddity even to wine connoisseurs. But the village is like so many in Italy: consciously reorganized to accommodate busloads of tourists.

The Locanda Rossa, in any case, is built into the old town walls, its bright rooms breathing the sea. The owners, Giorgio and Isabella Tridenti, are friends of Terni. Looking like a sharp junior executive on a day off, Giorgio is something of a wine enthusiast. During the day he flits around the restored *locanda* (inn) in colorful silk shirts, a voluble fount of Sirolo lore; but at night he is strangely reincarnated as The Owner, a bit like a younger, handsomer Basil Fawlty replete with bow tie, tuxedo, and cuff links, presiding over awkward Gourmet Nights in his little dining room.

From Giorgio I first heard the phrase "the Conero Riviera."

"Is every pretty coast," I asked, "a Riviera now?"

"It's always been the Conero Riviera. But I know what you mean. What will you drink?"

He suggested the Leopardi Conero Rosso. Count Leopardi was a strange man, Giorgio explained, but his wines were interesting.

"The Conero wines are booming. Or they will be."

It's easy to imagine that in a hundred years' time the entire globe will be circled by a kind of Riviera belt defined by Mediterranean climates, with the same restaurants serving Bonsai cuisine and probably a global wine brand called Seductive Bouquets. Strangely, the Conero Rosso of Leopardi seemed to have the same taste as Terni's. For piercing through the incredibly dainty constructions of Giorgio's food came that same laconic taste, which to my surprise I immediately found to be characteristically *stony*.

I explained to Giorgio that drinking Leopardi's wine alone was, at this very moment, the best way of getting to know both Count Leopardi and his stony wine. For there is a mood for drinking wine alone: a tender, solipsistically pleasurable mood which has nothing at all to do with misery. I told him that the ancient Greeks thought of drinking parties as voyages in a little ship, and the drinkers as sailors lost on a lonely sea.

"That's a drinking *party*," Giorgio observed solemnly. "And Italians don't even eat alone, let alone drink alone. For us it's miserable to drink alone." *Like a confession of failure*, he wanted to add.

I grew deliriously content. I began to tap my feet under the table and grin fiendishly at all the old ladies eating their snapper raviolis. Is there anything better than drinking? When the happiness of drinking overwhelms you, you cannot resist it. It descends upon you like a sudden fog, leaving you pathless and alone, just like the Greek drinkers who thought of their dining room as a storm-tossed ship alone on a sea.

The next day I drove up to Mount Conero. On this dreary coastal plain south of Ancona there are no other mountains at all, not even any hills, so Conero seems out of place. Thick woods cover it completely.

Near the top there is a military zone hidden in the scrub and a halfhearted tourist parking lot bordered by pizza joints. At the summit stands the early medieval church to which Terni's father had devoted so many years of his life. The Romanesque chapel stands apart, forbiddingly gray as befits a relic of the Middle Ages. Its carved doorways and arches melt back into the walls; in them can be seen the disintegrating figures of twelfth-century birds plucking grapes from vines. The nave is cold and stark, its columns flowing with worn carvings of flowers and serpents. According to Terni *père* there was once a stone at the edge of the sanctuary which read *Qui non possono passare le donne sotto pena di scommunica* (women may not pass through here under pain of excommunication). He also tells us that in the year 1038 Count Cortesi di Sirolo, descendant of a German mercenary of Belisarius, granted the land to the Benedictines, most of it "woods and vines." Other lands were given later by Gouhobaldo Leopardi, proving that both wine and the Leopardis have been here for a thousand years.

But even this remote sanctuary cannot be left unmolested by modern enterprise. Incongruously, a section of the ecclesiastical courtyards and outbuildings has been turned into a hotel. The gloomy mall-like restaurant takes advantage of the hillside to gaze out over the sea. From inside came a refrain of Snoop Dog playing on the bar's sound system.

Later that night I walked along the beach to the lonely church of Portonovo and at a restaurant nearby I drank a cold green Verdicchio. Wine is 99 percent psychological, a creation of where you are and with whom. I sat in the shadow of the odd mountain and drank my Verdicchio alone, feeling the first snail-like tendrils of my own taste asserting themselves through an unusual chain of associations: the Greeks, Visions of Johanna, the Zen of juggling, and the incomprehensible postulates of chaos theory.

The following day I drove to nearby Sassoferrato. Sassoferrato is a walled medieval town like a thousand others, sitting on a hill like a thousand others. I walked into a bar and ordered an Azzurro. I immediately began thinking that Sassoferrato was something of a desperate place, a place you would want to get out of if you were young. I was there because Sassoferrato, an old sulfur-mining town, is where the Mondavi family came from.

The Mondavis are the most powerful wine-making dynasty in California. Indeed, their patriarch, Robert Mondavi, can be said to have single-handedly invented the American wine industry back in the 1970s. And Robert Mondavi's parents had been born in Sassoferrato. In fact, they had been married there.

So I went out into the street and looked around. I had never drunk any of Mondavi's wines, but I had read about Sassoferrato in his recent autobiography, *Harvests of Joy*. The grand old man of American wine had written quite a bit about the hardships of Sassoferrato in his book. And he had written quite a bit about the Marches, too.

The Marches, Mondavi writes in *Harvests of Joy*, are the West Virginia of Italy. He describes going back to his mother's house on the outskirts of Sassoferrato (as if the town could even have outskirts). It strikes an odd chord in the old and extraordinarily wealthy American patriarch, returning to his Italian roots. The older Mondavis ate organically off the land, making their own olive oil and wine. This is the rural idyll, fiercely cherished by Italians. The reality was an oppressively feudal system known as the *mez-zadria*, under which peasants rented land from a landowner and paid him a percentage of their produce. Poverty and the *mezzadria* forced the Mondavis to emigrate to America in 1906.

Where many from Sassoferrato wandered off to the colonies of Libya or Ethiopia, Robert's father made his way to the iron ore mines of a small town in Minnesota called Virginia. Wandering around the ruined maternal home, Mondavi sees a connection to Napa Valley, where the young Mondavi family moved in the 1920s. Both places are marked by terraced hills, an ordered nature. "In terms of topography and landscapes," Mondavi writes, "you can see the similarity." Emotionally, one place is a mirror of the other.

In reality, the Marches aren't anything like Napa Valley or California. And certainly nothing could be farther from Napa than Sassoferrato itself. For where Napa is a place of luxury malls and never-closing restaurants, Sassoferrato seemed quite dead in the still of the afternoon. Yet Sassoferrato is still a kind of driving idea behind Robert Mondavi because it's where the Mondavi wine odyssey began. The driving idea of California, after all, was to imitate the

Old World and then surpass it. Behind all of Mondavi's driving ambition lies the misery of Sassoferrato.

One thing that California does not have, for example, is the
agriturismo accommodation. *Agriturismo* rooms are rented out in
olive farms or wine estates to give travelers escaping from the cities
a rural retreat. They were invented in the 1960s as Italians first began to fear that their countryside traditions were disappearing. It
became chic to spend a week in a leaking farm with the kids. None
of this sounded especially chic to me, but it did promise the authentic Italian countryside. So I followed the recommendation of
friends and searched out the Serafina Agriturismo farm near Castelraimondo, run by a man called Cosimo and his wife, Bea. As I drew
up to a set of rambling concrete buildings lost in a valley, I thought
at once of Mondavi's parents in their grim house in Sassoferrato
circa 1905. So this was why Italians had fled to California. Cosimo
was not just a farmer; he was an activist, a radical, a slow-food
devotee, and possibly the stingiest man I have ever met. Radio Radicale was blaring on the family radio as I came into the huge stone
kitchen: the ominous words *Palistinesi insieme con noi!* A lean little man in slightly affected blue overalls, Cosimo looked me over
for signs of Americanism. I did not pass the test. His first words
were: "You're not a friend of Robert Mondavi, are you?"

It was clear that as far as Cosimo was concerned, Robert Mondavi hadn't made good at all. Far from it. He'd gone to California,
that hellish incarnation of American capitalism.

The Serafina was falling to pieces around our ears. In my room
the rain came through the ceiling. A greenish rot covered most of
the walls. Bea, as thin and bedraggled as her husband, seemed not
to care. What obsessed them was the electricity bill, and after dinner they immediately turned off all the lights and huddled together
in a tiny bedroom with a single bulb. And it rained all night long.
By every light switch was a sticker which read *Please turn me off.*

But dinner was a surprisingly embracing affair. Since I was the
only guest, Cosimo called over his friends on the telephone.

"He's writing a book about Robert Mondavi. Trust me, he's a spy for the Americans . . ."

So he had a sense of humor after all. Water dripped from the ceiling in the kitchen too, but we crouched by the enormous fire and roasted onions on spits.

Cosimo: "As you see, we Italians still have quality of life. That's what you don't have, if you'll excuse me for saying so."

I asked him if in his fifty years he'd ever been outside of Italy.

"Sure. I went to Marseilles once when I was seventeen."

"Why do you run an *agriturismo*?"

Cosimo softened. The shambling, miserable kitchen tinkled with water drops. And yet a fantastical meal was taking shape on the table, gnocchi with mussels and prawns, artichoke, and grilled eggplant bruschette.

"It's philosophical. Back to the land."

Cosimo blinked behind his Trotsky wire frames and handed me the olives. Radio Radicale blared on. There was going to be a general strike—a *Sciopero Generale*—at the end of April. The Left was on the move, marching as always. But what did it have to do with organic olives?

"Everything," Cosimo stated flatly. He looked nervously at his wife slaving away at the stove. "Whatever is organic is leftist!"

It's a mantra which has probably spread all over the Western world, but nowhere more so than in Italy. I had already noted large roadside billboards that proclaimed *Agricultura Biologica* as a kind of war cry. Cosimo's activism, of course, extended to making his own wine. Out it came. "Completely organic, *hombre*."

My heart always trembles when those ominous unlabeled bottles come out. As we sat down to the gnocchi, Cosimo's wine fell into our glasses and I smelled at once an odor of fungus, straw, and simmering insanity. It tasted even worse.

"So? What do you think of our humble production? No fertilizers, remember."

I congratulated him. I've found that nothing seduces a man's ego more than complimenting his wine, especially when deep in his heart he knows that it's undrinkable. Cosimo looked fiercely at his wife, as if vindicated.

"Well, of course," he began, "it's nothing special, nothing fancy. Not like what you get in *New York*. But if I say so myself—"

Bea: "It's complete shit, your wine."

"—if I say so myself, it has something, something *local*. It's a humble Montepulciano like the real peasants used to make, but a real one all the same."

Bea: "Complete shit, in other words." She let out a sharp, shrill laugh. "Except it doesn't taste anything like peasant wine."

"My wife, signor, is a little drunk. It's the excitement of the *Sciopero Generale*, you know!"

What followed was one of the best meals I've ever had—prawns and mussels and baby carrots tasting of ginger and honey. But the wine, already catastrophic, got worse with every bottle proudly carried up from the cellar. The rain intensified and began to seep through the ceiling in alarming quantities. Mice ran about under the table, slithering against my feet and nibbling at fallen prawns. I began to wonder if, once upon a time, the Italy that the Mondavis left was really like this, or whether it was all a restless vision invented by a rootless middle class. Where did Cosimo and Bea come from? I couldn't see any books in the house, nor any signs of average urban affluence. Did they even come from the Marches in the first place? During the night as I lay alone in the upstairs room with buckets catching the rain, I held the acrid taste of Cosimo's inept Montepulciano wine in my mouth. Did this rancid Château Serafina express something about this place all the same? Because a wine must always express something about a place, and often about a people as well.

Driving back to Sassoferrato with a splitting headache the next morning, I tried to imagine what people like Cosimo hated so much about America, and more specifically what they hated about people like Robert Mondavi. Wherever I went there seemed to be an ambivalent tension about Mondavi. They talked about him as if he were a Mafia don. And yet, I thought to myself, he's just a wine maker, isn't he? And if they hated *il capitalismo americano* so much, why were they so busily making wines that Americans would like? A profound schizophrenia hung in the air.

Perhaps the reason for this is that today's global wine business is driven by California, which is to say precisely by people like Robert Mondavi. The tastes, styles, fads, and prejudices of California determine a great portion of what the world both produces and drinks, and every wine maker in the world battles with the fact that wine today is the story of the Americanization of Europe and the Europeanization of America. Wine, which is usually written about as a straightforward consumer product, is in reality a strange and sometimes unflattering mirror of ourselves. While wine ties us to places and their spirits, we have managed to turn it into a capitalist fetish which is sometimes traded at Sotheby's for small fortunes larger than the annual salaries of some African dictators.

Before I left the Serafina, Cosimo gave me a wooden box with a bottle of his dessert wine in it, a sweet red which he made secretively in his basement on his days off. It looked like the coffin of a mummified baby. To my surprise, he had no hangover whatsoever and was busy plucking baby carrots from a patch of dark gray earth dominated by a ragged teddy bear serving as a scarecrow. He was still a little suspicious. After I had paid for the room he asked me if I would be going to California.

"Most probably."

"If you see *that bastard*, tell him we still love our carrots!"

He held up an earthy bunch of them threateningly. I said I was sure that Mondavi loved organic carrots as much as he did.

"No, no, you tell him. We won't roll over and die!"

As it happened, I soon would be able to tell him: Robert Mondavi was about to invite me to lunch.

"Come back after the general strike!" Cosimo called after me.

In a field somewhere near Spoleto, within sight of that town's strangely Herculean aqueduct, I opened the dessert red with a piece of Gorgonzola and a peach and drank it for a while, lying among wet poppies. Later, walking back to the road, I laid the bottle in a garbage can and drove quite soberly into Spoleto. I found to my dismay that there was indeed a faint but sharply unpleasant taste of mushrooms under my tongue, and that I had no way of interpreting it.

Lunch with Robert Mondavi

Wine is not a source of ecstasy.   —Brillat-Savarin

The Robert Mondavi Winery was designed back in the sixties by the Los Angeles architect Cliff May in the Spanish Mission style once chicly popular in places like La Jolla's Mount Soledad. Its walls are adobe laced with lavish timber beams and huge hand-beaten Mexican lamps. Magnificent windows let in the shrill California light and through the sweeping arches of May's building I glimpsed an imposing sculpture of a polar bear standing outside among the cherry trees.

Robert Mondavi came in as if propelled on wheels, soundless but swift. Cocooned in a dapper multicolored knit waistcoat, he cuts an elfin but worldly figure in his corporate HQ office on Route 29. I thought him rather elegant in his suede-lined sports jacket and frosted pink shirt. Once upon a time, by his own admission, he had been something of an unpleasantly ruthless character. But time and heart disease had made him wiser and he had that spry aura of fantasy which all hale old men have. A glint in the eye, a sparkling waistcoat, the leprechaun effect: I immediately thought of Henry Miller in his old age, the American Methuselah who once wrote, "I have a motter—always merry!"

Robert was geniality itself, but also a man of tempered words. His eyes were those of a Roman emperor. Tiberius?

"Did you take the wine train?" he said at once, fixing me with that smile. "I remember when the Wine Train was a real train. It used to bring up the steel fermentation tanks."

"Difficult to believe," I said.

"Isn't it? We've come a long way, you know." And he sat back, smiling even more intensely, if even more strangely. "A *very* long way."

"That's easy to believe."

"Well," said Bob, as we must call him now, "we're going to drink some interesting stuff at lunch. I want you to say exactly what you think."

We walked over to the Mondavi restaurant in the middle of what seemed like a rainbow. It was unusual for Napa, all this rain, Bob said defensively. He peered up at the clouds as if he had personal control over them. As we strolled, he told me how much he loved the Cliff May buildings—it had been an inspiration back in 1966 to hire him. Mondavi had been working with his brother, Peter, at Krug just up the road, but family relations were tense and he was frustrated making what he regarded as run-of-the-mill wines. He cut free and founded his eponymous winery. It was the beginning of the Napa revolution, and May's grandiose architectural statement sent shock waves through the wine world.

The Mondavi operation was not only the first new winery to be founded in Napa since Prohibition, it was also by far the most flamboyant. The actual building was a deliberate expression of Mondavi's own booming personality. Its spare labyrinthine corridors and terra-cotta amphorae give it the feel of a Minoan king's lair.

"All right, you can say ego. I have an ego," the charming emperor said. "I wanted to found a dynasty. I had to say *I have arrived.*"

The company restaurant was a part of the original May vision, a splendid refectory redolent of the dining hall of a wealthy Mexican landowner. The interior is rich with deep wood, massive beams, and carved chairs. Olive trees glistened through the arched windows and a large tour group of Japanese girls came wafting past the windows snapping away with a hundred Instamatics. Mrs. Mondavi now joined us, a tiny sharp-tongued woman with brilliant platinum hair belying her years. If Bob made me think of Henry Miller—forceful, lusty—Bob's second wife, Margrit, made me think of Leni Riefenstahl. Her accent seemed more German than French and she had a sort of Riefenstahl energy about her, at once coquettish and dominant. The two clashed like a pair of toy triremes. While Margrit related something of her life to me, Bob fell silent. It was a wandering tale: married to an American army officer based in Okinawa, she'd passed through Napa one summer in the early sixties and decided to stay, though without the officer. She got a job as a two-dollar-an-hour tour guide at Krug, where she first glimpsed Mondavi from afar. Most of her colleagues were retired firemen, so the glamorous Margrit caught Bob's eye.

"Didn't I?" she said.

"You could say that."

The meal began. Aside from a wine class being conducted at a nearby table, we were alone. I glanced over. A long line of somber faces sniffed at huge glasses of white wine.

"Do you feel this is grassy?" the instructor was saying.

"I do think it's grassy," a weak voice piped up from the back.

"How grassy is it?"

"Pretty grassy," a thin woman in glasses whispered doubtfully. "I think there's some grassiness in it."

The instructor nodded, satisfied. "It's definitely grassy. I don't think we can say it *isn't* grassy."

I wondered if they were tasting one of Mondavi's wines. We ourselves began with a pricey 1999 Reserve Chardonnay and a 1997 Latour Corton-Charlemagne with which Bob had decided to pair it. It was an impish competition to see if Gallic presumption could be humbled, and whether, for that matter, their guest could make some kind of intelligible comment about his tastes. I, the guest, was in a funk. It was bad enough getting things wrong with friends, but in front of the world's most powerful wine baron my expressions of nontaste were bound to be embarrassing in the extreme. The bottles stood side by side like duelists, avatars of Franco-American rivalry and one-upmanship. I would have to choose one over the other, time after time.

At once, I had the feeling that Bob was setting up a playful re-enactment of a famous tasting which he describes with relish in his autobiography. On May 24, 1976, a group of French critics gathered on the patio of the Intercontinental Hotel in Paris to judge a panel of American and French wines. The panel had been assembled by the Parisian wine merchant Stephen Spurrier as a kind of mischievous fantasy. The British-born Spurrier had traveled to California himself to pick out the best American entries, which included Chardonnays such as the 1973 Château Montelena and other Chardonnays from Chalone Vineyards and Spring Mountain, as well as Cabernets such as Winiarski's 1973 Stag's Leap and similar offerings from Ridge, Clos du Val, and Heitz.

The Chardonnays were, logically enough, matched against white Burgundies, while the Cabernets dueled with top Bordeaux. The French side fielded its best: bottles of Meursault-Charmes from Domaine Roulot, a Puligny-Montrachet from Leflaive, a 1970 Mouton-Rothschild and an Haut-Brion from the same year, a 1971 Leoville Las Cases from Saint-Julien, and so on. The judges were all French and included some illustrious wine names: Aubert de Villaine, owner of Domaine Romanée-Conti; Christian Vanneque, sommelier at the Tour d'Argent; Jean-Claude Vrinat, owner of the Taillevent restaurant; and Odette Kahn, editor of *La Revue du Vin Français*. The French, of course, expected a walkover. Just like the Wehrmacht at Stalingrad.

What actually happened at possibly the most famous tasting of the twentieth century was that among the Chardonnays three of the top four were from Napa. And among the reds, the top position went to the 1973 Stag's Leap (although the next three were all French). Worse, the tasters made fools of themselves. As a journalist for *Time* gleefully recorded, one of them cried, "Ah, back to France!" as he sipped a 1972 Napa Valley Chardonnay. Another declared that a Batard-Montrachet was "definitely California."

The repercussions of this upset were enormous. For one thing, the prices of top California wines quadrupled overnight. As Mondavi relates it in his autobiography, before the Spurrier tasting a bottle of Stag's Leap Cabernet Reserve had sold for about six dollars. He even recalls the outrage in Napa Valley when Heitz hiked the price for one of its bottles to an unprecedented nine dollars. After the tasting, however, Napa suddenly decided that it had the right to charge as much for its wines as the great estates of Bordeaux and Burgundy. After all, they'd beaten them in the shoot-out at the Intercontinental Corral, hadn't they? "It was a blow to Gallic pride and presumption," Mondavi writes. "So why not start charging more?"

Our own version of the Spurrier tasting now got under way. We all swirled, nose-dipped, and gurgled. Then Bob smiled fiendishly and sat back, looking at me with that Tiberius gaze.

"So. Mondavi or Corton-Charlemagne?"

With a slight panic, I bought some time by sticking my nose back into the glass.

"Well," I burbled, "they both have their qualities . . ."

"I think," said Bob, "that the Corton-Charlemagne is terribly good. But ours is just, uh, a *little more pleasing*. Don't you think?"

Struck dumb, I think I emitted a kind of deliberately ambiguous groan. I was saved, surprisingly enough, by Margrit herself.

"No, no, Bob," she started up defiantly. "The Corton is more complex. It's just more complex. Smell it. It's more com*plex*."

Bob shrugged mildly, as if to himself. "Complex, yes. But is it more pleasing? I think ours is more pleasing in the end."

The Corton was more complex and therefore more pleasing, but the Reserve was a nice drink. I said it was a nice drink.

"Nice?" Bob said.

The food was bright Californian fare with the expected Italian twist, a far cry, I supposed, from the restaurant food of thirty years ago when Mondavi first set up shop. He was quick to point out that his peasant Italian roots, his family's roots in Sassoferrato, had brought a gastronomic revolution to northern California. So in a way, I said, he had Europeanized California?

"That's exactly what I did. In 1960 the only food you could get in Napa was hamburgers. I knew that if Americans didn't eat seriously they wouldn't drink seriously either." The Mondavi winery was therefore conceived from the first as a kind of educational temple of cuisine which would show Americans the road to gastronomic salvation. Built close to the road, it was also a tourist facility from day one.

We moved on to reds. A 1999 Carneros Pinot Noir from the Byron vineyard paired with a top burgundy, an Échézeaux from the same year made by Jean Gros. Échézeaux is a wine that comes from parcels of land not far from the famed Romanée-Conti vineyards in the Côte d'Or, and it can be one of the great red wines of the Côte (though not, some would say, in the hands of a producer like Jean Gros), comparable to its pricier and more glamorous neighbor.

Bob took some time to savor both, as if he was evaluating both of them for the first time. Over the rim of his glass he shot a look at me.

"So," he said. "You have a developed sense of taste. I'm curious to know what you think."

The nose of all Californian Pinot Noirs I have drunk so far always reminds me of a honey-flavored candy we used to eat in England in the seventies called Toffee Crunch. It's an indescribable scent, a kind of chemically musty honey. But such a comment was out of the question, so I tried with great effort to remember some of the innumerable phrases I had come across in my wine encyclopedias. Needless to say, I drew a blank. Pinot Noir, I tried to recollect. *Feminine.*

"I think," Bob pondered, "that without question the Échézeaux is a very fine wine. A marvelous Burgundy. A good example of what Pinot Noir is all about. Oh, no doubt about it." He paused and his head tilted to one side, his eyes shifting as he rolled over in his mind a definite conclusion. "But, hmm . . . , I have to say that I find that our Pinot Noir is . . . sort of . . . well, a bit more fruity. Don't you think? There's a bit more fruit. It's just that bit more fruity, don't you think? Just a bit *more pleasing.*"

"No, no," Margrit chirped without the slightest hesitation. "You're quite wrong, Bob. The Échézeaux is more complex. Don't you zink it's more complex?"

I said that the two wines were "two sides of the same coin."

"Eh?" croaked Bob. "How's that?"

I wasn't about to expound on Pinot Noir, so I said simply that the two wines seemed to express two sides of the same grape. Fruity *and* complex.

"But vich is more complex?" Margrit cried.

I began to perspire. "The Échézeaux . . . I think."

Bob laughed. Were they playing Good Cop, Bad Cop?

"It's all a matter of opinion," he said gaily. "The Échézeaux might have an extra dimension somewhere. But I think ours is not only more fruity, but somehow purer, more—" He searched for the right word. "Bright. It's a brighter wine."

"Oh, bright," Margrit sighed.

"Yes," I said, "it's definitely got more brightness."

But what did he mean? I went back to the glass.

The brightness of Mondavi wine, Bob explained, came from technology. Especially from a computerized monitoring of a wine as it went through different phases of fermentation and aging.

This was quite a revelation. But then again—the dark thought occurred to me—didn't the greater complexity of the Échézeaux preclude its being "bright"? Perhaps you couldn't be both.

"Well, you can," he replied. "But it takes time. We're working on it."

This was undoubtedly also true. *Brightness*. There, I suspected, was a key term. Bob had used it with such conviction. And wasn't brightness, in fact, the overriding quality of this actual place?

Sitting in this immense restaurant with the Japanese tourists floating past under the cherry trees, I had a vivid sense of power and calculating industry coming together in an effect of burnished brightness. The hedonism and relaxation were surface distractions beneath which a steely ambition constantly agitated. Had it been otherwise, Bob would not have been so proud of his considerable achievements. But this did not prevent him from touting the civilizational angle of wine: the Greek symposium, the tradition of generations, the value of the land, the arts. And now our conversation suddenly adopted a different vector.

The arts, in fact, were where Margrit came in, for it was she who had brought in the sculptures, the paintings, the terra-cotta amphorae.

"Americans are not Puritans," Bob suddenly said, as if it now needed to be explained. "But we still have the Puritan framework. It's the Puritan framework which we're trying to break down. It's a vision which my family, for one, never understood. Wine for them was just business."

He then leaned over and gave me an even more flinty Roman look. "Have you read Petronius?"

I nodded.

"You know what he wrote two thousand years ago?"

I wasn't sure—

" 'Wine is Life.' "

Bob tapped his glass with a forefinger nail and it rang like a miniature glass bell.

From early on, the Mondavis deliberately set out to establish a wine dynasty and to portray themselves as American royalty. Robert Mondavi's own life has mirrored the American century perfectly. His father had opened a saloon in Virginia, Minnesota. But even this modest living was soon threatened by the 1919 Volstead Act, which inaugurated Prohibition. Prohibition was incomprehensible to Italian immigrants, but in fact the new law allowed families to make two hundred gallons of wine for their own consumption—a sop to these same immigrants. Cesare Mondavi, the boy from Sassoferrato, had meanwhile become secretary of the Virginia Italian Club. And it was as its official secretary that the club sent him out to California in 1919 to prospect for the grapes with which the Minnesota Italians intended to make their two hundred permissible gallons. Once arrived in California, however, Mondavi fell in love with the land which must have so reminded him of the Marches. In 1921 he closed the Virginia saloon and moved his wife and four children to Lodi, California, where he decided to become a grape merchant.

Just south of Sacramento, Lodi was then the grape capital of the United States. The Mondavi grape-exporting business quickly flourished. In 1946 they established a family corporation, with the parents owning 40 percent of the stock and the rest divided among the children. Bob became a star football player at Lodi Union High, a restless character obsessed with besting others and being, as he puts it, the Most Valuable Player. After graduating from Stanford, he took wine-making classes from Professor Vic Enriques at UC Berkeley. Meanwhile, in 1943, Cesare had bought the historic Charles Krug Winery in the Napa Valley, an ailing concern run since 1933 by Louis Stalla. Charles Krug had founded the winery in 1861, making it probably the oldest vineyard in the valley. But after Prohibition, it had a prestigious name and not much else. Bob and his brother, Peter, settled in to run the winery together, a partnership that would end in disaster.

Ambitious from the outset, Bob was to run up inexorably against his family's desire to maintain the status quo of making potable commercial table wine. In his autobiography he uses phrases like "a passion for perfection," "turning your dream into reality," "a desire to excel," and "setting clear goals." He writes:

"Whatever I chose to do, I wanted to be The Best. I also wanted recognition; I wanted everyone to know that in this endeavor or that Bob Mondavi was the best." Unsurprisingly, this attitude did not endear him to gentler types like his brother.

Mondavi's rise occurred at an opportune moment in California's wine story. Between Prohibition and the end of the 1960s, California wine experienced its dark ages. This dismal epoch was largely due to Prohibition itself, which allowed Napa growers to make sacramental wine for churches in San Francisco but precious little else. In 1960 there were still only twenty wineries in the valley, and of these only half a dozen were even trying to make fine wines. Production was dominated by names like Italian Swiss Colony, the Roma Wine Company in Lodi, and Ernest and Julio Gallo in Sonoma. The historical thread that connected older wineries like Beaulieu and Krug to their nineteenth-century roots had mostly been broken, but Mondavi saw that a new tradition could be conjured up out of the blank slate that Prohibition had created. What was needed was a vineyard-cum-laboratory.

His idea would be to turn Krug, which the Mondavi family was already running, into just such a viticultural laboratory, where dozens of experiments with fermentation techniques, varietal plantings, and vineyard management could be carried out. But the other Mondavis were horrified. The cost of such experiments would be exorbitant; the investment per acre needed to change table wine into fine wine was unthinkable to the Napa of 1965. So Bob decided to leave Krug and buy a vineyard a few miles down Route 29. Outside of the tiny village of Oakville, he found a place called To Kalon. In fact, the Mondavi corporation had already bought a 325-acre parcel of To Kalon for Krug in 1958. For To Kalon had a mythic reputation in Napa.

At this point Bob detached himself from his Pinot Noir and pointed rather lyrically through the luminous windows. A sea of vines undulated over a mild hillside bathed with sun.

"There it is," he said beatifically. "To Kalon. Beautiful, no?"
"Very."
In his book, Bob describes his visit to To Kalon in 1965:

It exuded an indefinable quality I could not describe, a feeling that was almost mystical. . . . In its whole expanse of vines and greenery, I could not see a single blemish or man-made intrusion. . . . It perfectly captured my guiding ambition and spirit. In Greek *To Kalon* means "highest quality" or "highest good." To me, that meant, simply, The Best.

To Kalon was also perfectly placed to draw tourists on Route 29. The winery as experimental tourist laboratory was born, and To Kalon became the launching pad for the new Napa Cabernets which have soared to the top of the global wine market. It was one of the most important vineyard purchases of the twentieth century.

But the new vineyards didn't produce only reds. In 1969 Mondavi put out a white wine called Fumé Blanc. With its cute pseudo-French name, it was the first American white wine to make a mark on the mass market. With Fumé Blanc the Mondavi juggernaut began to roll forward.

Bob waved a lofty hand. Desserts had arrived.

"Tell me," he said, "what wines from California do you really dislike?"

I had to be careful here, so I said I didn't have much experience with them. I'd once tasted a fabulously expensive Helen Turley which I had thoroughly disliked. But it was not that I had disliked it so much as that I had had the impression that *it* had not liked *me*. At 17 percent alcohol, it had merely made me wonder what it would do to my liver. Since Helen Turley has often been called the queen of American wine makers and since her wines often sell for over two hundred dollars in restaurants, I was curious to see what Bob would say.

"Completely agree," he sighed. "I do get so tired of these huge Californian wines. They're so tiring. They leave you battered. I want something delicate. Don't you want something delicate, Margrit?"

"Absolutely."

"These so-called great wines," Bob went on a little more fiercely. "We're looking for fineness." He paused magisterially. "Without residual sugar!"

Recently the Mondavis had had a sharp difference of opinion with the all-American critic Robert Parker. Parker, the self-appointed Ralph Nader of wine consumership and author of the omnipotent *Wine Advocate*, had lambasted Mondavi for failing to produce the usual monster Cabernets which Napa is supposed to produce. A similar reaction had come from Jim Laube, the *Wine Spectator*'s Napa correspondent. There seemed to be a certain amount of confusion among these writers. If Mondavi could produce jammy monster Cabernets, why didn't he?

And yet hadn't Parker formerly showered Mondavi with gushing overtures? "When is the President of the United States," he wrote in the 1999 edition of his *Parker's Wine Buyer's Guide*, "going to give this man our highest civilian honor for the profound and positive influence he has had on wine, food and American culture?"

"But then," Bob said, "we had the temerity to go in a different direction. We got tired of the usual hyperbolic Napa style. We wanted to make wine you could actually drink with normal food."

"So your Parker scores went down?"

Declining Parker scores are the kiss of death for many wineries from Tierra del Fuego to the Langhe Hills. Parker's 1-to-100 numerical ratings are the most influential in the world.

"Our Parker scores did go down." Bob nodded. The eye twinkle had reappeared.

"Did you care?"

"It's not the point. A change is under way in Napa. American taste is outgrowing the critics who used to dominate it."

Afterward we walked around the winery, dipping in and out of May's grandiose arcades, slipping across what look like small plazas in Brasília. A commotion of tourists overwhelmed the vestibule, but none of them appeared to recognize Bob himself as he floated merrily among them. We had moved on to the delicate subject of taste. At last, some tips about taste!

What is a taste for fineness? I asked him.

"It's an interesting question. I ask myself if I had any taste before 1962. That was my first trip to Europe, you know. Did you read my book? It's all in there."

The sixties were a watershed for American wine culture. The people who created American wine taste first traveled to Europe in that decade: the critic Robert Parker, the importers Kermit Lynch and Neal Rosenthal, and of course Mondavi himself, who visited the Mosel, Tuscany, Bordeaux, and the villages of Burgundy. "I left Europe," he wrote, "elated."

It was a question of taste.

"Taste is a funny thing, isn't it?" Bob said cheerily. "I'll always remember that restaurant in Vienne in 1962. La Pyramide."

His meal at La Pyramide was a revelation and provided a new impetus for the driving Mondavi ambition. His description of the experience borders on the religious: "I'd go so far as to say that the food and the wine transported us into a world of gentleness and balance, of grace and harmony."

I asked him if that mental world was specifically European.

"At that time, yes. It was astonishing to us."

And was that what wine should offer, the transporting of our minds into a world of gentleness and balance?

"Well, I would say so. Wouldn't you?"

Perhaps, then, taste is a reflection of an altered state of mind, one in which those two qualities are paramount?

"Two things," I offered, "which don't surround us most of the time?"

"No. But back in 1962 it was even worse here in Napa. We had to struggle to make the *gentleness and balance* of wine felt. That came from France. We do owe them an enormous debt, you know. Even though we are surpassing them in many ways."

The imperial eye twinkled.

But now, I asked, do you really feel that you've surpassed them?

"Well, we often like to say that here in California. But in reality it's more complicated. When I was in France in 1962 I was amazed at two contradictory things. First, how beautiful the top wines were, how much better they were than anything in America. But on the other hand, how bad much of the average stuff was. There were a lot of bacteria defects, dirty practices. They used old oak barrels while the top châteaux in Bordeaux were using small, new barrels with much better results. So there was a contradiction."

And it was a contradiction that California—that Mondavi—thought could be exploited. America would use her technological know-how to make better *average* wines than lazy Old World traditionalists.

Cleanliness and technology?

"We learned from the French that different varietals had to be treated, even fermented, in different ways. There had to be subtlety of touch. Gentleness and balance. But we knew we could teach *them* how to make their wines cleaner, crisper."

"Brighter?"

His eyes lit up.

"Brighter, if you will. We knew that we could technically purify the whole process."

Gentleness and balance are states of mind; they are a condition of inner grace. I often wondered whether Californians didn't confuse this with its technological equivalent. In other words, they seemed to think that technological subtlety could create human subtlety. I wasn't at all sure that Bob himself thought this; but it seemed to be in the general Californian air all the same.

Our tasting had now wound down and I was off the hook.

"So," he said by way of a planned farewell. "You're going to visit To Kalon with our wine makers tomorrow? You'll see what I meant when I called it mystical in my book."

I looked at him standing in the suddenly hard sunlight and I thought I recognized in that Roman face with its aquiline nose the same tough faces I had seen pruning fruit trees in the villages around Castelraimondo. I told him that I had been to Sassoferrato myself and a kind of swift, childish pleasure came over the face. Had I liked it? Had I gone to Colmeroni just outside, where his mother was born? Had I drunk any Marches wines? As a matter of fact, I said, I had. A Conero Rosso. He shook his head, smiling. It wasn't clear that he had ever heard of it.

Napa is a strange town, as bedraggled as it is prim. A motionless river winds through it, cluttered with cranes and the exposed roots of uprooted trees. Riverside factories and brick banks recall a prosperous agricultural past based on walnuts and prunes, and so do clean Methodist churches and pale blue Victorian clapboards looking like ornamental Ottoman kiosks. Even the anarchists sprawled on the downtown Salvation Army lawn have the look of suspiciously tame garden gnomes.

The fantastical mansions with their wooden turrets, cavernous porches, and barricades of cherry trees are like the high-water mark of a tide of wealth which receded decades ago. For between the wars, Napa declined. The nineteenth-century waterfront grew decrepit, the mansions emptied out. But Napa's new wealth, driven by the wine boom, has created a second wave of construction, a second downtown. Needless to say, it's a roofed-in mall.

Built in purple and turquoise tones, it's like every other California downtown mall: boxed trees, Shades of California, a branch of Settings home furnishings. But inside the Napa Valley Art Association, the grape-inspired schlock begins. Cupids and putti in grape leaves, still lifes with Chardonnay bunches, acrylic vineyard landscapes. Piped music wafts around the corridors, the Vintage Golf Design table lamps sit in immaculate windows, and the golfing equipment stores brim with boxes of Titleist balls and Koolaburra hats.

Not far from the river, too, is Robert Mondavi's new Copia Center. This is Napa's latest wine and food museum, and a monument to the career of Mondavi himself. A plaque lauds him as "founder, visionary, philanthropist and believer in the art of life." *Wine and food, it goes on, are carriers of culture and celebrants of life, returning us to the world of the senses, of memory and imagination.*

Inside, Copia is a little bewildering, packed with its artworks, video exhibitions, and food. Julia Child has a restaurant franchise here, Julia's Kitchen, and there is a Wine Spectator Tasting Table stuffed with bottles of Chalone, WillaKenzie, and Mer Soleil. Unable to resist a quick drink, I settled in at the bar and ordered a glass of Atlas Peak Sangiovese. It was bustling that day: there was a major exhibition on the theme of mustard, for it was apparently mustard month in Napa and scores of decorated mustard pots were everywhere. Taking my glass, I wandered upstairs, anxious to get away from the mustard and amazed that security had not spotted me drinking *and* walking.

There was an impressive piece by Mario Mertz of the Turin-based Arte Povera group, a man best known for his minimalist igloos and tables. Impossibly, it was called *L'Horizont de Lumière Traverse Notre Vestibule du Jour.* It was a wine, steel, and honey installation, all tubes and phials filled with dark red liquids. Nearby, Art Guys had set up their "match installation #19," a film of ten thousand matches fixed into a wall being set alight. "This disrupts the norm and challenges many of our notions about the sacred space of the museum." Perplexed winers and diners stood around and yawned.

Before long, I too became quite aimless. Perhaps it was the Atlas Peak Sangiovese. I passed a superb photograph of Elvis snacking at the Hotel Jefferson Coffee Shop in 1956, but I somehow couldn't imagine Elvis drinking wine. The retail shop was filled with the gastronomic fluff of the emerging sophisticated classes—Mario Batali and Jacques Pépin cookbooks, translucent lemon chopping boards, and Burt's Bees peppermint shower soap. Immense jars of zucchini and oil lined the walls. At a video installation called Circle of the Senses, I learned how to make an artisanal pizza from scratch to a growling Tom Waits–like soundtrack. Then, as I was staggering tipsy around the vast Beringer Atrium past a bronze statue of a turkey, I realized that I was actually inside a new kind of gastronomic city. Julia's Kitchen was more tightly packed than any restaurant in downtown Napa and the Wine Spectator Tasting Table was equally thronged. It was a bold concept on the part of Mondavi: the culinary mall.

That evening I drove up Route 29 to the Don Giovanni restaurant to see if California wines really were as astronomically priced as their French counterparts. Don Giovanni is one of those Napa restaurants that use Italian substance to fill out a very American style: sweeping bar, tropical fans, Mexican patios. I had a pizza. The wine list was mind-boggling. Araujo Cabernet for $140; Paradigm Merlot for $160; Marcassin Blue Slide Ridge for $225; Mondavi's Opus One for $130. Amid this cacophony I spied a Quintarelli Valpolicella at a humble $59, a wine that I was sure was more beautiful than anything else on the list. It struck an odd note among the other Europeans there, Gaja's $300 Barberesco or Marchese Antinori's Solaia at $280. But out of curiosity I ordered a half bottle of the wine with the most preposterous name: Blockheadia Ringnosi Zinfandel from Lorenza Lake Winery. Blockheadia Ringnosi? It sounded like an Eastern European horror movie actor from the 1920s. The wine itself was pleasant enough, simple and rounded, fruity and clean. Not complex, but drinkable—in a word, presentable.

Curious about Francis Ford Coppola, I wanted to try the Niebaum-Coppola Edizione Pannino at $80, but at the last minute I balked at the price. Compared to the Gaja and the Marcassin, it was a steal. But the prices already seemed like a psychological game that some unseen power was playing with me. One could call it "Pay or Not Pay?" If you paid and the wine was good but not extraordinary, what did you do except swallow the charge on your credit card and move on? Could you really tell what a $225 bottle should taste like?

I doubted that Gaja's $300 bottle was really worth the price, even though it has an immense reputation in Piedmont and beyond. More to the point, did the Blue Slide Ridge merit its tag of $225? I doubted it even more. Naturally, however, such questions are beside the point, for those prices are a game played with people for whom money is a fluid thing, not something finite and carefully measured. Thus wine operates in the same dimension as Cartier watches, diamond rings, and rare Moroccan trilobites. It seduces our profligate subconscious and humbles our powers of caution.

The Vinelife

Do not do unto others as you would that they should do unto you.
Their tastes may not be the same.   —George Bernard Shaw

Some things had gone unmentioned at lunch with Bob
Mondavi, prosaic statistics on the consumption and status
of wine during the past century. The rise of American wine
has not been merely a matter of changes in taste. Perhaps more fun-
damentally, it has been a matter of America's changing rank in the
table of global consumption decade by decade, and the precipitous
rise of drinking itself as a social pastime since the high noon of ab-
stention in the 1920s. A nation of angry Prohibitionists had become
a nation of accidental connoisseurs.

In 1934, for example, Americans consumed just 33 million gallons of wine, which averaged out at about a quart a head. By 1966,
when Mondavi opened his Cliff May winery, the figures were 203
million and a gallon a head, respectively, which shows that Americans had continued to vigorously explore wine in the Eisenhower
years and had opened their wallets accordingly. Total annual consumption soared to 506 million gallons in 1981, by which time every
American was drinking an average of two gallons of wine a year. The
peak year of the century for American per capita wine consumption

was 1986, with two and a half gallons downed per head and 587 million gallons overall. Thereafter, wine consumption declined.

The 1990s, of course, witnessed a health food craze, a trend that was only reversed at the end of the decade by the allegedly scientific news that red wine contained chemicals friendly to the benevolent form of cholesterol. By 2000 American drinking was back to two gallons a head, with 565 million gallons for the nation as a whole. But the long-term trend was obvious: from an abstemious fraction of a gallon a head to two a head in seventy years. Each American today drinks eight times as much wine as he or she did in 1934.

It was this change that made Mondavi's fortune, and it was also the catapult that hurled California onto the world stage. But—for those of us who find these kinds of statistics irresistible—there are also the figures for overall national wine consumption, which show a significant shift in world drinking patterns. Taste, it turns out, is as much a matter of markets as of personal cultivation.

For example, the world's top wine-consuming countries are France, Italy, and the United States. And compared to France and Italy, proportionately far more of what the United States consumes is imported. Whence an obvious fact arises: the American wine scene now wields an unprecedented influence.

In some ways, this is surprising. The United States is not, after all, the foremost wine importer in the world, either in volume or in dollar value. (Germany imports the most wine, about 20 percent of the world's total, with the United Kingdom a distant second.) But the United States is still the third biggest importer in dollar value, claiming 14 percent of the world's total. France, by contrast, accounts for only 3.7 percent of world imports, and Italy for only 1.7 percent. Import power, then, rests with only three countries, who together make up half of all the world's sales. It would not be surprising if the United Kingdom, Germany, and the United States shaped the taste of what the producer countries end up selling to them.

Thus there is a great paradox in the wine world. The French and the Italians are by far the largest producers and consumers. They are also by far the largest exporters. (France generates an amazing 42 percent of all the world's exports by value.) But France and Italy are puny consumers of other people's wines. Overwhelmingly, they drink what they make themselves. And this makes them curiously vulnerable to influence from the outside. Because France is such a potent exporter, she cannot afford to ignore the dictates of her customers' tastes, and Anglo-Saxon tastes, as she is discovering, are not necessarily her own.

Of the three importer giants, meanwhile, only the United States and Germany are *simultaneously* major producers and exporters. Americans are both the fourth-largest exporters of the world and the fourth-largest producers. Hence of all the countries which produce, export, import, and drink wine, the United States is the one that has the most relative clout in all four areas at once. She can influence imports with one hand and with the other bring her weight to bear on questions of production. She is the only country that drinks other people's wines as extravagantly as she drinks her own. And it is this fact which has helped make Napa the cockpit of global wine.

From the Mondavis I wandered idly over to the Niebaum-Coppola winery just next door. Its long driveway is adorned with voluptuous iron lamps brought from Paris, and as I drove down it a preposterously Gothic mansion swung into view. Edgar Allan Poe amid palms.

Formerly known as Inglenook, the winery founded by the Norwegian sea captain Gustave Niebaum in 1886 rose to improbable heights in the 1940s under the direction of wine maker John Daniel. Inglenook Cabernets made by Daniel are now rare collectors' items, but the winery declined after his death and was bought in 1976 by film director Francis Ford Coppola. The Gothic mansion must have appealed powerfully to him—a Dracula touch. Coppola wanted to restore the wine estate to its former glory and make commercially successful wines at the same time. The result, among other things, was Rubicon, a potent red ubiquitously present at your local wine store. Following the Mondavi example, Coppola thought to revive the old Niebaum place by making it into a tourist attraction, a mixture of enological airport boutique and personal shrine to his own electrifying personality. People love it.

I walked around the mansion. The staircase is carved with wooden grape clusters, lit with stained glass. The first floor is devoted to memorabilia from Coppola's films—the Godfather's sinister desk, a gaudy maroon Tucker "Combat Car," Oscar statue reproductions, Dracula costumes. Downstairs, Coppola celebrates his father, the composer Carmino Coppola, with sheet music from hits like "Gelosia" from the film *Amore che Uccide* and the score for Abel Gance's silent *Napoleon*.

The rest of the ground floor, however, is pure wine mall. Now I saw the dreaded *Apocalypse Now* T-shirts on their racks, as well as a bewildering cornucopia of mad knickknacks, things like Coppola's favorite four-dollar pencil sharpener and Coppola's favorite Parisian notepad. And there was even a wine called Apocalypse Now. It was a three-liter magnum bottle of the 2000 Director's Reserve Cabernet, hand-painted, with a slip-out CD underneath it. The two-hundred-dollar price tag was somewhat apocalyptic too, but I was curious about the CD that came with the wine. Did you play it while sipping the Director's Reserve? I scanned down the titles of the tracks: "Search and Destroy," "Waiting in Saigon," "Helicopter Attack," and so on. Perhaps this was wine music. I tried to remember "Helicopter Attack." It sounded like a Helen Turley wine, or for that matter a Coppola one. I wondered if I would have the guts to order a bottle of Apocalypse Now in a restaurant. *That* would be a wine you couldn't send back.

Tom Wolfe has made the point that American places are now part of what he calls the "psychological economy." That is, they are no longer actual places at all, but charged, fleeting tourist impressions that exist to give us momentary experiences for which we pay hard cash. But what exactly are these experiences? Are they the same as those provided by films? It's easy for Wolfe to point to places like Times Square as the epitome of this trend; he remembers having lunch with Marshall McLuhan in the garden of the New York restaurant Lutèce in the 1970s and McLuhan saying (as he gestured toward the skyscrapers all around), "This will soon all be Disneyland. People will come here just to look at it." But Niebaum-Coppola, like many Napa wineries, is also a part of the psychological economy. It's a winery which you *look at* while buying a pencil sharpener and a Dracula baseball cap.

Five minutes' drive north from Niebaum, another historic winery, Beringer, also feels like a railroad czar's fantasy, but this time in the timbered Elizabethan style.

As at Niebaum, the intensity of the tourist ambience at Beringer is overwhelming. Around a giant mossy tree and sappy Bacchic garden nudes, visitors wander about with Beringer purchase bags. Inside at a splendid bar of carved wood with stained glass windows I stopped and had a cold glass of Beringer Chardonnay. So people were drinking; but of course they weren't really drinking. What they were really doing was shopping. For gift ties, baseball bats, ceremonial candles, and the *Oxford Companion to Food*. Then there was the wine. The $100 bottles of Reserve Cab, which the critic Robert Parker describes as having "a super nose of smoked herbs, melted licorice and cassis jam" (*melted* licorice?); the $80 bottles of Howell Mountain with a score of 91 from the *Wine Spectator* and scents of "mocha, herbs, coffee." People were buying basketloads of them, smacking their lips at the thought of a glassful of smoked herbs and melted licorice.

I slipped into the room next door and found myself standing before a gorgeous stained glass window which I now perceived portrayed the balding head of Shakespeare. The bard looked a little tipsy, not to mention multicolored. To one side, I spied a glass of wine standing all alone on a table. Perhaps someone had left it there on their way out, but it looked pristinely untouched. Could it be a glass of the enormously expensive Reserve Cab ladled out during a tasting next door? I couldn't control either my schoolboy curiosity or my simple greed. I went over and grasped the stem, ready to lift it quickly to the nose and sniff.

But at that moment I looked up at the face of the bard and saw eight Japanese faces peering through it. It was a surreal collage, to say the least. And they were looking straight at me, just as I found that the wine and the glass were both plastic and that they were nailed securely to the table. My body must have performed a strange twitch, because the Japanese began laughing uproariously. To them I must have looked like an outsized alcoholic Charlie Chaplin. I fled to the bar, where I was able to buy a copy of Oz Clarke's *Essential Wine Book*. I was sure it would come in handy.

At To Kalon, the vineyard manager, Mitchell Klug, was waiting for me. He was like so many Napa farmers: rugged, bearded, and likably canny. The Homeric helmsman look. And like many of them, he didn't seem quite of the land. There was something urban and scientific in his verbal undertow, a hint of university intellectualism.

"In the wine world," he said, "we now have these stars who have been manufactured entirely by the magazine industry. It's like hip-hop, Hollywood, anything else. The magazines create cult celebrities and with them a culture of novelty." He didn't want to name names. "You can see it everywhere, this culture of instant change. But with wine you hit a problem. Our culture is fast, but wine is slow. It takes decades. The irony with all these novelty cult wines—"

"Like Screaming Eagle?"

"—if you like. But the irony with all of them is that wine has a different mentality from commodities that can change very quickly. It isn't music or fashion or software. You can't change a vineyard overnight."

But was the problem just magazines and their trendy manias?

"Not at all. Look at Bordeaux. Bordeaux is interesting. You know, Bordeaux was in the doldrums thirty years ago. Then there was a revival in the 1980s. There were many factors behind it, but in the end a new business model for wine happened. Lynch-Bages was the first Bordeaux estate to reinvent itself by turning itself into a business machine. You had to create a *business* that flowed smoothly, which cut out all the quirks and uncertainties. Vineyards require huge amounts of capital. They're capital investments. The higher the quality you're aiming for, the higher the level of capital investment needed. Spend or die! But once you've spent all that money, you need to earn it back. It's a self-maintaining cycle. So you charge high prices for the wine. You can't do it all haphazardly, it has to be cost effective."

But what kind of wine, I asked, comes out of all this?

"Ah, there's the rub." Mitchell suddenly looked like Hamlet. "As far as I can see, when you buy a bottle of Lynch-Bages you're not just buying a wine, you're buying a theoretical model. Is it genuine? Who knows."

We arrived in the heart of To Kalon. The rain had cleared and squeaking larks appeared over the dark yellow haze of thousands of mustard flowers. Long-eared rabbits darted in and out of the Cabernet stalks as if a Lewis Carroll tale were about to begin, and at the end of the monumental rows of vines wind machines turned in silence. The vineyard was spacious, consciously grand, and orderly; a *royal* vineyard, I thought. We crept between the rows, turning the leaves with our fingers. Mitchell began to talk about vine spacing and the lessons of Petrus: the ultimate symbol of Bordeaux's glamour and power.

But Mitchell wasn't talking about glomming onto French glitz. He was talking about wine technicalities:

"We use the vine spacing that we saw at Petrus when we went to Bordeaux. It's one meter by one meter. So you have each vine planted a meter apart longitudinally, and then placed in rows which are a meter apart. In Napa, to do it like that was a revolution twenty years ago."

Until the 1980s almost all American vineyards were planted according to a scientific formula devised by the School of Viticulture and Enology of the University of California at Davis and championed by one Professor A. J. Winkler.

The wine faculty of UC Davis, located in a small town fourteen miles west of Sacramento, has been by far the most important academic influence on American wine making over the last fifty years. Its graduates have fanned out over much of the country, forming and reforming American vineyards from the vines up, while its faculty have profoundly shaped the outlook of generations of wine makers.

Winkler's formula postulated that vines should be planted eight feet apart and in rows twelve feet apart. This arrangement yielded exactly 454 vines per acre and was judged to be ideal for bulk wine growing. The space between the rows was just large enough for tractors to pass through, and the small number of vines per acre meant that more fruit would grow on each vine.

Widely spaced vines are "unstressed," which tends to make them larger and more productive. The more unstressed a plant is by nearby competitor plants, the more relaxed and happy it feels. And the more relaxed and unthreatened it feels, the more energy it puts into growing leaves and fruit. Conversely, the more stressed a vine is by being too close to a competitor, the more energy it puts into reproducing itself—that is, it pours its energy into the grapes. It doesn't produce more of them, but the grapes it does produce have greater density and complexity.

Thus, in Burgundy and Bordeaux vine spacing was always far closer than in California. In France, a spacing of one meter by one meter, or three feet by three, would yield 4,046 vines per acre. The vines were stressed, probably neurotic even; but they would produce a rich, high-strung fruit which in turn would yield a denser, more layered wine.

The Americans understood that closer spacing was the secret of places like Petrus. But it was also one of the reasons for Petrus's price tag. For its commercial glitz, in other words. Tending 4,046 vines per acre as if each one is a needy child is exhausting and expensive. A tractor can't pass down a three-foot gap, except $120,000 Bobard machines, which are the tractor equivalent of Porsches. And if you were paying two dollars a vine, your outlay would go from $2,000 per acre to $8,000. Your vines might have increased fourfold in number, but your net yield for an acre would only be 20 percent higher.

Per plant, the yield goes from twenty-five pounds of grapes a vine to about eight pounds. It's unsurprising, then, that Napa growers were initially outraged by the French system; UC Davis and the college scientists denounced it as extravagant.

So long as Californians were growing bland Thomson seedless grapes for tank wine and fruit bowls, there seemed no reason not to do it Winkler's way. It was cheaper and easier. But then To Kalon came along and Napa had a laboratory for the Petrus way. The Mondavis decided to spend the money and replanted with the close French spacing and 4,046 vines per acre. A shock wave passed through the valley. Mondavi was turning to Bordeaux instead of to UC Davis? (Perhaps Mondavi himself had not yet tasted a great Château Davis.)

Moreover, as the Mondavis entered into a partnership with Philippe de Rothschild, the wine maker from Mouton-Rothschild, Patrick Leon, came to Mondavi to supervise the replantings in close, Bordeaux-like formations.

So the influence, I asked, had also gone from France to California in very recent memory? Close spacing began at Mondavi in 1984. So was the basic vineyard technique here lifted wholesale from Bordeaux?

"Of course. But being number one we like to keep that fact a little under the carpet!"

Leon also advocated thinning the leaf canopy to allow more direct sunlight onto the grapes. This was also standard Mouton-Rothschild practice: light produces more tannin and color.

According to Mitchell, a similar revolution took place at Petrus several decades ago.

"It destroyed the monopoly of the Bordeaux aristocracy, who were wrong-footed by this change in practice. Then they all imitated Petrus. Close spacing became the norm."

Surely, though, Bordeaux was the very definition of ancient tradition in wine?

"Petrus began close spacing in the 1950s. The new concentrated Petrus wine began appearing in the 1960s. At that time, the stuff from Pomerol (where Petrus is located) was like chicken blood. Petrus itself was nowhere in the 1950s. Now Pomerol is the most expensive land in France—it's $13 million an acre. That compares with about $260,000 an acre for top land in Napa."

I said that one of the myths that California and France held about each other was of a younger nation transforming an older one in the way that a child transforms a parent. A struggle between innovation and tradition. Youthful energy jousting with stodgy prudence. At least, that's the way Americans like to see it.

"That's what's strange about Bordeaux: it's a recent invention, not an ancient tradition. We adopted their spacing only about thirty years after they did. Not centuries."

Like Bordeaux vineyards, To Kalon has the feel of a high-powered agricultural showpiece. Yet I was struck by how vehemently Mitchell decried corporations. It was part of the Mondavi mythos: the family against corporate America.

Still, I had to remark, things seemed to be going very well in the golden domains of the Napa Valley. They seemed to be making a lot of money.

"Oh, look around you," Mitchell said.

Along Route 29, a convoy of black stretch limos suddenly appeared like a funeral cortege. Madonna on a wine spree? The forested

Mayacamas now looked far more manicured, more arranged, than they had before, and it seemed to me that sometimes the influx of money from nearby Silicon Valley is literally tangible.

"There's nothing you can do about wealth," Mitchell said, with a faint air of satisfied resignation, as if you could either take wealth or leave it. "All you can do is tend your vines. The money takes care of itself."

Back on Route 29, I stopped at the Dean & DeLuca store a step away from the Flora Spring Winery. Dean & DeLuca's wine section is an economic graph of the Napa Valley, as is its palmy parking lot brimming with Saabs, BMWs, and Mercedes. So what kind of wine do people come to buy at Dean & DeLuca, a fashionable grocery store whose New York branch doesn't even have a liquor license? I scratched out a frantic list on the back of a Mondavi brochure:

Caymus magnum: $500
Cask 23, Stag's Leap: $400
Diamond Creek Red Rock Terrace: $270
Ridge Montebello: $132
Dunn's Creek 1988: $100
Opus One 1980 (gigantic bottle): $2,200

And so on.

Most surprising was a casual wire basket of Opus One standing unceremoniously near the door priced at $120 each. It was a "sale."

I also saw for the first time whole classes of hyphenated wines with names like Cal-Ital and Cal-Rhone. These are Californian wines made with regional French or Italian varietals, like Jade Mountain's Mourvèdre, which is dubbed a Cal-Rhone, or Bonny Doon's wittily named Old Telegram, which apes the composition of Vieux Télégraphe from Châteauneuf-du-Pape and could also be called Cal-Rhone.

This begs the question as to whether French wines could one day call themselves Rhone-Cals or Burgundy-Cals. The case for calling some Bordeaux Bordeaux-Cals has already been made, but soon every wine in the world might be hyphenated. There will be Chile-Cals, Pinot-Argies, Americo-Provences, Australo-Barolos, Kiwi-Loires, Cal-Mosels, and so forth. My guess is that the Saab crowd would rather relish this. It's the same principle as the two hundred different coffee styles at Starbuck's, all of which taste like Starbuck's coffee, which is to say ingeniously undrinkable.

Opus One is the most expensive winery ever built in Napa, or indeed in the world. Mondavi and Philippe de Rothschild's joint venture started in 1979 is the *ne plus ultra* of high-technology wine making. Seen from the road through its imposing gates, it looks like a nuclear missile silo. Only when you get closer do you see the circular themes, Mayan temple decor, and toadstool lamps of architect Scott Johnson's 1990 creation. When Mondavi and Rothschild met in 1970, they decided they wanted to make a winery that was close in spirit to a Bordeaux château, not just in terms of its wines but also in terms of its physical presence. They wanted grandiosity, cool elegance, hauteur. If they couldn't reproduce the Louis XIV mansions and sculpted hedges, at least they could have an atmosphere of technical high purpose. They decided that terroir had to shine through. They were going to exploit forty different lots with different soils and stones, different yeasts, and they were going to make twenty-five thousand cases of Cabernet which would rival Mouton-Rothschild itself. That is, after they had spent $27 million on the winery itself.

I was met on the grand white staircase by Ralph Ewing, Opus One's guest relations man. It was the first Napa winery I had been to that had no tourists, no buses or cars. Instead, there was a single stretch limo in the lot. That, said Ewing, was because Opus wasn't open to visitors.

"We preserve a sense of peace here."

Subtext: no hoi polloi.

We stopped for a moment among the rippling olive trees and looked out over the valley. There are moments when California slips into an unexpected ancientness; and the quirky Pueblo-Mayan architecture had a hint of Atlantis about it. The lack of mass tourism was in keeping with a priestly vocation, a hieratic attitude to the making of elite wine, and the resulting peacefulness turned the mind away from wine and drinking and jollity and more toward the nature of the place itself: a somber temple to innovation and style.

We went up to one of the airy adobe-style balconies and a pergola of redwood stained to resemble metal. From here the composition of slopes, rotundas, and arcades attained their desired coherence. Scott's inspiration, it seems, had been old Parisian tollhouses rather than Mayan temples, but the walls of Texas cream limestone did not recall gray days by the Seine.

In the pergola, piano music seemed to be flowing out of unseen pipes.

"California," Ralph said, "spent years trying to deny the existence of terroir. I suppose because terroir isn't scientific. Back in 1966, the first California winery to put the name of a vineyard site on its label was Heitz. The site was Martha's Vineyard, and that was an unusual thing to do back then."

Was that because Americans are basically nomadic? They didn't grasp the idea of place?

"That's a factor. But who knows? Perhaps it just goes against our deepest prejudice, which is that technology determines. How could technology not be able to do what simple soil does? How could medieval monks know better than *us*?"

But terroir was all the rage now, I said. Wasn't it?

"It's all the fashion. But how many people really work with terroir in California? I mean *really*?"

We went down to the Salon, the reception room. Here there was definitely a whiff of Marie Antoinette. A huge gilt-leaf mirror, Bacchic-themed armchairs also smothered with gilt, gold satin drapes, and a stupendous glass table. The Bonnard on the wall was clearly an original. Margrit had picked it out herself.

We peered at the Bonnard and hummed. The vestibule next door, however, was all severe white beehive minimalism and ghostly echoes. Downstairs, it's a cross between a military bunker and a chic hotel. We passed high-tech labs equipped with skylights instead of fluorescent lamps—natural light reveals more subtle colors in the examined wine. Then a hand-sorting bay where technicians fondle red grapes to see if elusive sunburn can be detected on the skins; with white grapes, they look for a telltale black bull's-eye buried in the fruit.

I was struck by a contradiction. Opus One couldn't be more opulently technological. But the technology seemed to me to be as much invested in the decor—the beautiful lighting, the purring corridors—as in the wine-making apparatus itself. There were the labs, but these were more for verifying chemical qualities in grapes that had already been grown and wine that had already been made. The steel fermentation tanks were indeed awesomely futuristic, as well as preciously designed. But everything else in the wine-making arsenal seemed pointedly medieval and rustic. Old-fashioned press baskets stood under the tanks with no pumps connecting them, just as they might have done in a French village winery a hundred years ago.

Ralph admitted that this was so. It was an irony of Californian technology. While California wineries had been tyrannized for decades by the Davis faculty and its technocratic ideas, as well as by the general lure of gadgetry, Opus One had quietly gone back to French technical tradition.

It was, indeed, almost monastic in its simplicity: gravity instead of pumps, hand selection, ultrasensitive Marzola presses, a seeming plethora of earthy wood and stone. Again, it was the quest for gentleness of touch. Even the surreal-looking de-stoning machine looked more like a sculpture than a piece of industrial machinery. Did they, like many French wine makers, time some of their operations according to the phases of the moon?

"Some in California," he said "are doing just that."

This was a strange kind of luxury product. But then again, perhaps it was in keeping with the Zeitgeist: minimalist environmentalism.

On the other hand, couldn't all this high-tech low technology have been nothing more than the wine-making equivalent of an elaborate word game? Certain words were fashionable at the moment and crucial to one's credibility: terms like handmade, artisanal, terroir, boutique, traditional, gentleness and balance, organic, natural, environmentally friendly. It was a lexicon which the old sixties generation was very comfortable with.

After the gung-ho techno-nightmare of the seventies, it must have been something of a relief to use such words again. But that didn't necessarily mean that these words actually meant anything. Who knows what words people will be using in thirty years' time? The vocabulary of Brave New Wine might abhor the term "handmade."

We stood in the underground tasting room, looking out through a window into an immense, curved cellar, or *chai*, as the French call them. Opus's wine maker, Michael Silacci, had joined us.

"Ever drunk an Opus One?" he asked.

"I'm far too poor," I said.

"No? Well, shall we start with a '98?"

We sat on iron-and-wicker seats. In this half-lit subterranean chamber, I felt once again that I was in a Minoan palace, just as I had in the Mondavi parent winery. But when Michael showed me the label of the '98, it was not the Minotaur I saw on it but Janus: a two-faced head made up of the profiles of Bob Mondavi and Baron Philippe de Rothschild.

The stone had come from Rothschild, Michael explained as he pulled the cork out of the '98, as had the handsome wall lamps. He poured into our glasses.

"Benjamin Netanyahu came here, you know. He knows his

wines. He really does. So does the president of Nicaragua, Alemán. He bought $28,000 worth of our wine."

"Rather a lot for Nicaragua."

"He didn't care. Must have been for presidential entertainment."

"What did he buy?"

"Half sweet. Half Reserve Cabernet."

We let the wine sit for a bit, then drank together silently. Michael continued talking after an appropriate pause for taste sensations to sink in.

"Know which country is the biggest alcohol consumer in the world? China. The wine business is just starting out there: they give away a free bottle of lemonade to every client who buys a wine. The Chinese hate Cabernet, it's too acid for them, too dry. They like sweet Moscato. The Mexican middle class is coming up and the elites in Chile are a true wine class now. A lot of Brazilians are into wine too."

We peered into the great arc of one thousand barrels below us. It seemed a mighty collection of Cabernet indeed. I thought of the Chinese emperor's famous horde of clay tomb warriors. The Seguin-Moreau barrels of French oak were all carefully stained around the middle with wine, giving them an elegant pale red band, and finished with painted willow rims to deter wine-loving parasites called bore bugs. The color scheme was perfect. The whole complex was a visual feast, immaculately ordered and spotlessly clean. This was indeed part of the Mondavi commercial concept: hiply designed winery space replacing expensive ad space in magazines. It was more economical, they explained, to bring tourists physically into the winery than to seduce them with commercials. People remember visits, not ads.

In the cool quiet of the *chai*, we pondered the '98 Opus, which was drier than I had expected. It is quite a leap to go from drinking $10 bottles whose names you can hardly remember to $120 bottles of Opus One *in situ*. I wondered what I should say. It seemed to me that by now the words "dry," "stony," and "austere," which are taken as compliments these days, were a bit exhausted. I could add "elegant," but that seemed decidedly platitudinous. Nor could I perorate on red fruit and the wine's famous "complex nose of lead pencil." Toasty oak, perhaps? Finally I tried this:

"In the mouth"—I had learned this phrase from the encyclopedias—"it's incredibly silky. It's soft . . . uh, cushiony. I think I can taste violets—"

They stared at me for a moment.

The '98 did indeed strike me as a Netanyahu wine. They added that there was a slight hint of violets. Crushed or fresh though? One couldn't deny that it was silky, or generous in spirit.

"It's a generous wine," Ralph said. They nodded.

Meanwhile Michael continued considering the glittering prospects of the global wine market: he saw it as a constantly expanding universe. "A decade from now, first-growth Bordeaux will cost $5–6,000 a case. They're already at $3,600 to $4,000 for the 2000 vintage."

"So it's rather like the market for Lamborghinis," I said. "Economic cycles only graze it."

"Strange, isn't it?"

"Wine as a brand?"

Ralph made a sweet face. "Well, you won't hear Bob saying that. But everything in capitalism now is a brand, isn't it? Brands and their consumers."

"Who drinks wine, then?"

Ralph had very definite views on this subject, as well he might:

"In the $100-plus category, Parker rules. It's your white middle-aged male Ritz-Carlton crowd. Between $40 and $60, it's the *Wine Spectator*. But, you see, women actually buy 65 percent of all wine, and women are *much* stingier about how much they'll pay. Women will pay between $15 and $20, rarely more. Women don't fetishize wine. It's true across the world. Women motivate the consumption of wine—the romantic dinner—but not the collecting of it."

Five guys, went the saying, will order beer. Five women will order a mix of wine and beer, while four guys and one woman will invariably order wine.

"Wine is a sexual gift. It's a seduction. Even though the wine-drinking age group is the forty-to-sixty-five-year-olds."

"So there's hope," Michael muttered.

"Well, we'll see."

I looked around at the huge hand-hammered Mexican lamps and the grape motifs of the benches in the Tasting Room. Was this place also an attempt at seduction? What kind of seduction? Had Benjamin Netanyahu succumbed to it, or President Alemán when he had purchased $28,000 worth of Cabernet? I naturally wondered to myself if I would spend $28,000 on Opus One grape juice if I had at my disposal the expense account of the Nicaraguan nation. It must, at the very least, have been an exhilarating check to write.

As we strolled back up into the afternoon sunlight and the eerily rippling ornamental olive trees, I saw the same stretch limo in the parking lot and detected at once the same ethereal piano playing a Chopin étude.

"Well," I said, "I'm off to see Copia and then the Auberge du Soleil. Or maybe it's the other way around."

They looked at their watches.

"Auberge du Soleil first."

"The foie gras is very good," Michael said earnestly. "And the medallions of lamb. Oh, the medallions of lamb."

We all meditated on the medallions of lamb for a moment.

As we descended the grand staircase like three Atlantean priests, I had a sudden feeling of exhilaration which had nothing to do with the thought of writing enormous checks. It was just the sense of space, a distant field of mustard slowly switching off for the night. A man-made extravagance set among those same ochre mustard flowers, with all its sleek buried machinery, its inbuilt austerity, its priestly superiority, its artificial silence. One could call it the severe poetry of the technological dream.

Oh Brave New Wine!

❦

There is nothing to be done about it now; civilization has ceased to be that delicate flower which was preserved and painstakingly cultivated in one or two sheltered areas of a soil rich in wild species which may have seemed menacing because of the vigor of their growth, but which nevertheless made it possible to vary and revitalize the cultivated stock. Mankind has opted for monoculture; it is in the process of creating a mass civilization, as beetroot is grown in the mass. Henceforth, man's daily bill of fare will consist only of this one item.

—Claude Lévi-Strauss, *Tristes Tropiques*

With his mass of untidy and spiky gray hair, Leo McCloskey brims with an insatiable energy that borders on the manic. As he shook my hand, he seemed on the brink of either a tremendous discovery or a nervous breakdown. The headquarters of Enologix are on quietly suburban Seventh Avenue West, a mile from the center of Sonoma, and as McCloskey whisked me through the corporate vestibule, all carpets and plants, I felt as if I had arrived at a mortgage company for a felicitous appointment. We swept into a bright Californian office in which, being a canny drinker, I immediately spied a bottle of Plumpjack. McCloskey offered me a chaste coffee instead. Perhaps he had noted the unstable alcoholic look in our touring enthusiast's eye.

"Don't get me wrong," he laughed. "I like a good drink."

"Coffee's fine," I lied.

Enologix is one of the most influential cogs in the wondrous machine of California wine, consultants to Mondavi, David Bruce, Randall Grahm, Paul Draper at Ridge, and many other stars. It has revolutionized the way wineries plan their futures and continually overhaul their "product lines."

McCloskey has created a unique digital database, derived from the cellars of dozens of Napa and Sonoma wineries, which catalogs such information as barrel type and age (including the subtly differing qualities of different woods), cellar conditions, grape varietals, climate and vintage analyses, and the usual chemical elements in the wine itself—sugar, phenols, tannins, and so on. Using this information to create a "digital image" of any given cellar, Enologix can run hypothetical experiments to predict the best wine that cellar can possibly make. Everything coming out of the cellar can be predicted: average scores, optimum prices, volume, aging potential, and the wine's fit to any given terroir. The software, says McCloskey, can tell a wine maker what he can do to produce any wine style in his cellar with the simple click of a computer button.

Seated before the computer screen, McCloskey gave me a demonstration.

"Say we have a cellar in Napa—"

He brought up the digital profile of a cellar filled with vats of Cabernet Sauvignon and Viognier which had been fermenting for about two months. Long columns of statistics suddenly unfurled across the screen.

"—so, there we have the two wines they're trying to make. We see that the vats are steel, with some American and French oak barrels. Concrete floors, correct temperatures, average humidity. Fine. It's a so-so cellar doing reasonably good stuff. But they want to up their Parker or *Wine Spectator* scores. The Cab is at about 86 in Parker and about 89 in the *Spectator*. They need to get up into the 90s."

Looking at the keyboard I now noticed that there was a button marked "Blend Now." He tapped it triumphantly and the software began flickering its combinations.

"If we *choose* to be Eric de Rothschild," McCloskey said, rather astonishingly, "we can be."

Sure enough, the system had almost instantaneously come up with a series of recommendations for the owner of the cellar. To get a 92 with Parker or the *Spectator* he had to make this or that refinement. It was as simple and rational as calculating his income tax, though probably a little more expensive: wineries pay $300 to $400 a month to use the Enologix database.

"See?"

He turned to me like a magician who has just nimbly plucked an egg from behind your left ear.

"Incredible," I said, but my eye went back longingly to the bottle of Plumpjack.

"So we've set up the blending model. Let's call it 'My Dream Wine.' Say I want to bottle in ten months. The software sets up the blend for me. I can choose what style of wine I want to make."

"Eric de Rothschild—"

"Well, exactly! Lots of people come to me and say, hey I want to make a Lafite-Rothschild style of wine. No problem."

McCloskey did just that with our sample cellar. The software instantly provided a Lafite profile, an aggregate of all the elements that go to make a typical Lafite. In fact, Enologix uses Bordeaux as its benchmark for assessing Napa wines because, as far as prices go, that is exactly what the market does. Digesting all the variables, the program then came up with its recommendations for making the faux-Lafite out of the raw materials in the digitalized cellar, then calculated what McCloskey calls its "quality number." This is the maximum quality level which the projected wine can reach; it was 0.39 for My Dream Wine, where a 0.5 would be equivalent to a 90 rating in the *Wine Spectator*. It wasn't bad for a first try. But a real Lafite came in at 0.59.

I said it was almost like designing a building on a laptop or engineering a car using software. Exactly, he said. You could get a five- or six-point increase within eighteen months of starting the system.

"We have all the engineering specs, if you like, of a Lafite or a Latour in our database. That is, all the chemistry which makes them taste the way they taste. We're part of the digital age so now we should use this tool. It's creating a producer-based sense of reality."

I wasn't sure what this meant.

"Taste equals intensity," he went on.

"But isn't taste individual, unpredictable?" I asked.

"Not really. It can be calculated logistically."

Ah, I thought: the machine in the mind!

But needless to say, McCloskey is in fact most articulately against the machine in the mind in all its forms. In fact, nothing gets him so caustic as the machine in the mind, even though he seemed to be consummately practicing the machine in the mind.

"Oh, I think we have to take back wine from the scientists," he said breezily. "Give it back to the wine makers. You know, I think of myself as a kind of replacement for Davis!"

McCloskey told me that in Napa there were now effectively two parallel wine industries. One was a mass-production machine (closely related, one assumes, to the variety which exists in the mind), while the other was "traditional." The traditionalists being those who had "gone back to European norms." They cared about real wine, the arts-and-crafts wine makers as opposed to the mass-production geniuses like Kendall Jackson or Jacob's Creek. McCloskey placed himself in the artsy camp. In McCloskey's view, these two opposing camps were now clashing in the marketplace.

"So you're at war with the machine in the mind?" I asked.

"Most definitely I am."

"And which camp is going to win?"

"Well, we have the critics on our side. But it's Hollywood versus independent films."

I said that these days I couldn't much tell them apart.

"It's a question of mentality," he said. "It's a question of who occupies the central ground. In the New World, we need to defend quality against the Australians."

By now I had already heard "the Australians" referred to as the ultimate wine spooks. They were the gimmick-technology spoilers whose Coca-Cola wines were like a bad parody of California, but they were armed with even greater marketing chutzpah. A perceptible scorn was directed at them and their gadgets: *they* were the real avatars of the machine in the mind!

"Critics," he said, "support uniqueness. So proprietary components must dominate in a wine."

"You mean there has to be an author?"

"If you like. But today's wine is dominated by a few giant food corporations. In France—"

And here McCloskey became visibly intense, filled with a vast, pungent sincerity. The French, he said, had done a wonderful thing back in the socialist 1930s. They had passed laws protecting small farmers and wine makers from the predations of large companies. They had created appellations before the rise of the modern corporation, Madison Avenue, and cutting-edge marketing. It was why Château Lafite could exist today. I took this to suggest that without some kind of activism our handmade wines would disappear down the throat of Moloch. Except that "activism" has all the wrong connotations; fine wine is never going to be defended by the average left-wing activist or even the average right-wing one. It's going to be defended by the average drinker. And by the average statistician, I felt moved to add.

"Well," McCloskey said, drawing himself up a little, "the fine wine business, you know, is totally driven by quality metrics."

Any product could be rated metrically, just as Amazon.com does. Barrels can be rated, yeasts can be rated . . .

"We generate $2 million a year selling metrics to wine makers! It's a matter of thought leadership!"

"Everything's going mad," I said.

But I think he didn't hear me. Pretty soon, he added mournfully, the guys at Davis were planning to change the colors of wine artificially by a technique called co-pigmentation.

"That really is mad," I sighed.

"I tell you, it's a struggle to keep things real."

I looked at my watch and suddenly felt the age-old yearning for a good old-fashioned drink, metrics be screwed.

As we walked out into the arc-lamp sunlight, McCloskey turned yet more philosophical.

"Our techniques would be completely recognizable to a wine maker of the 1850s. It's the irony of Californian technology."

"I've heard that before."

"Because we're all coming to realize it. All this technology—spinning cones, filters, evaporators—it's all voodoo."

He threw up his hands and laughed, and I laughed as well. *A drink, where was that drink?* I thought about the bottle of Plumpjack, but then again I probably would not have enjoyed it.

"I'm going for a drink," I declared.

"There's a very good hotel in Sonoma with a bar. I can't really give you a rating, of course."

"I can do without a rating for one afternoon."

"It's your choice!"

California's preeminence in the wine world is due mostly to her scientific approach to farming. The critic Matt Kramer calls it "agriculture shaped by the machine." This new form of agriculture arose in the period between 1870 and 1930 and was assisted by the nation's agricultural colleges, which set out on a crusade to standardize and systematize farming practices. But why did Americans embrace these new methods more than Europeans?

Kramer thinks the huge size of American farms, as well as a national fondness for "tinkering and a fascination with machinery" had something to do with it. But it was also, he suggests, because Americans need to constantly remake and dominate their landscapes.

Although Europeans like Louis Pasteur and Hans Buchner were the ones who had unraveled the science of wine making in the late nineteenth century—establishing that yeasts cause fermentation, that bacteria mixed with oyxgen turns wine into vinegar and that enzymes are the agents of fermentation—European practice itself remained "unmoved by the revelations." Americans, on the other hand, had "no ingrained tradition." They needed to make bulk wine rationally and they had no hangups about applying the science to the vine. The men in white coats at Davis duly went to work.

Of course, there is another reason why Californians so eagerly turned to science and machinery when they finally decided to make serious wine: American wineries were in horrific condition. Andrew Barr, in his social history *Drink*, tells us that even in the late 1930s there were rats swimming happily in the vats of Sauvignon Blanc at Beaulieu and vinegar flies in the other wines. "The wine is so excellent," the resident wine maker cooed, "that all the flies go to it. It doesn't do any damage." Open fermentation tanks let off clouds of carbon dioxide which got birds flying overhead drunk; stunned, they would fall into the vats and stay there.

Prohibition, which demolished the American wine industry between 1919 and 1933, left California in a technological vacuum by the mid-thirties. One consequence of this was that Californians stopped looking to Europe for their inspiration. They were forced inward. And although most of the new technology came from Europe, Americans did not take Europe as their wine-making model. Instead, colleges like UC Davis set the tone. In the end, this enabled California's technology to overtake Europe's by the end of the 1960s.

Ironically, California's usurpation of wine technology was due to a man who could not have been more quintessentially Old World. The enologist André Tchelistcheff arrived at Beaulieu in 1938, hired as a reforming expert to put California's leading winery in order. He was a Nabokovian figure, a courtly Russian exile fond of cigarette holders and elegant clothes, and like his great literary contemporary he fused fastidiousness with an encyclopedic grasp of a narrow field of scientific expertise—not butterflies, but wine making. He set about rationalizing Beaulieu.

Tchelistcheff first observed that Californian wineries had not yet learned how to tailor their varietals to their soils. Beaulieu alone made twenty-eight different wines: it was a free-for-all. Fresh from a France which had just instituted a codified system of appellations, or wine-growing districts, the Russian was struck dumb. Later, in the 1950s, he oversaw the introduction of novel techniques such as cold fermentation, in which vats made completely out of stainless steel were equipped with double walls between which a coolant could be passed. Fermentation of white wines could now be rescued from the scorching temperatures of the valley, and this made for much fresher, lighter American white wines. This stainless steel and cooling technology led to the white wine boom of the 1970s.

Tchelistcheff was not the only reformer. On the budding wine faculty at UC Davis a few miles west of Sacramento, the legendary enologist Maynard Amerine and his colleague Dr. Albert Winkler were apostles of no-nonsense scientific viticulture, perhaps *the* apostles. In the 1940s they devised California's classification system for determining climatic zones, from Region I, the coolest, to Region V, the hottest. It was the first attempt to systematize grape growing and make it comply with a scientific model. Winkler and Amerine created a kind of heat index for vineyards which enabled growers to compare conditions in wine estates all over the world.

Amerine's most famous book, *Wines: Their Sensory Evaluation*, published in 1976, is mostly a work of statistics. In it he penned an astonishing sentence which beautifully sums up his attitude:

Our basic premise is that wine consumers and professional enologists alike will enjoy their wines more and will make more intelligent decisions about wine quality and value if they understand how and why they make such decisions and how to determine, when necessary, the statistical significance of those decisions.

Before we assume that technological artificiality is the characteristic sin of the American "air-conditioned nightmare," as Henry Miller called it, it's worth reflecting that various duels between artifice, machinery, markets, nature, and authenticity are hardly new; moreover, they are hardly uniquely American. It could be argued, in fact, that the French nineteenth century, which gave birth to our most cherished notions of a wine tradition, was itself a prey to the same tensions.

Surely the inspiration for Winkler and Amerine's rationalization of California's viticulture, however distantly, was the great Bordeaux classification of 1855. And there are parallels between the Napa wine boom of the 1990s and the golden age of Bordeaux in the last half of the nineteenth century, which rested foursquare on that very same classification: the first of all attempts to rationalize wine and make it *marketable.*

Prior to 1855, the wine markets of Europe were what could be called reasonably chaotic. But in the Medoc region of Bordeaux, an informal hierarchy of quality and prices had nevertheless emerged over the generations, with exporters and merchants gradually arriving at a gentlemen's consensus with regard to the region's best wines. At the top of this informal list, decade after decade, were the so-called Grand Crus, of which there were only four: Haut-Brion, Lafite, Latour, and Margaux. Below these were the lesser wines, known as Second Growths, Third Growths, and so on all the way down to humble *vins bourgeois.*

In 1850, an English Freemason, Charles Cocks, and a French bookseller, Michel Feret, brought out one of the most influential wine books of all time, *Bordeaux et ses vins, classé par ordre et mérite.* Cocks and Feret, as it is now widely known, is still printed as a standard listing of Bordeaux wineries, but back in 1855 it was the model for the Bordeaux Chamber of Commerce's official classification when Napoleon III asked it to represent French wine at the Paris Exposition Universelle of that year. The *Classement*, then, was a commercial ploy intended to make Bordeaux wines more rationally intelligible to brokers and buyers during the industrial boom of the midcentury. It gave them a fixed hierarchical list which they could cross-reference easily. And it worked. The Exposition Universelle was a triumph for the Medoc, while the *Classement* itself has remained remarkably constant ever since. The Grand Crus have remained just as they were in 1855; only Mouton-Rothschild was added in 1973. "No single document," Hugh Johnson writes, "can ever have done so much to publicize a product, and indeed keep it in the public eye, as a matter for discussion and debate, for over 130 years."

The *Classement* also coincided with the railway age. When the Paris–Bordeaux line was opened in 1853, Bordeaux ceased being a rural backwater. The vineyards became a Parisian social scene, flooded with millionaires, aristocrats, and entrepreneurs. It's worth recalling that there were virtually no "châteaux" until the boom created them. A so-called château was not a specific vineyard, nor even a great house of any kind. It was simply a method of wine making, for within an estate one vineyard could be exchanged for another as long as it fell within the classification. As Johnson adds: "The only word that really rings true is 'usage': a chateau is what it does. There is a word that fits rather neatly: a brand."

So the classification was a kind of brand-creation system. And shortly thereafter, preposterous "châteaux" began springing up to make these brands monumentally material in some way—and, too, to make them into alluring tourist experiences. Bordeaux launched itself on a half-century-long boom which found its biggest export markets in Argentina and the United States, and by the 1880s ancient practices were succumbing to the science of Pasteur and new editions of Chaptal, while newfangled machines rocked the ancient calm of the fields. (The anti-hail cannon, for one, was a monstrous weapon which shot missiles into clouds to precipitate a hailstorm onto other people's vineyards.) Wine had gone age of industry.

In his great 1884 tirade against nature, *A rebours*, Huysmans praised the artificiality of the new nineteenth-century wines and their perfect inauthenticity:

> Thus it is well known that nowadays, in restaurants famed for the excellence of their cellars, the gourmets go into raptures over rare vintages manufactured out of cheap wines treated according to Monsieur Pasteur's methods. Now, whether they are genuine or faked, these wines have the same aroma, the same color, the same bouquet; and consequently the pleasure experienced in tasting these factitious, sophisticated beverages is absolutely identical with that which would be afforded by the pure, unadulterated wine, now unobtainable at any price.

For Huysmans's artifice-loving dandy Des Esseintes (who prefers artificial flowers to real ones), drinking such wines was like going to the Bain Vigier moored to a pontoon in the center of Paris and relishing an illusion of sea bathing. And so he reflected:

> There can be no doubt that by transferring this ingenious trickery, this clever simulation to the intellectual plane, one can enjoy, just as easily as on the material plane, imaginary pleasures similar in all respects to the pleasures of reality.

Could there be a more poignant summing up of the seductions of artifice? And if technology is that same poignant artifice, how does one taste its fruit?

Huysmans has here described the sultry and addictive subversions of our own simulated tastes. For surely taste itself normally rests upon a belief in the superiority of what is "natural" over what is fake—yet technology itself believes in no such thing, and nor do we. Thus every engineer is a Des Esseintes. And perhaps, nowadays, every citizen is as well.

I went to Sterling Vineyards in pursuit of the elusive enigmas of the technological dream. It's one of Napa's landmark wineries, but as soon as you are in its shadow you begin to fear and loathe that very phrase, "landmark winery." Sterling is a place unlike any other, and in fact I was immediately struck by this bizarre construction perched on a high hill above Route 29 like a medieval castle. It's a sugar-white avant-garde keep connected to the parking lot and reception areas below by a cable car. The cable car is almost as famous as the winery itself: a technological wonder! The winery was actually founded by the don of the British Sterling paper empire, Peter Newton (I instantly remembered all my school work copied out on endless sheets of Sterling paper). From paper to wine: Newton had wanted a château, and he wanted a château in the best 1960s Austin Powers style. Furthermore, he wanted to survey his domain. Like a true lord, he had to be high up *above the fields*.

Newton's fantasy of being a gentleman California wine maker did not pan out. Coca-Cola bought Sterling in the late seventies and then sold it to the Seagram Company in 1984. The current owner is the Anglo-American corporation Diageo, the world's largest "drinks business," as its happy brochure has it, and owner of such illustrious brands as Smirnoff, Johnnie Walker, Malibu, and Guinness.

I staggered off the funicular and into the confines of the white castle on the hill. Diageo's sunny corporate slogans ran through my head: *We possess the drive to create positive energy in others!* The company even funds the International Center for Alcohol Policies.

The sun was indeed shining, and glowing positive energy and constant improvement seemed indeed to be radiant in the air. I suddenly felt like one of Snow White's energetic dwarfs, singing,
shoveling, prancing my way along immense tunnels and corridors.
Hi ho, hi ho, it's off to drink we go. A few operatives in company
vests floated by and I felt like saluting them in the Roman manner.
Eventually, however, I was met by Gregg Fowler, Sterling's wine
maker, who offered me a warmly positive handshake full of emotional energy and a vigorous pace to whisk us up to the tasting
room. On the way, the bell in the mission-style tower began ringing
(or so I thought) and we peered out at sublime valley views.

"I suppose," Fowler said, "you're wondering if I like working
here? Silly question, silly question." Robust and sanguine, he seemed
to be bursting with pleasure at the mere idea of driving up to this
monasterial complex every morning. It wasn't the usual commuter
schlepp. "Shall we go quickly through the facilities? I think you'll find
them interesting."

I did. We wandered through a maze of bunkerlike chambers:
bins of citric acid, enormous oak vats, the air thermostatically controlled. In the *chais* of reserve wine, small chandeliers glowed in the
dark. As we strolled through the rows of barrels, I asked him about
oak. Oak is a vast and thorny subject to wine makers, because it is
one of the principal means of modulating their wines. Modern fermentation barrels—or *barriques*, as they are sometimes known—
are made from a variety of oaks from around the world. The
chemicals in oak impart to fermenting wine a whole spectrum of
flavors, which wine makers often call their "spices."

In the eighties, the use of oak became a fashionable gimmick,
giving cheaper wines a superficial vanilla-tasting gloss which often
disguised their inner faults. The practice of throwing oak chips into
fermenting wine has mercifully lost much of its respectability, but
oak remains a blunt weapon in the vintner's armory. Fowler was
proud of Sterling's willingness to experiment with kinds of oak

other than the traditional French sources, such as the Alliers forest northeast of Paris, which are expensive. Sterling used wood from all over. There were Appalachian oak, Russian oak (from a cool climate, with a tight grain, similar to the French but less expensive), Hungarian oak, Oregon oak ("smells like bug spray!"), Czech oak, and even Chinese oak.

"Chinese oak?" Never had I heard of wine fermented in Chinese oak.

Fowler was enjoying his mischief. Was this what joyful corporate strategists called "thinking outside the box"?

"You gotta upgrade the spice box," he said. "Why not Chinese oak? Oak is a spice."

We went down to another cave, slightly cooler. Here were the Reserve Merlots and Cabernets from vineyards such as Three Palms and Selby Creek. I asked him what he drank at home.

"Our stuff. Or whatever we can swap."

The Sterling team went to Bordeaux regularly, tasting at Haut-Brion, that sort of thing, but the juice was too pricey for them.

He laughed ruefully. "Well," he began, "I'd say that at Sterling we practice active instead of passive wine making." He paused. "Our Reserve Merlot is our most hedonistic wine."

He explained that although they made a hundred thousand cases of the Reserve, they could still cleave to high quality. "We're a small large vineyard," he added.

"What's your passion?" I then blurted out.

"Cleanliness," he said intensely, looking me in the eye. "Our passion is cleanliness. Cleanliness and attention to detail."

"Well, it's important to be hedonistic," I said fatuously.

"Definitely."

And so we went up to the airy tasting room on a higher floor of the castle, determined, I assumed, to be hedonistic.

The tasting room was itself spotlessly white, with radiating beams. We were met there by Evan Goldstein, Sterling's PR man.

"Marriott and Disney are our biggest clients," he said with a touch of awe. "Then TGI Friday and Legal Seafoods in Boston."

"As opposed to illegal?" No one laughed.

"Then there's Capital Grill, the Kempton Group, Drew in New York. You know that all these restaurants in the main cities are mostly controlled by two or three big groups?"

"Like wine, then."

I looked around the room. There were some extraordinary artworks in it: Picasso's *Dance of the Fauns* (1957), Renoir's *Woman of the Grape Vine*. They were drawn from the Seagram Collection, the Sterling Collection of Arts, Wine and History. Meanwhile, the Sauvignon Blanc 2000 was being poured and Fowler was explaining how they had decided to go in a new direction with this wine, to pick the fruit when it was much riper, giving a more fruit-driven end result.

"We're going for a burst of fruit. The fruit character is going to be the foremost thing—"

"Not that we want to be tutti-frutti," Goldstein put in quickly.

"—oh not at all. Varietal character is what we want. Now the fruit is strong enough we don't have to add Semillion to it." Semillion had been added in previous years to bring the acidity level down and flesh the wine out a bit. "Now we add a little Pinot Grigio instead—it adds spice."

"It's like our secret sauce," Goldstein said.

We drank.

"Seduction? Oh yeah," Fowler said at once.

The wine was creamy, fruity, as promised. But perhaps also a tad tutti-frutti after all.

"And not too tutti-frutti," Goldstein said.

"So you see," Fowler added, "we drove our fruit element up . . ."

Next up was a Chardonnay from the Russian River, an area of Sonoma not far from the Pacific coast. We swirled and spat with maximum attention, but the phrase "tutti-frutti" was ringing in my brain like a Swahili battle cry. Was I being betrayed by my inept papillae yet again or was this a full-scale assault of the tutti-fruttis? The tutti-fruttis were now clambering all over me, and in particular over my quivering and abject tongue, scaling the walls of my mouth and launching blitzkrieg strikes into my nasal passages. And to accompany this, my drinking companions were conducting a chorus of self-praise which I felt sure they had sung before.

"Real nice tropical influence—"

"Mangoes, yeah, pineapples—"

"It's a Southeast Asian fruit market!" Goldstein finally cried.

"Seduction? Oh yeah!"

I too felt myself getting carried away.

"A Bangkok paddy field!" I whooped.

A little later, after tasting the Platinum Cab 2000, we fell to talking about yeasts. They add various yeasts just as they add various oaks. One in particular, derived from Tuscany's prized Brunello, was employed to "highlight the jammy fruit aspect." For their aromatic whites they used two different yeast strains which "brought out the floral elements."

"Yeasts—" Fowler began, just as a Pinot Grigio was being poured.

Our lips touched the glasses, and something odd happened. The room's speaker system suddenly erupted with loud music. I thought I heard a burst of Mozart piccolos before Goldstein, leaping up at once and asphyxiating the sound at its source, brought back silence. A few moments later, as we went back to a Cabernet, it happened again: Beethoven's Fifth, I thought. Was this wine-activated music? Piccolos for Pinot Grigio? Beethoven's Fifth for the Cabernet? When we had regained our composure it was time to talk about wine trends. For wine trends are, in a sense, the most important subject of all. We talked about Chardonnay. Wasn't Chardonnay moldy old hat these days, especially the butter-and-toasted-oak variety?

Fowler shook his head.

"Not as much as you might think. It's still *the* white wine in the United States. And Australian Chards are dominant here. There's still double-digit growth in the Chard market."

"Even for those awful tutti-frutti specimens?"

"Most people here have sweet palates. Sauvignon Blanc is still way too dry for my daughter, for example."

"And the New Zealand explosion wines," Goldstein put in, "go great with Asian food."

I said that I had never heard of explosion wines. Were they dangerous?

"They're yum," said Goldstein. "That's onomatopoeia."

"Love your lexicon, Evan."

We were all rather jolly by now, downing glasses of the Merlot. Merlot, Fowler said, was Sterling's core wine: 1.2 million cases of it. "What I love about Sterling," he added, "is the scale possible here!" The Merlot accounted for a quarter of their overall production. But I wanted to get back to explosion wines. Did Sterling make an explosion wine? But this was really a question of palates, wasn't it?

"Are there different palates," I asked, "on different continents?"

Fowler: "Absolutely. There's a French palate, a Californian palate, a New World palate. The New World palate is all about Asian fruit."

Goldstein: "Yum."

Fowler: "High-alcohol varietal descriptors."

I wasn't sure what this meant, but somehow in my bones I knew that it fit psychologically with what we were drinking. "Is that explosive?"

"The heavy fruit bomb era of the seventies," Fowler went on, "is over." (So perhaps *there* was the explosive element.) "In the eighties we had to bring the sugar levels down, make more balanced food wines. So now New and Old Worlds are much more blurred.

After all, we share all this technology with Europeans now. All these so-called artisanal, artistic wines . . . well, I mean we're seeing the lines more and more blurred."

Did the term "so-called" imply that he didn't believe in artistic wines?

"I think the lines are more blurred, that's all. We're all making artisanal wines now. For example, we work on each individual lot, we pick by flavor, we examine each parcel of soil minutely, we work closely with the terroir."

I nodded, feeling a little drowsy. Outside, we wandered around the white terraces, looking out over forested slopes. Was that Robin Williams's house over there? Joe Mantegna's place? Behind Mondavi's lands, stupefying mansions rose against the trees. Fowler nodded to himself, as if giving the land his silent approval. Where was it all going, I wondered. Soon the valley would be a giant arboreal bedroom with wine factories and golf courses landscaped between the mansions. But would that necessarily be a bad thing? It wasn't a question I could answer without sounding like a Luddite. It was clear, in any case, that the people who actually lived and worked here didn't necessarily think it would be a bad thing.

But at the same time I felt a rising need for something primitive, roughshod, and archaic. Looking into the distance you think you see the older, prehistoric, frontier California: porcelain blue mountains, a whiff of chaparral, the heat of violent suns. But that land is always, somehow, on the horizon, in the distance, *pale*. In the foreground all is smooth, flesh-colored, and tranquil.

"Well," I said, "I'm going for a walk."

"Really?" everyone said.

Where, they wondered aloud, does anyone "go for a walk"?

I said I wasn't sure.

Driving me down to the parking lot at the foot of the funicular, Goldstein said that going for a walk wasn't generally a great idea in these parts. Going for a *hike* might be a better idea.

"Unless," he said, "you walk through a vineyard."

I thought this was a fine idea. And as it happened, I knew a wild vineyard I could walk through.

"I'm going to Wild Horse Valley," I said confidently.

The arrival, in recent years, of so-called garage wineries, imitations of the *garagistes* which have grown up in Saint-Émilion in Bordeaux, has been greeted with a blast of media hype. The principles are trendy enough: low technology, back to nature, small scale. Production limited, literally, to one's own garage. It's an exultantly hippy idea. Of course California was going to adopt it.

Most *garagistes* in California, however, are nothing of the sort. True garage wine makers are few and far between, impossibly rare relics of another age. One of them, however, is Tulocay on the outskirts of Napa village. It's run by an unhippyish independentalist named Bill Cadman, a somewhat legendary figure among Napa wine makers, as I had been told often enough. Whenever I dropped Cadman's name into the middle of any conversation with a Napa wine maker, however glamorous, their eyes would shift from side to side, they would break into a snorting, mysterious laugh, and they would shake their head and mutter, "Ah, Cadman! What a character!" As if the word "character" could only denote qualities as dubiously complex as those sported by Cesare Borgia.

The inference was that Cadman drank too much and that he was a curmudgeon and a loner. Sure enough, Cadman was outside under the trees, drinking alone. He looked a little like the art critic Robert Hughes, with a weather-beaten, craggy face on which subtle expressions of intelligent disillusion played at high speed. He had the clear, bright blue eyes of an all-too-aware drinker, a kind of burly charisma which came from a great apartness. It was clear at once that this was no trafficker in commodities or brands. It was something of a shock and I wasn't sure how to act. Normally, maybe? But Cadman himself is not the ill-at-ease sort.

"So you found me," he said flatly. "A bloody miracle, eh?"

"Your neighbors don't know you."

He waved a hand. "Doesn't matter. This place has changed out of all recognition anyway."

Tulocay began life in 1975, at around the same time that Cadman was working for Mondavi. He bought his first two acres here in 1971, when Napa was a hick town and its wines were mostly hick wines. His career in wine began at Krug.

"Before that I traded stock. So I *know* how absurd the prices of wines are today. It's a great fraud, really. The price-quality relationship is almost nonexistent."

A dry laugh, and the pop of new corks. Cadman poured one of his Zinfandels.

"The sick thing is," he said, "that people *want* to spend more money. It makes them feel reassured. I mean, how sick is that? It's pure consumerist exhibitionism. Thirty years ago, wine in San Francisco was cheap as shit. You could get second-growth Sauternes for three dollars! Of course—and this is my no doubt nostalgic and biased view—in those days everyone in Napa had much more fun than they do now. Before corporate fetishism took over."

The Zin was an Amador County 1998, a rustic wine of deep raspberry flavors. Drinking it so suddenly, just sitting in the sun amid electric blue butterflies, gave me more pleasure than anything I'd drunk yet. We were now on the back patio of the house overlooking a lemon-colored field, dry and fragrant, in which two white horses stood in the shade of huge mulberries. And we were drinking it normally, that is, with chunks of dry pecorino cheese and olives and saucers of Italian oil.

In some ways, I was wary: it is always too easy to search out the "authentic" lost-soul wine maker living troglodytically in charming medieval squalor and raving at the corruption of the successful. I remember reading Kermit Lynch's *Adventures on the Wine Route* for the first time and laughing at the photograph in which a young and raffish American importer is standing in a cellar with the

Rhône vignerons Raymond Trollat and Gerard Chave. They look like a gathering of anarchist bomb makers loitering in a sooty cave. And Lynch's delicious book is delicious precisely because of its atmosphere of *Cold Comfort Farm*, with absurdity, squalor, and sublimity harmlessly mixed into Dionysian alchemy.

But that was fifteen years ago. We are a little less patient with the archetype of the peasant now—perhaps because we know that half the time he is a cunning con man. But Cadman does not fall into the category at all. He isn't trying to be schoolboyishly authentic. On the contrary, he seems to have landed where he is because of various dark forces, mistakes, passions, truculent convictions. And his view of Napa's evolution came from the inside. It rang true.

"I look at Napa, the *Wine Spectator*, and I realize that it's a lifestyle thing ultimately. Wine and wealth follow each other around in the most obnoxious way. You have rich people building cellars with spotlights aimed at the bottles of Yquem and Petrus! And the wealthy *like* being told what to like. They need their Parkers."

I asked him why Napa felt so confident.

"I'll tell you what it is. In Napa they think, 'Hey, the French make great wine, *we* make better great wine.' After all, deep down they're just stupid smelly Frenchmen. Anything they can do, we can do better. So we charge *more than they do*!"

I said, in parenthesis, that Napa wine makers always offered you their Zinfandel as their most humble offering and worked their way up to their Pinot Noirs. But the Zinfandels were often the best wines.

"I'm no different from anyone else. I have a Pinot Noir hangup. So how is the Zinfandel?"

"I like it. The old way, eh?"

"Yeah. *That* sure didn't last, did it?"

Having finished both the Zinfandel and a bottle of Tulocay Pinot Noir (Toffee Crunch), as well as a crisp Wild Horse Chardonnay, we went for a drive up to Wild Horse Valley. The road wound through a North Italian landscape made only more ethereal by a passing polo field. It was noticeably cooler—which is precisely what draws Cadman to the Chardonnay here. The pursuit of coolness: it's the paradoxical Grail of the serious California vigneron. Coolness which brings out the delicate acid, which mitigates the Asian spice market effect.

"What happened," Cadman said, "to the old Italians in Napa who used to have such wonderful gardens? And the dairy farmers. It was all dairy farmers not so long ago."

We were walking under spacious terraces of vines, the air cooling rapidly and a sudden darkness appearing at the edge of things: a lone tree in an ochre field, miles of white fences around the ranches.

Did he like coming up by himself?

Every wine maker, he said, has a place like this. "A place that says it all."

"I often wonder," I said, "if they think about a place as they're laboring over a wine. As if they want to turn that place into something sensual, ethereal. To put it into the liquid."

"It's a weird idea, isn't it? But why not? What else is one supposed to do with one's life?"

Later that night I had dinner alone at Tuscany, Napa's sleek Italian eatery on Main, and drank at the bar a Banfi Super-Tuscan which the menu declared was a 96-point wine according to the *Wine Spectator*. Banfi is the estate in Chianti which all dutiful tourists go to see when they are in Italy; its wines are perfect simulations—but of what? I balanced it off with a Ruffino Al Sole Fonte, a wine in which the wildly energetic tannins of real Italian wines have been sedated by the thick sugar of a candy bar. I looked up at the windows of the restaurant, where I read backward an odd hymn to the real Italy. *This is the Italy of our dreams, the magical region we have read about. We can visualize it in our mind's eye.*

So place is no longer a fixed and stable thing whose qualities strike us with instinctual force. It has become a wobbly, vague parody that exists primarily in our mind's eye, an ever-fading copy of a copy. But then again, I have willed it so, have I not? As I walked home to the Beazley House through the rain, I paused for a moment by a monument at the heart of Napa which I had previously over-looked. It's a memorial to Peter Jensen and Edwin Pridham, forgotten inventors of the loudspeaker. There is a modest sculpture of this device above the following inscription:

1606 F Street May 1915
Napa, Birthplace of the Loudspeaker

The Spirit of Place

❧

Different places on the face of the earth have different vital efflu-
ence, different vibration, different chemical exhalation, different polar-
ity with different stars: call it what you like. But the spirit of place is a
great reality.   —D. H. Lawrence

If you read a memoir by a famous wine writer, say Kermit
Lynch's *Adventures on the Wine Route* or the more nostalgic essays of Gerald Asher, there always comes a moment when the wine expert confronts the awkward question: What
is the best wine you have ever drunk?

Our wine writer knows that if he says a Petrus '61 we will groan
and think, "Of course, what else?" So he cannot say a Petrus '61 or
a Lafite '29. He could try something more exotic, a rare Chambave,
something Argentine, an ancient imperial Tokay from the czar's
Massandra Collection. But he is being watched carefully, for after
all he is the wine writer and his pronouncement is momentous.
Then something interesting happens. The wine writer decides to dip
into deep memory, to reach back into his youth.

In an essay called "Remembrance of Wine Past," Asher mulls
over the most memorable wines of his life. He recalls a 1791 Château
Margaux, "a vibrant strawberry color and astonishingly fresh," a

wine made from Malbec and strangely perfumed with orrisroot, totally unlike today's much denser Cabernet Bordeaux. Asher admits
that this exotic wine tastes extraordinary because psychologically
he cannot quite reconcile twentieth-century Los Angeles with "calories transmitted in solar energy that had also warmed the faces of
Thomas Jefferson and Marie Antoinette." He also remembers a
1981 Barossa Valley Cabernet Sauvignon from the Hill-Smith estate drunk after helping a friend move from an apartment. But then
Asher seems to think harder and throws a longer line into memory.

> But *most* memorable of my life? Were it not that people ca-
> sually met might assume I was making fun of them, I would
> in fact explain that it was, and still remains, unidentified. I
> drank it at a mountain inn near the Simplon pass in the early
> summer of either 1962 or 1963.

At that time Asher was a young man visiting producers all over
Europe for a London importer. He was on his way to Verona and had
just drunk a flowery white Fendant, a local wine of the Swiss Valais.
At the Simplon Pass he had the kind of mystical experience available
only on roads (Saul of Tarsus being the model). First of all, the experience was a place: snow, wildflowers, the road to Domodossola, a
midday sun, the inn. There was the lunch, veal scallops, buttered noo-
dles, and then the wine, a "light red wine poured from a pitcher." He
tried to finger the Alpine grape varietal—Bonarda? Ruche? Brachetto?

> The wine was sweetly exotic: lively on the tongue, perfectly
> balanced, and with a long, glossy finish. It was the sort of
> wine that Omar Khayyam might have had in mind for his
> desert tryst. The young woman who had poured it for me was
> amused when I asked what it was. She said it was *vino rosso*.

Asher says that he has searched for that wine for thirty years
and never found anything remotely like it, before admitting that

perhaps it was he who "created" it in the first place. "But the pleasure in any wine is subjective: we each bring something to what is there in the glass and interpret the result differently."

Asher seems to be suggesting that place itself is twofold: on the one hand, it is terroir; on the other, it is what is going on around you as you are drinking. The first is geological, the second psychological. And taste was presumably a high-wire act balancing itself precariously between the two.

I wanted to find the geological spirit of place. Accordingly, I decided to travel to the remote Central Valley estate of Chalone, perched in the mountains called the Pinnacles above the hamlet of Soledad. It was reputed to be a "special place." A place where *place* was alive and mysteriously well. Did its wine, I wondered to myself, match its location?

I first read about Chalone in a piece on Edna Valley by Gerald Asher himself. I was struck by his lyrical appreciation of the town of San Luis Obispo, the nearest coastal hub and a town which all lovers of Hitchcock venerate for the tower scenes in *Vertigo*. Asher described how the white wines of the nearby Edna Valley came to prominence. It began with a place called Chalone, even though this remote winery was actually a hundred miles north of Edna Valley itself, nestled in the forbidding Gabilan Range. Chalone was founded by an eccentric Harvard-educated musician named Dick Graf. It had become a cult enterprise in the late seventies, when a prominent San Francisco wineshop called John Walker had sought a private Chardonnay to bottle under its own label. A bistro called Le Central on Montgomery Street was looking for much the same thing. As Asher writes, the remoteness of the place only added to its mystique:

> The last part of the three-hour drive leads up a twisting road
> through miles of parched mountain landscape resembling
> nothing so much as a Dutch primitive's idea of Saint John

the Baptist's habitat. In the early seventies, what's more, the
winery itself, eerily remote and virtually without water or
electricity, did indeed have an almost religious austerity
about it; its domestic-type well and small generator didn't
come close to supplying its needs.

Something about that mention of John the Baptist made me sit
up. But who was the John the Baptist figure who had set up such an
improbable operation in the first place?

In 1960 Chalone was still an artisanal wine made without electricity (it was fermented in old port barrels bought from Paul Masson
for fifteen dollars each). The labels were made by a Berkeley callig-
rapher named Arthur Baker and printed by the restaurateur Narsai
David on parchment paper. Everything was handmade and impro-
vised, as low-tech as anything in the Middle Ages. In a way, it was
a quietly sixties countercultural place built nail by nail by urban ro-
mantics looking for something their professional lives couldn't pro-
vide. Making wine in 1960 America was little more than a quaint
pastime, like weaving Tibetan carpets or making jasmine joss sticks.

But the resident wine maker, Philip Togni, an Englishman who
had started out as an oil prospector, had met the reforming enologist Maynard Amerine on a trip to Madrid. On Amerine's recommendation Togni went to Château Prieure-Lichine in Bordeaux to
study wine making. The significance of this connection is hard to
miss. Then one day in 1987, a dapper visitor named Baron Eric de
Rothschild drove up unexpectedly from Soledad and paid a short
visit to Chalone. As with Mondavi, the Rothschild effect was about
to globalize a Californian enterprise. For California's most desper-
ately poor winery has since become one of the most powerful wine
corporations in the world, a corporation which now includes
Château Lafite in its far-flung portfolio. A Chalone, after all, had
been among the Chardonnay winners at Stephen Spurrier's famous
tasting at the Intercontinental Hotel in Paris. Graf, who was killed

in a plane crash in 1994, had once planned to erect giant statues of the great composers around the vineyard like so many Easter Island heads, while his mad organ playing used to keep terrified locals awake. It was an unlikely place for a global corporation to be born.

After spending a sleepless night in the guest house, I found myself inside the winery at an early hour with Chalone's wine maker Don Karlsen. A wind of incredible frigidity howled around the wooden structure, moaning in a way that made me shudder.

"I don't drink at 8 a.m.," I confessed. "I mean, not usually."

"Really? Then you're not a pro. Wine writers always get started at 8 a.m. It's the best time—your palate's wide awake."

"My palate may be wide awake, but I'm not."

"Well, can you taste the Pinot Blanc?"

The wind howled; I stared balefully into the cool liquid. Could I have some salami?

"There are brands and there are places," Don boomed as we went upstairs to the simple tasting room. "Chalone is a place, not a brand."

He uttered the word "brand" as if it were flatly detestable, much as one would use the word "tapeworm."

Are some places brands?

"Some are, sure. But here we're selling the site, not the wine making. We try to be invisible."

Through a door I could already see some impressive-looking machinery. Military machines, I thought irrationally.

"Most American wine making," Don went on, "is based on climate. That was the Davis rule, Maynard Amerine and all that. But here terroir is created by high minerality in the soil, as in Burgundy. Rodney Strong always said this was the most Burgundian wine in America."

Karlsen is a portrait of robust dynamism and Viking-like good health, all reddish blond locks and equally rose-tinted cheeks. He was originally a marine biologist. And once again I was taken aback at how many wine makers here were scientists or ex-scientists. We stepped outside, glass in hand, to peer at the rock spires towering over slopes of vines.

"There are only two terroirs in America," he continued with mathematical certainty, lifting his glass toward the Pinnacles. "The limestone shelf here in Chalone and the soil around Rutherford, what we call Rutherford dust. It looks like powdered cocoa. Everything else—"

"But isn't terroir just a sense of place?"

"No, it isn't. Typicity is not terroir. Look at Carneros. Carneros is a definite place, but it doesn't really have terroir, in my opinion. If you plant the wrong varietals in a place you end up with antiterroir. But our marketing idiots just grab the word 'terroir' and run with it." He made a running motion with two fingers. "But then again, an easy wine creates an easy return. You play it safe."

And who determines what an "easy" wine is?

"Market researchers and wine magazines. I could say the market, but the market is a tricky thing to define."

Parker?

"Oh, Parker likes us. He's said that Chalone is the only terroir in these parts. But it's also a lack of sites. Why is Napa Chardonnay such shit? Because there's not enough fruit intensity to match the oak they're using. And that's because they don't have any great sites. The fruit doesn't have any pronounced character."

We walked onto the fermentation floor and out through a back door with solemn views. A cold wind now plowed across the mountain sides, numbing our ears. Karlsen said that he could not understand why wine prospectors were not up here scouring the hills looking for undiscovered new sites. In the end, he had decided that it was something in the national character. The first wine explorers here had been French; Americans, he said, didn't like quirky or difficult endeavors. They preferred quick, easy solutions.

"We're obsessed with quick fixes, with what we call *processes*. Have you noticed that we hear that word every five seconds these days? Process. Process this, process that. Everything's a process. But wine isn't a process. Making spam is a process."

We strolled along a row of vines and Karlsen touched the leaves and stalks with the tips of his fingers. He touched them as if they were kittens or precious baby minks. Was this something wine makers did instinctively or was it a show for me? I had already noticed that in America wine growers and wine makers were actually two distinct breeds of men who usually kept their functions far apart. This was contrary to European practice, in which grower and maker are as often as not the same individual—often a person with a poetic bent. In California, on the other hand, the scientist wine makers had a harder, more pragmatic temper. They were not growers, so they did not descend so poetically into the vines as their European equivalents. Karlsen did so, however. I wondered if this was his individual feeling or whether it corresponded to some corporate desideratum about nature which the very location of Chalone somehow made inevitable.

Karlsen certainly wanted to "let the land breathe."

"You mean," I ventured, "that most American land remains in some sense undiscovered?"

"In a way. It hasn't been discovered yet. Because it takes time. Centuries, maybe. Land doesn't reveal itself quickly."

"And Americans hate all the waiting around?"

"It's undeniable, isn't it?"

I said that depended which Americans you talked to.

"What I'm talking about," he said, "is our attitude to technology. Americans have a sore time trying to think their way *out* of technology. We believe in it so ardently. The shadow of the wine maker is what counts." I looked down at his shadow flitting between the rows.

Of course, I said, people have been moralizing about the American love affair with technology since day one. And anyway, modern technology was invented in Europe. Did Europeans also suffer from a love affair with the dreaded machines? Since when did Europe become a symbol of frolicking swains and meadow-loving bucolics?

Karlsen was unfazed. "Technology for us is basically a matter of ego. It's an ugly love affair, if it is a love affair."

"What do you have against egos?"

"Well, in wine you have to let go of the ego. You have to drop all this crap about being a wine maker. Let the wine tell you what to do."

So, I tried again, it was this attitude of passivity (if that was the right term) which Americans couldn't accept? It wasn't their nature to be passive.

"But 'passive' isn't the right word. It's . . . what is it? Restraint? Humility?"

But Karlsen had another thought: the American education system.

"Much of the problem lies with these university faculties like Davis. These Davis graduates, they have no clue how to enjoy wine. The enjoyment—it means nothing to them. Wine today is being made by technicians who have no idea how to enjoy wine."

Just as literature is being taught by people who have no idea how to enjoy a book?

"Because they think it's a technology. They can't imagine something which is not a technology."

These were statements with which it was hard to disagree. But at the same time I had to question whether people here did what they preached. Karlsen told me that for him the quality "buttery" in a Chardonnay was a defect, and I believed him. But the Chardonnay I was tasting with him now seemed a little, well (I hated to think it), buttery. Perhaps, I thought dismally, it's my inept palate which cannot under any circumstances be trusted. Nor could I "feel" the place itself in the wine, as I was so earnestly trying to do. The Chalone Pinot Blanc, however, was another matter. Seeing that I had liked it more, Karlsen rubbed his beard as bearded men often do when they are overtaken by a feeling of flattering irony.

"Of course," he said, "that's the wine that nobody buys because it's not a Chardonnay. Is it the best white wine in America?"

He laughed Viking-style. Or was it marine biologist–style?

"It's a bloody nice glass of wine," I offered, shivering in the cold.

"What do you taste?"

"Grapes," I said.

"Good, good. That's what's in it!"

After a while, he added, "In any case, aromas are not what matter. It's texture that matters. Texture is all, I say."

Through the air came a taste of herbs. Around us the leaves were yellowing, becoming crisp. The olive trees had turned gray and I began to regret downing my glasses of Pinot Blanc with such gusto. Black olives lay embedded in the mud between our feet.

"Who the hell would want to live up here?" But it was clear from his tone that what he meant was "Who the hell *wouldn't* want to live up here?"

"At least it keeps the corporate types away," he added. "I mean, we're a corporation of course." He paused. "But we don't cut any corners . . ."

As I took my leave, I couldn't help feeling how strange the whole place had been. That dry grass hissing in the winds, the golden vines, the hills bristling with thorns, and the polished winery machinery shining in bursts of sunlight. Perhaps *this* was the technological dream after all—the wild place artfully enclosing the machine like a menacing children's fairy tale. Karlsen loved living out here because it felt like the frontier. It was where there was change, and he said so. What, then, was changing? The wine, of course.

Hadn't Parker recently praised its new Pinot Noirs made with increasing amounts of new oak? They were "softer," more "charming," but also "more forward than the old style Chalone Pinots." The old Pinots, Parker wrote, were acidic, shrill, and tart. The new ones were sweet, succulent, sexy.

So that was progress.

Down in Soledad, I ate a huge lunch of flautas and tacos *al pas-*

tor at La Fuente restaurant among the Mexican farm workers. With relief, I ordered an *agua de jamaica* and forgot the taste of wine altogether. A dry wind whipped against the windows as if the desert were nearby waiting to wither our faces. The vineyard workers from the nearby *estancia* likewise drank their jarritos in silence, pausing from time to time to pop a pickled carrot in their mouths.

I kept waiting for the moment when I'd unexpectedly stumble across a recognition of my own taste. I could not shake this feeling of blindness on my part. At Applewood's—a slick woodland hotel on the Russian River—I was sitting at the bar waiting to be seduced by glasses of Rocchioli Pinot Noir and other such luxuries served up with priestly gravity. And yet I always found those very same glasses of Rocchioli Pinot Noir to be like an exercise in calisthenics. I am drawn to the gloomy forests of the Russian River and the wooden houses on their stilts sitting in the mist; but I could not find their equivalent in a glass. Should one not expect such things in the first place? But then it is in the nature of the accidental connoisseur to expect them. And why should we not expect them? I took another sip, looking for Russian Riverness.

It could not be said that the ambience was not conducive. A fire roared; the tables were empty, rain beating at the windows. I was alone at the bar but for a shabby little European tourist in a blue windbreaker, poring over what looked like pedantic monographs on motel rates. From his pinched red nose and appalling English, I knew that he must be French, or at least Belgian. Since I now saw that he too was drinking the Rocchioli Pinot Noir, I couldn't resist striking up a conversation. Perhaps he was a wine trader or importer who could give me some gossip? Perhaps he'd be grateful for a few moments of his native tongue.

Maurice Delgado wasn't a wine trader; he was a tourist. His wife was grounded with a stomach bug in their hotel bed across the courtyard. So he had come to the bar with a bunch of wine notes from a variety of French newspapers and magazines, all of them pertinent to American wines, and had started his tab rolling with a Rocchioli Pinot Noir. Ah, American wines, Monsieur: they are something of a secret, are they not? And they are fabulous, Monsieur, fabulously opulent and opulently fabulous. It said so on page 14 of that week's *L'Express*.

"Are they really a secret?" I asked incredulously.

"For us they are a secret. Especially this Russian River. I have here, Monsieur, some notes on what to drink on holiday, and voilà! I have found Rochioli Pinot Noir."

He unfolded a filthy photocopied sheet on the bar and made me read it. Sure enough, it was a French tasting note for the very wine we were drinking:

Robe grenat foncé, bordé d'orange. Nez direct et séduisant, débordant de notes florales, de pain d'épices, de cacao, de cerises confites. Bouche sphérique, sexy, charnue, au boisé de haut niveau. Veloutés, les tannins s'enroulent autour des arômes de fruits et de terres humides, longueur épatante.

Translation: Dark purple robe, bordered with orange. A direct and seductive nose overflowing with floral notes, gingerbread, cocoa, candied cherries. A mouth which is spherical, sexy, fleshy, with refined wood. Velvety, tannins flowing around aromas of fruits and moist earth, astonishing length.

He tapped the photocopy and winked.

"Not bad, eh?"

" 'Spherical mouth'? Is that French?"

He sipped and rolled his eyes. Well, the papers didn't lie, did they? If they said it had a spherical mouth, then it had a spherical mouth. He for one was prepared to believe that it had a spherical mouth. Didn't it have a spherical, sexy mouth?

Disconcerted, I tried again. Surely these lyrical tasting notes could not be entirely delusional? But try as I might, I could not find anything specifically spherical, let alone sexy, in my glass. As for the cocoa, that was also a no-show, as was the gingerbread and the moist earth. Candied cherries, however, there were.

"Yes, floral notes," the visitor was saying, half closing his eyes and appearing to swoon into a state of Port Royal ecstasy. "Floral notes, floral notes . . ."

But which flowers?

I have a fondness for sententious people. There is something weirdly charming and seductively vulnerable, something all too human, about the sententious. They are trying to establish some higher truth. And they are only sententious because they are out of their depth. But then, did I not always feel out of my own depth with wine drinkers? And did not my own pronouncements on this subject also have a willy-nilly sententiousness which I could never escape? So I rather liked this Delgado (whoever he was) for his hopeless sententiousness, which was also that of the French, which always sounds dated and provincial to American ears, but which is therefore all the more endearing. Floral notes, floral notes, he kept repeating, as if they were ringing in our ears. Why *notes*? Is wine a form of music?

I decided to prick this balloon at once.

"To tell the truth, Maurice," I said, "I can't taste any floral notes whatsoever. Nor any gingerbread, nor any moist earth nor cocoa. I can taste a bit of candied cherries, but is that a good thing, I ask you? Don't candied cherries belong in cocktails?"

Maurice's face dropped and he looked a bit put out. He cocked his head back and forth—okay, I'll think about it—and returned his gnarled red nose to his glass. Inhalation, knitted brows. Jesus, it said in the notes there were floral notes. And if we couldn't find them that was certainly our fault. But then again, maybe he had been a little too effusive, a little too—how shall we say?—pro-

American? He had thought to flatter a local. And now the local might be prepared to confirm his true unspoken prejudices. So his eyes narrowed. Was it safe? We were alone, and moreover chatting in French. No one would overhear us.

He refolded the photocopy and tucked it away.

"Well, Laurent, I see your point. I didn't want to say it straight out. Yes, I'm prepared to assert that there are floral notes. But it's a little *flat* after all, isn't it? I didn't say that I found it sexy."

"A sexy wine?"

"Oh I've had a sexy wine or two. The wife and I like a sexy wine on Saturday night. Especially on vacation. But this is not a sexy wine, is it?"

"If wine is sex," I said, "this is yoga."

"Yoga? You're saying it's like yoga?" He swirled, sniffed. "I'm not sure I get you there. You mean athletic?"

"Virtuous. Unsexy."

He suddenly laughed viciously. "Ah, you mean American!"

Suddenly a psychological lode was opened up. We were on familiar territory: Americans and sex. If wine was sexy, and American wine unsexy, then we could now talk about how Americans did not have sex. Americans did not have sex just as they did not have culture. Oh, they were fabulous people, of course, *formidable*. Excellent engineers and software designers. But sex, love, sensuality, theater, state-run TV, wine . . . well, there they came unstuck.

He leaned over, man to man.

"In all the time I have been here," he whispered, "I have not seen a single sexy woman. What do you *do*?"

I shrugged. I said traveled a lot.

"We may be fucked up," he added, "but at least we have women. The women here are like nonfat yogurts."

This was an alarming direction for the conversation, and I wearily tried to steer it back to wine.

"Just as this wine is a kind of nonfat wine," I offered.

"Ah, nonfat!" he cried with extraordinary energy. "Everything here is nonfat. It is why my wife has diarrhea. We cannot find any normal yogurt. Always this nonfat. Nonfat yogurt, nonfat women, nonfat wine. Of course, we are speaking metaphorically. Actually, they are very fat."

I stared at him blankly.

He had now come 180 degrees from his original position. Perhaps we all have this chameleon instinct in us, a gift for self-prostitution, and at a given moment we will put away our photocopied received opinions and utter our real prejudices (which of course are also received opinions). For this reason, I couldn't hold it against him. I much prefer the suggestible type to the implacable type.

Still, there was nothing "Russian River" about our Russian River wine, and I was now more curious than ever to see if I could nail down a spirit of place in a wine.

"But," Maurice offered at last, holding up his purple-robed glass of gingerbread tones, "at least it's definitely Californian!"

I thought of Samuel Butler's utopian Victorian novel *Erewhon*. I had loved that word when I was a child, *Erewhon*. Was it a lost Indian tribe like the Mohicans? It was a long time before I realized that it was merely the word "nowhere" spelled backward, or almost. That was Utopia: nowhere backward. So I would have liked to say to an uncomprehending Maurice, "You know, Maurice, this is an Erewhon wine, candied cherries or no candied cherries."

Perhaps I simply didn't know anything about the land it was from. That, alas, was equally possible.

We clinked glasses and I bought him another round of the Rocchioli.

"Does it always rain here?" he asked dismally.

If there was one place in California where I thought I might be able to find a kind of "somewhereness," it would not necessarily be here in Sonoma or Napa but in the Santa Cruz Mountains, which rise west of Palo Alto and Silicon Valley, an hour south of San Francisco. The Santa Cruz Mountains: the most austere of the California wine regions, the highest and coldest, the most endowed, so it is often said, with terroir. It is in and around Santa Cruz that some of the brightest minds in American wine brood on these very questions.

At the end of the nineteenth century, the Santa Cruz Mountains were explored by European wine prospectors like the Frenchman Paul Masson, who established a vineyard called La Cresta high up on the slopes overlooking what was then called the Santa Clara Valley—a place of prune, walnut, and apricot farms. In the 1880s Masson brought over bottling equipment from France. He built a rustic mountain "château" and made a national name for himself with renowned champagne. The Belle Epoque vaudeville star Anna Held famously took a bath in it at San Francisco's Palace Hotel.

Masson was a curious character. Highly cultured, with connections to San Francisco's high society and San Jose's exclusive Saint Claire Club, where he was quaintly known as the Duc de Cognac, Masson was a hedonistic gentleman farmer in a place where such exotics were virtually unknown. He was not at all like the loggers who made an arduous living felling the coastal redwoods. His was a self-created European microcosm of pianos, carriages, champagne cellars, and stand-fall collars, all of it erected on a wild mountaintop populated by loggers.

Masson was eventually ruined by Prohibition. In the dark 1920s, however, many of his Italian field workers made a handsome living bootlegging a strange "wine" which they made by adding the intensely dark juice of the local Salvador grape to water and mixing it with sugar. Eventually, the Salvador became the grape of choice for bootleggers nationwide and surreptitious Salvador trade sprang up between Santa Cruz and generous East Coast buyers. An outmoded Masson was scandalized.

Masson's adopted heir was the burly, volcanic Martin Ray, who took over the Paul Masson Champagne Company in the 1930s. Ray, the son of a fire-breathing prohibitionist minister, passed much of his youth on the Masson vineyards and took to wine making himself, building up such a reputation for himself that by the forties he had become the de facto prince of American wine. "Rusty Ray," as he was known, also became a kind of human synonym for the mountains themselves. "Rusty Ray country," John Steinbeck called it. But his name is largely forgotten now. I came across this telling passage in a biography of Ray written by his widow, Eleanor:

> In accounts of winemaking history Martin Ray's name isn't mentioned much nowadays, and sometimes not at all. During his lifetime, by refusing to play the necessary politics and public relations of the highly competitive trade, he alienated various influential wine writers and wine associations. They considered him obstreperous, difficult, arcane, a zealot in his fight for authentic varietals—against the phony wines supposedly containing at least the minimum of the variety so labelled. . . . He himself provoked controversies in his continuous, relentless war against the bogus "varietals" that damaged California's prestige on the world market.

Ray instigated the first American "wine revolution" by producing and marketing the first 100 percent varietal wines. (As recently as 1962, the *New York Times* could write that "Alfred Knopf, the publisher, has bottles of a fine California wine from the Martin Ray vineyard to show visiting Englishmen and Frenchmen what can be produced in this country.") He was also an outsider, a Jeremiah, a mountaintop moralist and iconoclast.

But what did he moralize against? Against philistinism, against impure wine posing as pure? It isn't entirely clear until one remembers that in the 1940s American "Pinot Noir" contained no Pinot whatsoever. Like Masson, however, Ray was a "lusty bon vivant."

Guests to La Cresta included the likes of Prince Vasili and Princess Natasha Romanoff. Jeremiah liked to mix with the champagne crowd.

As I drove up to his house, I wondered whether people, or their ghosts, lend themselves to the spirit of place. Outsiders, iconoclasts: do Masson and Ray, who died in 1976, still suffuse Table Mountain, where they lived? The estate descended from Masson's and Ray's old holdings, the Mount Eden Vineyard, is today an elite American domain.

Like Chalone, it sprawls over the top of the mountain, at the end of a spiraling mountain trail under the peaks of the Chaine d'Or around it. Rows of vines tilt over the steep gradients garnished with blue milk cartons to scare off rabbits. And at its center still stands the slightly grandiose chalet-style house where Martin Ray lived as the reigning prince of American wine half a century ago. At the top I looked back down at Silicon Valley, half submerged in pink light and fog: the ghastly stucco mansions which litter the foothills had fallen away and a dense Californian bush of toyon and madrone trees had taken over. From here El Camino Real—the old Spanish silver route—was almost silent. Its tributary malls, computer complexes, and parking lots appeared as inoffensive as the plastic hotels on a Monopoly board. Intel, Apple, Silicon Graphics: they had all receded into a delicate and transforming fog.

Since 1981 Mount Eden has been run by Ellie and Geoffrey McPhearson, self-confessed ex-hippies who—much to their own surprise—have garnered eloquent accolades from none other than Robert Parker. This alone has made them successful. Ellie was there by herself, a tallish blonde with more crisp elegance about her than most ex-hippies, and as she showed me around Ray's woody house, which still exuded the handsome chic of the 1940s, she told me that coincidentally enough, Mount Eden had once been owned by the Chalone Group.

"California," I had to admit, "really is a small place."

"Very small. Dick Graf was the wine consultant here back in 1972. But by 1981 this place was a wreck. The cellars were in ruins."

No equipment, no lab: it was perfect for the McPhearsons.

We went into the tasting room and Ellie disappeared in search of some bottles to drink. The walls were decorated with framed poems of the Native American–Earth Summit variety—

> *as i walk across the mountain*
> *i am on sacred ground, on holy ground*

Ellie came back with a '97 Pinot made from the last of the old Martin Ray vines, a Cabernet, and a 2000 Chardonnay which has won accolades from Robert Parker. Mount Eden is known more for its Chardonnays than anything else, and these have brought the winery much of its kudos. "Almost impossible to distinguish from some of France's grand cru white burgundies," Parker declared of the 1998 Reserve. "The single finest Chardonnay made in California," the *Spectator*'s Matt Kramer has pronounced.

I asked Ellie about the soil here. It was "Franciscan shale," she explained, with shallow topsoil.

Did it have terroir?

"You tell me," she said.

The wines, I thought, were lively, very pure, very clean. It struck me that this, in essence, was what the conscientious American wine maker does best: a clean, honest purity of fruit. I thought to myself, "mountain wine." But sacred ground? One obviously couldn't expect that kind of thing to be in a wine. The Cabernet was lean, dry; not a Napa wine. Did she agree?

"Well, we came from Burgundy. That was our reference. And many wine makers in California have never actually drunk a Burgundy, incredibly enough. Their palates are entirely structured around American wine."

"Is there an American terroir?" I asked.

"Most Californians would be insulted even at the question. But actually it's a good question, a painful question. There's not as much American terroir as people here think. It's rarer than we think. I think we have it here because Masson and Ray *brought it into being*."

"So terroir expresses the legacy of fathers and sons—"

"Or daughters."

"Naturally. Daughters too."

We laughed. There aren't many women wine makers in the world.

But is it mystical to say that you can feel such things in a drink? The thought and feeling which passes between father and son, even symbolic fathers and sons like Masson and Ray?

Ellie was unsure. "It *is* a little mystical."

But then she caught me glancing at the walls.

"Then again," she said, "why not be mystical?"

I confessed that I liked being mystical occasionally. "Besides," I said, "it isn't *that* mystical."

In fact, it made sense. Wasn't that the ultimate meaning of that much-derided word "tradition"? A cultural telepathy.

We walked for a bit in the vines. It was strange being so distinctly above the fog line. Here you were confronted with the collision of two worlds: Silicon Valley and the older wine landscape. I asked if they were now feeding off each other.

"Well," Ellie advised, "just go down to Palo Alto and check out Draeger's supermarket. It's quite an education."

Unsure what this might mean, I swept down to Palo Alto for an hour and made my way to Draeger's, the elite supermarket of the town. Not far from the frozen foods section stand $900 bottles of Château Latour and fashionable $600 Le Pin, a cult Bordeaux, looking almost innocent on their shelves, their labels a little wan and sickly like the statues at Madame Tussaud's. It's in places like this, amid a rummaging for cabbages and chocolate bars, that the uneasy fraudulence of wine strikes you most forcefully. Do valley executives really sweep through here with carts of frozen pizza and piles of Château Latour 1990? Nothing else in the supermarket aisle, not even at Draeger's, has its price determined by speculation and the impregnable charisma of fame. Thus, unsurprisingly, these bottles looked a little guilty, as if they were about to be unmasked by a passing Mexican housewife. The whole wine system is nervous about the prospect of such a defrocking because it knows that its reputation, like its profits, hangs by a slender thread. To pay six hundred dollars for a bottle of Le Pin is little more than an act of superstitious faith. The people at Le Pin know this, and so do the importers, distributers, and retailers who place it on the shelf at Draeger's. But what is in the heart of the tremulous, danger-tempted, overpaid, but unsure drinker who makes his way toward it and lifts it with a shaking hand from its niche?

On the Skyliner highway, flashing past Alice's Restaurant, I was now on my way to Ridge, another cloud-bound vineyard high in the sky and the lofty queen of American wineries. I was met when I arrived by Paul Draper, Ridge's star wine maker, a quiet gentlemanly vigneron who has long presided over America's most aristocratic Zinfandels and Cabernets. He was dapper in pressed denims and a sleekly clipped white beard. We walked out across the parking lot to the back of the winery, where an unforgiving wind whipped across the slopes of vines.

"Cool climate, poor soils," he began as we wrapped ourselves in scarves. "Not at all what you think of as California. And we have limestone." He made a rather princely gesture toward this shivering land. "Limestone equals terroir!"

Ridge is descended from the labors of yet another errant European dandy—in this case, a doctor named Perrone who migrated from the Italian North to San Francisco and then trekked into the hills looking for shelves of limestone. The cellars were carved out of this rock in 1886, a place of soft troglodytic gloom in the depths of which an air pump emitted a slow *pop-pop-pop*. By now I was getting used to cellars and was even beginning to relish them: they are a mixture of Gollum's cave and what I imagine to be the gadgetry in the bunkers of the Maginot line. The air is humid and menacingly lulling, with a cool whiff of fungus.

Draper took out his pipette and began stooping carefully among the lines of Radoux and Mendocino barrels, occasionally plucking out the corks and dipping the pipette deep into the barrel to suck out a sample for us to swill. When the Sterling men described their array of oak barrels as a spice cabinet, I had been skeptical; most cooks are profligate with their spices. But Draper clearly loved to tinker and explore with the different angles of oak. He told me that he appreciated the clean white oak of the Appalachians: it was unique. Bordeaux *barriques* were only six gallons bigger than American ones but double the price—still, they too had a quality which couldn't be gained by any other means.

Straight from the barrel, a raw young wine is difficult to taste. One has to imagine its deeper potential, Draper said, rather than simply wincing at its crude sourness. But the diverse spectrum of oak tones could be felt even in the 2000s. I had the feeling of being inside a scrupulously controlled and private experiment, for Ridge doesn't work with outside vineyards and uses only its own grapes. Everything is grown on its own properties, whether Monte Bello, Lytton Springs, or Geyserville.

"Do you taste the differences?" Draper asked. "Not just the soils, but also the oaks. It's like hitting baseballs at different angles."

We were gurgling some juvenile Zinfandel. Inevitably, perhaps, the question of elitism came up, for Ridge is known for making very expensive wines. A bottle of Monte Bello Cabernet can go for $130.

"I would say," Draper began, "that wine has to express a place or it's basically just grape juice. How do we do that cheaply? There's no way. We depend on people who can taste, I mean really taste."

I said that this probably excluded me. He smiled sweetly.

"I'm sure you can taste," he said.

What could I taste in his Zinfandel? The overripe prunes and copious glycerin which I had slyly looked up in the *Wine Buyer's Guide* beforehand? Plums and cherries? Draper had dropped me a little cue to say something, a passing thought on his wine perhaps, but I was tongue-tied. Yet it seemed to me that I *was* beginning to sense something about Californian wine now. I thought, for one thing, that I could draw a line connecting the Santa Cruz wines. I didn't have the vocabulary to express the exact quality which linked them, but the connection was nevertheless there, even if it remained difficult to articulate.

"The enemy of place is the wine maker as star," Draper continued, "as an Emeril-type figure. The wine maker who 'creates' miracles in his little lab. And the other enemy is the consumer consensus model—Gallo, say, or the Australians. Do you really feel a spirit of place in Australian wines? Of course not. You could manufacture most of them on Mars. Wines are like children, you can't really impose yourself on them. They have a stubborn inner warp. You can let them speak, that's all."

So there is such a thing as a high-altitude wine, a mountain wine?

"Naturally there is. Just as mountain people differ in temperament from valley people. Because of our cold nights here in Monte Bello the wines have very high acidity. Then there are other imponderables."

I said, finally, that if I could really taste anything it was *that*.

"Not the smoked prunes?"

"No smoked prunes."

In the folksy, wood-bound upstairs tasting room, we set to consuming a few bottles. A 1999 Geyserville Zinfandel, a 1993 Monte Bello Cabernet, and a 1999 Chardonnay, a surprisingly dry version of an otherwise overworked genre, with no trace of pineapple or mango. It had been made with indigenous yeasts and American oak.

Then we tasted a 1997 Cabernet which was too rich and a 1998 which was not. Draper was now relaxed. He had been a philosophy major at Stanford and there is still something of the quaffing don about him. We fell to talking about the powerful Piedmont producer Angelo Gaja, a man whose wines garner all imaginable praise (and price tags). Draper is a friend of Gaja and admires him; but at the same time he sees in him exactly the tensions I had felt myself in Antonio Terni, and indeed in Italy in general.

"I tasted a Gaja wine recently mixed from Nebbiolo and Cabernet. And I have to say, I was stunned, but not in the delightful way. It seemed to be a monster of a thing, a Parker wine if ever I've tasted one, a Beringer almost! And I respect Gaja enormously. But I thought, what the hell is *this*?"

"And he's getting three hundred dollars a bottle, isn't he?"

"He certainly is. It's the tragedy of Bordeaux too. Look at the really great Bordeaux from way back. The greatest wine I've ever drunk was an 1864 Lafite. The most complex and perfect I've ever tasted. Now they're making juicier and fatter wines with every year."

"But isn't that democracy? People drink what they want?"

"Oh, you can't argue with that, can you?" He looked over with ineffable irony and stroked the white beard. "I just want to say that I think it's a tragedy that the French themselves are leading the charge toward these crasser wines."

I asked him if he thought the Santa Cruz Mountains were the future of American wine, of American terroir.

"More than Napa? Oh, for sure. Not that we've found it yet necessarily, because it's trial and error over centuries that settles these questions. But I suppose you should go to Bonny Doon and talk to Randall Grahm about that. He'll tell you that American terroir is a myth. Of course, he's in downtown Santa Cruz, where there isn't any terroir at all." Draper smiled like a master wizard who has just jinxed a friendly rival. "Randall is an urban creature, you see. But he *is* the resident iconoclast of Santa Cruz. One should always have an iconoclast somewhere in the cupboard."

Perhaps it's the air of seaside towns. Santa Cruz is half left-wing college town, half raffish boardwalk, a cross between Wellesley and Coney Island. A drive down Mission Street takes you past sullen Taco Bells and Pleasure Pizzas, a trailer beach with the sign *No Dogs, No Refunds*. A huge roller coaster winds along the shore, blocking it from view so that town and ocean are artfully alienated from each other. An estuary, low hills, beach equipment, empty sidewalks under the rain: they call it Silicon Beach because of the nearby concentration of digital genius. I ambled past a giant Neptune's Kingdom entertainment complex complete with wet doormen, casinos, and bike storage lockers; the closed tamale joints of Beach Street; and motels with names like Capri and Peter Pan, *In-Room Jacuzzi Included*. A little farther on, pastel Victorian mansions line the bluffs, shaded by bedraggled palms.

Bonny Doon itself is not situated on any wine land; it's an urban winery squeezed into Santa Cruz's industrial downtown at the end of a cul-de-sac called Ingall Street. Around it lie vegetable packing sheds devoted to the Brussels sprouts business and an old railroad line with quays giving onto warehouse bays.

Randall Grahm is perhaps the single most easily identifiable figure in American wine. Over the years, he has created his own persona: the enfant terrible of a staid business, the flagellator of lax minds, the Puck of the American branch of Vinimundo. Bonny Doon is famed for its coruscating and relentlessly punning newsletters which send up the world of wine with freewheeling abandon. Advertising his Rieslings, for example, Grahm sets out on a small jeremiad mixed with a dash of despair. It is called "The Riesling Asylum":

We can view this little corner of Himmelreich as a place for asylum seekers, a refuge from the cold and oppressive winds of conformity. Yes, give us your tired, your huddled masses of corpulent/oaky/buttery Chardonnay yearning to breathe freely in a Riedel riesling decanter.

The Asylum also serves as the official meeting spot for the Santa Cruz chapter of the NRA, the National Riesling Association—an ancient and mysterious order of international terroirists dedicated to the advancement of killer grape varietals.

Grahm makes serious experimental wines by blending both rare and common varietals from all over the world and decking them out with splendid names like Cigare Volant (Flying Cigar), Critique of Pure Riesling, and Big House Red, a sort of parody of the glut of crass wine names now visible in bars all over the world: Big Fat Bastard Chardonnay or the Old Tart sold by Sainsbury's in Britain. But for Grahm it's not an attempt to get cozy with Crocodile Dundee consumers, it's more an argument that American wine takes itself too seriously—too seriously for wine which is usually, in his words, "simple, fun and one-dimensional." Bonny Doon isn't a traditional winery at all; it's more like a hiply earnest blending laboratory.

Grahm is a lanky, bespectacled figure with an extravagant ponytail fastened with glinty hippy beads. A sixties figure, all the way.

"Welcome," he bowed, "to glorious *Ingellstrasse.*"

We sauntered down the seemingly abandoned rail tracks and over to a hidden Chinese restaurant called O'Mei, which turned out to be one of the best in Santa Cruz. By the time we got there we had covered the early part of his life. Born in Los Angeles, he had taken philosophy at UC Santa Cruz, a "paradise" back in the early seventies. His mentor had been Norman O. Brown, the great philosopher of psychoanalysis then resident on campus. I said that I was a fervent admirer of Norman O. Brown, and Grahm looked suddenly relieved. He replied that he and Norman had often gone for long walks together. He himself had specialized in Heidegger. There our common admirations ended. Hadn't old Heidegger and his pet

concept of *Dasein*, or Being-in-the-World, been a bit unbearable?
I asked.

"Well I suppose he was," he said. "I was certainly drowning in
Dasein."

"I have trouble with it myself."

"—so I decided to turn to wine instead."

"That's what I do when I get bogged down with *Dasein*."

"So I got a job in a wine store in Beverly Hills."

This seemed like the perfect remedy for a doctoral thesis on Heidegger, and Grahm thought so too.

"It turned my life around. One minute I was drowning in *Dasein*, the next I was drinking free bottles of Comte de Vogue. It was
the moment of initiation."

In Beverly Hills, Grahm quickly noticed how Hollywood stars
bought and consumed wine. The cash flow was stupendous. Grahm
graduated to salesman and some of the stupendous flow began to
bend his way. After hours, the owner cracked open bottles of La
Mission Haut-Brion, Château Palmer, and Lafite. The young salesman recently liberated from *Dasein* decided that, since he could
never afford to buy the stuff, he would have to make it himself.

"So I went to Davis, God help me. But I really dug it. It was my
awakening. And look at me, I'm Jewish. I mean—a Jewish farmer?
A Jewish wine maker? It's a Woody Allen farce. I used to prune in
the fields in a suit and tie. I'm a Jewish urban cat, but those pruning
shears, man, oh, they were incredible, it was like sculpting, it was
meditative . . . pruning vines is like making a work of art. It's intellectual, satisfying. Even a Jewish farmer could understand that."

"But wasn't Davis," I asked, "worse than *Dasein*?"

"Davis *is* *Dasein*. Except it was also so provincial, so smug,
parochial. Oh those poor froggies in their *filthy* cellars! From people
who'd never drunk *anything*."

We were now seated and drinking a bottle of Flying Cigar from
the wine list. And very jolly too.

"They'd never traveled anywhere. Not *anywhere*. They told us that terroir doesn't exist, that cleanliness is next to godliness, and so forth. But you can't blame Americans for all this crap in the end. Let me explain why."

By now I had already heard plenty about New World and Old World palates. Grahm stated flatly that New Worlders could no longer drink European wines. The bifurcation was total. People drank one or the other. But it was a strange tale in the end, because this so-called New World palate had actually come about for purely economic reasons.

"Terroir wines," he explained, holding a dumpling suspended in midair on a fork and fixing me with surprisingly prophetic and un-mad eyes, "are just too expensive if you're starting from scratch, as we Americans were and are. Helen Turley tells me that it costs $60,000 an acre to make a terroir wine. Low yields, withholding water—it's ruinous for us, impossible. And you're spending all this money with no certain outcome, on land with no history. We didn't inherit thousands of ancient vineyards like the French. So the fruity American style was created by this dilemma—how do you make money?"

The dumpling vanished and I shrugged. "How do you?"

"Time is our enemy here. Italians don't think about corporate restructuring while eating lunch, do they?"

I said I didn't really know what Italians thought about at lunch. Their second homes?

"It's actually a natural physiological disposition to like food that is ripe. It's natural. Our tongue naturally goes, like, Ripe and sweet! Yummy!" This, he added, was why Californian wines regularly won competitions. "But then, why do *we* not like these yummy wines? Because we can't find any mineral depth in them. Now, the mineral depth of European wine doesn't show up in chemical analyses. Remember, six pounds of fruit per vine in Europe, thirty pounds in California. What does that mean? More minerality in European fruit. Less quintessence of fruit, more extracted mineral. But it's not scientifically provable. It's only on your tongue!"

An American wine, in other words, is all fruit, alcohol, and oak. There is usually little else. It stands to reason that what we call place is also a matter of hidden minerals. But was this taste for minerality over ripeness therefore a biological perversity?

"Shit, isn't civilization a biological perversity?"

"You mean it's getting away from what we *like*?"

Loud laughter.

"No, no. I'm not one of these purists who insist that it's only authentic, you know, real, if it tastes rank and ugly. Not at all. Perversity should be delicious, no?"

I mentioned Paul Draper's comments about Gaja and Grahm rolled his eyes.

"Yeah, he's 'compromised.' But Gaja's wines—excuse me, they're delicious. Yummy. So perhaps I've been corrupted too?"

But how did he sell wine to Americans who wanted yummy-yummy and no touchy minerals?

"*Ach so*, big neurotic problem. Well, we kind of fall between two stools. We're bridging the gap. We're in between. We *have* to be. We try to swing both ways. After all, we have no choice. We're terroirists." He pronounced the word as "terrorist." "That is, we are not working with any real terroir."

"Why not?"

Grahm sighed: the big cosmic question. How could he put it simply over lunch?

"Paul Draper is always considered the apostle of terroir. Its high priest in America. I'm his opposite because I'm the agnostic of terroir. I'm like the agnostic who's agonized by the absence of God. I *wish* we had terroir. But we don't. I'd like to make a terroir wine before I die. But who knows if I will. I think Americans babbling about their terroir is—as yet—utter bullshit. It's marketing psychobabble, okay? So I—I go another way. I'm doing what Americans should be doing. I'm experimenting, I'm free to make stuff up, I'm using *other* elements. I'm playing with fruit. Why not?"

Was that more resonant with the American personality—pushy, booming, irresistible?

"It's not that. It's that we have no choice. What else is interesting? If we don't have terroir let's cast around and see what else we can do. Our great advantage is our freedom from tradition. In a way, this very *lack* of terroir. We could do something funky with that!"

I told Grahm that I used to drink his icewine at Temple Bar on the Bowery in New York City, and that I had many memories of miserable winter nights redeemed by that single chilly glass of Bonny Doon on the bar. We ambled back to the winery through chilly sunshine, sifting through groups of Mexican workers. The winery itself seemed empty; we strolled past rows of immense Vicard vats coated with white insulation, stopping for a moment at a spigot which disgorged a few mouthfuls of rawly foaming bright purple Grenache (Cigare, for example, is one-third Grenache mixed with Syrah). Past a few more Definox taps, we came to vats of Sangiovese, Malvasia, Barbera: Grahm loves Italian varietals and mixes them like dabs of paint on a large palette. Oxygen pumps and tubes lay strewn about—Grahm loves the technique known as *micro-bullage*, or microfermentation, whereby extra oxygen is pumped into the liquid during fermentation to hasten the chemical conversion of hard green tannins in the grape pips into softer, riper ones. The technique was invented by Patrick Ducorneau in the Madiran region of southwestern France, where the powerfully hard wines are often difficult to sell. *Micro-bullage* imitates a long aging—that is, the natural process whereby the elements in wine, such as tannins, alcohol, and acid, settle down and meld over time, gradually forming something balanced and equilibrious. *Micro-bullage* artificially hurries this process along, giving a facile smoothness which only great age usually confers. The technique is a shortcut, in other words, and has been called a dark art, a Faustian bargain. But why is it important to Randall Grahm in Santa Cruz?

"Because—how can I say this?—because it enables me to sort of *imitate* the spirit of place. It extracts a sort of pseudo-terroir out of the grape. Because, you see, we can get everything out of the grape, everything, even if we don't have deep minerality from a complex soil. With a chemically balanced grape, we get a lovely wine—but it's a wine that has no real place. It's a grape-driven wine. And that's the American vice, normally. But we turn it into our virtue."

"So your wines are agnostic wines. Wines *pining for terroir?*"

"Yes. I mean, so long as they're genuinely pining they're not a complete fake."

Inside the vats are shelves where the lees sit at a higher-than-usual elevation, so that they can mingle more saucily with the juice as it ferments. This makes for a more soy-salty kind of wine, because the bitter lees impart more of their acidic flavors, thereby bending the wine gently away from the simpler sweetness of the fruit's sugar. Meanwhile, Grahm explained how he had just found a fantastic little plot of land near a town called Tracy at the head of the Central Valley, a true mini-terroir which no one had yet discovered.

"So you see, I'm still looking for the Holy Grail of terroir! I'm still looking for that special *place.*"

We went back into the office, where a disco ball hung from the ceiling, sparkling with mad seventies lechery. Grahm's fingers were now stained purple from his excursions with the pipette and his endless dipping into puncheons. For some reason we were in a rather high mood—perhaps it was the foamy Grenache, as pure and powerful as something brewed in a primitive vat in ancient Corinth. And now in this altered state I began to see unmistakably Dionysian characteristics in the man dancing madly around me playfully wielding a baseball bat as he took swings at imaginary balls lobbed at him by his (half-terrified?) staff. There was a fierce glee, a light-footedness, an I-don't-give-a-shit glitter in the eyes. I realized that he must have made a formidable Beverly Hills salesman for crates of Château Palmer. Who could have said no? *That Cab from Tracy,* he cried, *it's whacked out, man, it's totally whacked out!*

As he saw me out I asked him if he was just a Francophile.

"Francophile? Well, the French are so damn provincial. They're so absurd. But at the same time . . ."

"They have a sense of place, don't they?"

"It won't save them," Grahm said grimly. "The explosion wines are coming."

"But still—"

"Yeah, yeah. And no it's not some stupid lefty I-hate-America thing. It's a serious question, dead serious. Are you going to France soon?"

I said I was off to confront my own long-festering Francophilia, which was simultaneously a festering Francophobia.

"Peculiar," Grahm said. He put down the baseball bat and shook my hand. "What," he mused on, "if wine was the last thing that the French do really well? I mean, better than anyone else. What would the French do to fuck it up?"

I said that was anyone's guess. That was why I was going to journey through France alone for a while. I told him that I had lived there for nine years.

"Ah! So you're revisiting the scene of the crime, so to speak?"

"So to speak."

As I pulled away from the Bonny Doon parking lot, I looked in through the brightly lit office window and caught a brief glimpse of Randall Grahm with his stained hands executing a perfect John Travolta move under the shimmering disco ball. Dionysus on Silicon Beach.

An Idea of France

❧

Taste is the feminine of genius.   —Lord Edward Fitzgerald

When I was destitute in Paris, I had a favorite walk. Getting up in the middle of the afternoon in a small room on the rue Saint-Denis, I set out across the city. I made my way to one of the last remaining covered *passages*, those glass-roofed remnants of the fantastical enclosed shopping malls of the nineteenth century. In the depth of the Passage Vivienne I went to Legrand et Fils, Wine Merchants since 1822, to stare through the windows at magnums of Échézeaux and Gosset champagne. Standard-sized bottles were laid on their backs in little fluffs of straw or in pale wood coffins next to large red coffee-table books with titles like *Le nez du vin* and *Le nez du miel*, as if everything in the edible universe had its own specific "nose" and its own coffee-table manual.

As for the instruments of wine expertise, they were laid out like the hardware in a priest's supply outlet, if priests have such things as supply outlets, or the fantastical dissection tools in David Cronenberg's *Dead Ringers*. Silver screws with inlaid handles, ice buckets, decanters, funnels, thermometers, humidity controllers, cellar books, fresh editions of *Le nez du Bordeaux*, cognac glasses, polyresin bottle holders in the form of little leprechauns wielding bottles four times their size, and easy-to-install wine bars.

In the display windows of Legrand et Fils pleasure is organized, analyzed, and equipped. Recently I found the following declaration for a brand of wineglass known as Les Impitoyables, or The Pitiless Ones:

Les Impitoyables
Les multiplicateurs du Plaisir!

What other people can imagine pleasure being multiplied, as if it were a mathematical quantity? In what other country is pleasure so aristocratically organized?

My initiation into this epicurean system was facilitated by a pupil of mine at a language school on the rue de la Paix. This would be my first experience with what is called a man of the world. Monsieur Expert-Besançon was a raffish fifty-year-old silk merchant with a mistress in the capital and an appetite for snappy lunches at Beauvilliers.

A man of the world knows certain things: the wide and treacherous domain of business and politics; how to choose a shirt; how to choose cars, lunch venues, flowers—and of course *wine*. The desire to share is what made M. Expert-Besançon a gentleman and a man of the world rather than a mere connoisseur. He had decided to imprint something of himself upon me, namely (as he put it) his *theory of wine*. M. Expert-Besançon liked to talk about Jean Monnet and General de Gaulle, both of whom he admired. What is a good European, he would ask? A man who believes in a *visionary structure*. He arranged for the manager to show us around Bofinger, especially the upper floor, famous for its pictorial *boiserie*. We stood before the mysterious image of three ruined towers on top of a hill, the Alsatian castle known as Les Trois Châteaux d'Eguisheim, while the manager gravely pointed his finger at it and said, "As you can see, they are a kind of sundial for the villagers below!" M. Expert-

Besançon steered me around the paneled Second Empire rooms with their great silver serving dishes standing empty under chandeliers. The inlay of the walls showed scenes of the four continents, monochrome glimpses of aqueducts and pagodas. Downstairs, we sat under the oval glass ceiling bordered with wisps of purple glass convolvulus.

Expert-Besançon showed me how to handle the different-sized glasses, an etiquette which I still haven't quite mastered, and how to manipulate different forks, tongs, and strangely shaped knives. Occasionally he told a smutty joke, but in so severe a manner that I was never sure if it was a smutty joke or not. He demonstrated the opening of oysters and the slicing of sea urchins.

"Did you know," he would say, his eyes opening like a predatory creature of some kind, "that 30 percent of French women have confessed to peeing in a swimming pool? And that 17 percent of Communists are left-handed? What kind of champagne do you like?"

Flummoxed, I blurted out the only champagne brand I knew: Mumm.

Expert-Besançon took on the look of a malevolent wizard. His fingers rose upward.

"*Mumm?* Did you say *Mumm?*"

"Mumm." I remember blushing violently.

"You cannot mean Mumm," he went on. "We'll hear no more about Mumm." There was silence. "The champagne to drink is Krug. I have a *1959* at my place," he hissed. "It's for my daughter's wedding."

That secretive half-mad look. It was this look which was intriguing rather than the inside information on which champagne to drink. The connoisseur is always a little potty, but in the case of wine the connoisseur is more than eccentric: he is consumed by a ferocious pedantry.

"The *1959*," he repeated, and I began to think that maybe it was a one-word smutty joke. "The greatest year of all, in my humble opinion."

"Really?"

"Absolutely." His face suddenly went red. "It has beautifully *dimmed* already."

There has always been a tension in the American experience of France. Jefferson had it when he lived in Paris. Deep down, he worshiped everything French; he of course famously loved and collected French wine. But at the same time he was always writing pathologically unhinged letters home in which he ranted and raved against everything French. Against, that is, the spirit of aristocracy which infuriatingly was somehow in the Parisian air, like a toxic pollen.

Needless to say, what Jefferson treasured most in Bordeaux wines was their subtle artistocracy. Wine was no more a democratic drink in the 1780s than it is now. Jefferson paid serious money for his wine habit and urged comparably endowed Americans to do the same. But the denouncer of aristocracy could not extend such a denunciation into the nonmaterial dimension of taste, where aristocracy—the rule of *aristos*, the best—is inevitable. Intuitively, he sensed that wine would never be judged outside the aristocracy of taste, because if it were, its meaning would evaporate, just as poetry lost its meaning in the Soviet Union when it was judged according to its social usefulness rather than by its position in the glamorously imperious hierarchy of taste—a hierarchy which is as merciless and unforgiving as it is mysteriously spontaneous.

Nowhere does this tension emerge with greater clarity than in the complex persona of Robert Parker, Jr. After the ambassador himself, Parker is probably the most influential American in France today. And no one is more a Yank at King Arthur's Court than the man who has actually insured his wine-classifying nose for a million dollars. Whereas we have already talked about Robert Parker here and there, it is now time to look at this amazing person more closely—for Parker is perhaps the only American who is changing France's idea of herself, an idea that is naturally bound up with being the ultimate land of wine. That Robert Parker of Monkton, Maryland, now drives the market in Bordeaux's elite wines is for them a phenomenon of the highest perplexity.

Although there are signs that Parker's influence may be waning somewhat, and that the wine world is outgrowing his cheerful dictatorship, his reach is still impressive. British wine critic Jancis Robinson records the dismay of the novelist Julian Barnes when a wine he liked was panned by the great critic. Barnes was therefore confronted with the astonishing possibility that *he shouldn't like what he actually liked*. A crisis of faith in one's own tasting powers? "Clearly," Michael Steinberger has written, "this is not a normal critic-consumer relationship, but then wine unnerves many people."

But Parker is a paradox. At a recent Légion d'Honneur ceremony at the Élysée Palace, Parker was awarded France's highest civilian honor by President Jacques Chirac, the only wine critic ever so honored. In the splendid palace Parker stood stiffly at attention, a stocky fifty-something figure with bulldog features, and wept as Chirac pinned a medal to his chest. Parker later called it "an out-of-body experience." The citation called Parker the greatest ambassador of French wine in the world. But the reality is of course more irrational and fraught with all the neuroses outlined above. Who, then, is Robert Parker, Francophile extraordinaire, and why does he exist?

The most influential critic in the world today happens to be a critic of wine. He is not a snob or an obvious aesthete, as one might imagine, but an ordinary American, a burly, awkward, hardworking guy from the backcountry of northern

Maryland, about half a step removed from the farm. . . . he
has no formal training in wine.
　　　　—William Langewiesche, in the *Atlantic Monthly*,
　　　　　　　　　　　　　　　　　　　　December 2000

What I've brought is a democratic view. I don't give a shit
that your family goes back to pre-Revolution and you've
more wealth than I could imagine. If this wine's no good, I'm
gonna say so.　　　　　—Robert Parker, quoted in the above

Robert Parker was born in 1947, the son of a Maryland dairy
farmer. He grew up in the small town of Monkton, later studying
history and art history at the University of Maryland and then at-
tending the university's law school. After graduating in 1973, he
practiced law as an assistant general counsel for the Farm Credit
Banks of Baltimore. Wine might seem to be an unlikely career for a
stolid provincial farm lawyer, but in fact Parker seems to have been
something of a dreamer, an academic drifter not quite sure of what
he wanted to do with himself. In his spare time he was tippling.
　　A trip to France in 1967, following his wife-to-be on a scholar-
ship in Strasbourg, had accidentally propelled him out of Maryland
and into the back roads of Europe. Like most of his sixties peers, he
tumbled into wine by romantic accident—or out of boredom at the
prospect of returning to Baltimore and managing farm accounts.
But unlike the more sophisticated and worldly Gerald Asher zigzag-
ging along the wine routes in his sports car, Parker seems to have
lumbered from tourist cliché to tourist cliché with hayseed feverish-
ness: Latin Quarter hotels, frog's legs at sundown, battlefields. But
then came a *fateful* dinner, according to William Langewiesche, author of the *Atlantic Monthly* profile.
　　Parker was invited to the home of a Strasbourg doctor where,
unexpectedly, he successfully identified the principal components
of a Riesling as being scents of grapefruit and lemon. Epiphany!

"And Parker," declares his profiler, "is said to have understood at that moment that he had the talents of a prodigy." His modesty has never since deserted him. In a 2001 *Paris Match* interview, Parker mused: "It became apparent to me in the late sixties, when I began tasting wine, that I had a very sensitive sense of smell, as well as a precise palate. It became increasingly apparent in tastings with other like-minded wine enthusiasts, as I was able to focus and seemed to have an ability to grasp the texture and aromatics of a wine far more easily than many other subjects I have dealt with in my life."

What makes a critic a critic? Is it a physiological talent, a predisposition to sense things other people can't? Remarkably, Parker's reputation rests partly on certain purported properties of his own body. His palate is said to be equipped with a unique "cleft." The Cleft, as it is known, is (one imagines) a singular ravine over which the wine molecules play with happy freedom. One of the most unusual features of this remarkable anatomical eccentricity is its indefatigability. The Cleft never tires. By his own estimate Parker tastes approximately ten thousand wines every year and claims to be able to remember each one as if photographically. He will happily taste 125 cheaper wines a day, a number that falls to 75 a day for vintages of higher pedigree. The critic therefore is not just an intelligent man with a singular passion; he is a deformity of nature equipped with powers that you and I do not possess. Parker memorizes ten thousand wines every year and stores them in a cerebral filing cabinet whose intricacies are hardly subject to the skeptical probes of science. It's just a gift. And confronted with such an aptitude, we meekly throw in the towel. Who are we, deprived of a Cleft, to disagree with the pronouncements of such a thoroughly purposeful connoisseur?

Armed with an implacable palate, the young Parker leaped into the fray of the wine world—if such a sedate world could be said to be capable of frays. He began writing the *Wine Advocate* in 1978:

an earnestly independent consumer newsletter. He quickly built a reputation for integrity, a reputation which is mostly justified. In a business marked by incessant cronyism and toadyism Parker set himself up as an enological Jeremiah. In 1982, the wine media did not yet exist. Parker stepped into a vacuum. He became the mirror of his generation—a generation which was suddenly interested in "the finer things." As a true Boomer, moreover, he saw himself as a sixties liberal consumer advocate. After the 1982 Bordeaux vintage (which Parker hailed against received opinion), the *Wine Advocate* became a consumer cult and today boasts forty thousand sub-scribers in thirty-seven countries worldwide.

In 1985 Parker began writing books. One on Bordeaux, another two on the wines of the Rhône and Burgundy, as well as a series of monumental thousand-page *Wine Buyer's Guides*. *Le Guide Parker* is now a perennial best-seller in France. Parker himself has been made an honorary citizen of the legendary Rhône wine village of Châteauneuf-du-Pape, only the third person to be so honored, after Frédéric Mistral and Marcel Pagnol.

Thus it could fairly be said that Parker has entered the French pantheon, a remarkable achievement for a foreigner. Yet Parker had originally set himself up as a knuckle-rapper of French deviousness and pretension—the homey small-town boy with no-nonsense moral values who would tell the bewildered American consumer what was what—and that had involved taking the French down a peg or two. Burgundian wine maker Hubert de Montille wryly calls him "the model American citizen."

The wine world had always been a cozy, mildly scammy sort of old boys' network where mutual back-scratching was the norm. Parker emerged alongside the *Wine Spectator*, which many see as a shill for the California industry, and the British establishment rep-resented by magazines like *Decanter*.

With ordinary consumers, there is no question that Parker's 100-point rating system has been the key to his remarkable success.

It is based on the system used in American high schools and is actually a 50-point system: scoring begins at 50. Just as you score 50 just for showing up in class, a wine scores 50 simply for being in a bottle. Thereafter, it enters more mysterious territory.

The system gives the insecure consumer a canny illusion of scientific objectivity. In his *Paris Match* interview Parker was asked, "Is there a universal taste to wine?" He replied: "While I am not sure if there is such a thing as 'universal taste,' I do believe that quality in wine, much like quality in cuisine, art or music, can be quantified." He went on to point out that certain opinions were minoritarian for good reasons. If some people think Mozart isn't very good or that 1982 Bordeaux are lame wines, they are in the distinct minority for "quantifiable" reasons. The proof of this axiom for Parker himself? "The fact that my work has been successful in many different countries, and my books have been translated into numerous foreign languages, in many cases becoming best-sellers." Consumers worldwide, he pointed out, "have tended to agree with my thoughts." Therefore numerical ratings reflect a concrete reality. They are more or less exact representations of things which all men and women universally feel gliding across their tongues.

It's a remarkable view of taste. In his profile of Parker in the *Atlantic Monthly*, Langewiesche has an uneasy dinner with the former owner of Château Margaux, Bernard Ginestet. The account is interesting because it illustrates the culture clash which has nurtured the Parker myth. The Frenchman, Langewiesche writes, "had the demeanour of a disillusioned aristocrat, at once detached and self-abandoned. . . . He erected barriers." With his gray skin and chain smoker's voice, Ginestet is an American's caricature of an exhausted, evasive Bordeaux toff, grimacing and shrugging "in the Gallic manner."

At one point Ginestet comes out with an arresting phrase. He says, "Bob is an artisan of the globalization of wine." And then: "American taste is very standardized." What he is referring to is the monopoly of powerful critics over American taste, a phenomenon which is undeniable, as any harried Broadway director will tell you when discussing a bad review from the *New York Times*. Ginestet draws a square in the air. "Bob," he says, "has square taste."

Parker is only the latest in a long line of writers who have created a vocabulary of taste for wine. He is the most extravagant of current practitioners, but he is by no means the most eccentric. Over the last hundred years, indeed, the language of wine has evolved around shifting metaphors which can easily confound the novice: first social class, then sex, then fruits and vegetables. Parker, like most critics, assimilates all three into a lush rhetoric of taste. But can we do the same with a straight face?

The humble accidental connoisseur, trying as he or she is to acquire some taste, must at some point inevitably come up against this rhetoric and try to make some sense of it. Until the 1970s, wine writing mostly used metaphors of social breeding and sex to praise wine. Wines were described rather like people: they were either "refined," had "breeding," "finesse," and "distinction," or else coarse, ill-mannered, and unsubtle. And they could also be masculine or feminine. In Lichine's 1956 *Encyclopedia*, for example, wines are either male, that is, "hard," "assertive," and "big," or else (like Chambolle-Musigny's) they are feminine, "beguiling," "seductive," and "graceful." Wines, in short, were surrogate humans. Lichine insisted that they were sexed accordingly.

Maynard Amerine's landmark 1976 book changed all that. The human metaphors were largely swept away in favor of a more "scientific" vocabulary derived from the animal kingdom. Wines would now be described in terms of a vast array of foods, from cocoa beans and asparagus to almonds and citrus fruits, with just about everything from the grocery section of Balducci's thrown in between, if we except boring carrots and peas. But Amerine went further. In an early stab at political correctness, he claimed that the older terms were unpleasantly classist and sexist. The following words, he suggested, should be suppressed: "coarse," "elegant," "noble," "delicate," "ordinary," "well-bred," and "finesse." Wines, in other words, were no longer to be seen in terms of a snobby European-style class system; they were to be seen as fresh, democratic, healthy, and natural. In other words, American.

The core of the new vocabulary was fruit. In a brilliant article, Sean Shesgreen, professor of English at Northern Illinois University, has argued that this new lexicon ushered in a mood of pastoral idyll. The fruits it favored, writes Shesgreen, were invariably high in sugar, such as cherries, Asian pears, peaches, melons, plums, figs, tangerines, litchis, and pineapples. "While it also," he goes on, "shows a preference for exotic foods like papaya, quince, guava, passion fruit, and mango, its all-time favorite is the berry: straw-berries, raspberries, blackberries, boysenberries, mulberries, goose-berries, cranberries, blueberries and bilberries."

It also reflected the changing American kitchen, with its endless array of raw materials, from herbs, spices, and baking ingredients to things like olives, bacon, honey, marzipan, tapenade, coffee, and chocolate. To these have been added bizarre exotica: pencil lead, io-dine, saddle leather, and pig blood (as contrasted with "beef blood"). There is also, of course, smoke, tobacco, and wild game, now so common that they rarely raise an eyebrow.

This pastoral dialect has now swept the world. But what do these extraordinarily strange descriptions actually mean? Can a wine really taste of prunes, horsehair, caramel, and violets all at once? Or like sugarcoated strawberries, mocha, wild mushroom, expansive metal, and Asian spices?

Psychiatric metaphors are also increasing. Wines are said to have personalities that are diffuse, or "chewy." Do psychiatrists deal with chewy personalities? Conversely, I've often tasted wines I thought were schizophrenic, but I've yet to hear that word used in the critics' armory. I've never heard a wine called mad, but the world is actually full of mad wines.

Parker is a virtuoso of this language. He often talks of wines that taste like "melted asphalt," or "crisp stones," or "crisp cherries," not to mention "caramel-coated autumn leaves," "concentrated meat essences," and "crushed seashells." A Mongeard-Mugneret Burgundy, for example, has a "thick-textured chewy personality"; a Grand Échézeaux from the same producer exhibits "deep, sensual, spicy berry fruit aromas and an intense, concentrated, chewy, blackberry, dark cherry, currant and Asian spice-packed, velvety-textured palate leading to a long, rich and sweet finish."

This florid patois not only helped critics and marketeers sell more wine in the affluent eighties and nineties, it also coincided with a profound shift in the way Americans looked at Europe, and especially the way they looked at France.

If France has always represented a cultural model whose values were formality, aristocracy, urbanity, snobbery, and cynical artfulness, French wines reigned supreme because they expressed these qualities. But the Reagan years saw France gradually being toppled from her perch. For if Amerine didn't like words like "finesse" and "elegance," why should the new wine consumers like the way France herself embodied them? Americans began to turn toward Italy instead.

Unlike the French, Italians were spontaneous, unsnooty, casual, unpretentiously friendly, and family-oriented—that is, much more like Americans themselves. Italy was also a land which deep in the American subconscious offered a pastoral romance. The huge success of Italian-sounding wines like Gallo and Mondavi had much to do with this commercialized idea of Italy: the Italian family seated around Mediterranean banquets in golden sunshine. Somehow Italy, Shesgreen suggests, had the innocent energy of nature. Like fruit-and-veggie-packed wine itself, that sun-kissed land had about it a whiff of the health food store. Where these bucolic connections and vocabularies had been embraced by enophiles like Parker, the zest for all things Italian nourished and sustained them, bestowing on such pastoral allusions the naturalness and validity they needed to take root and flourish.

Thus, could it not be argued that the fashionable wine vocabulary of our time does a strange disservice to the French, even though it is also popular in France? But it also presumably does a disservice to us and to our wretchedly accidental palates. For even if we cannot understand Amerine, Parker, or the Shakespearean oratory of *The Wine Enthusiast*, we are bursting with repressed curiosity about our taste. How can it be described?

The new catchwords are now all drawn from the exhausted Western boudoir: "pillowy," "ravishing," "overendowed"—tender words which prove that Americans are actually far more interested in edibles than they are in sex. But one is still getting nowhere. One turns inward. Like everyone, even the most radically indifferent gastronomic amateur, I draw up lists of things which I think my mouth likes. These lists are of little interest to anyone else but I compose them anyway as I lie awake in idle insomnia. My list goes something like this: salt, chocolate, soursweet honey, minerals, chalk, shells, the sea. I like gritty, flinty, saline, minerally things with a hard core. I cover my food with mountains of salt; I like my chocolate as black and bitter as pitch.

In this respect I am like pregnant women with their pickles or like the queer rats studied by Thomas Scott at the University of Delaware, which, when deliberately starved of salt, found their sugar-loving neurons mysteriously switching to salt instead. We taste wine in exactly the same way that lemurs test leaves, passing volatile compounds over their Jacobson's organs (the passageway connecting mouth and nose) to detect toxins, sugars, salts, tannins. But do we love sugars in the way that animals do, as if it were hardwired into us by evolution, that is to say by the endless search for ripe fruit?

When fruit ferments into alcohol, animals are often attracted to it: the sourness of the fermented fruit signals to the Jacobson's organs that bacteria have disabled unpleasant things like cyanide and strychnine. It is thought that pregnant women love pickles because their sourness proclaims a kind of chemical purity which makes them safe. Our senses are millions of years old, honed by the forest. And the forest is a jigsaw of good and evil chemicals, sweet and sour—a complex mix.

The Department of Viticulture and Enology at Davis has helped American vintners set up their wineries for years by means of a scientifically determined wine aroma wheel devised by the "sense scientist" Ann Noble. This simple device, which looks like a bright frisbee, helps the inexperienced new wine maker to collate his or her tastes in an orderly way. Every imaginable taste sensation, every possible aroma of wine, is arranged on the aroma wheel in sequences that establish family relations among them. For example, one section of the pretty wheel is labeled "Herbaceous or Vegetative," and includes things such as *bell pepper*, *mint*, and *eucalyptus*. Another is labeled "Chemical" and subdivided into Pungent, Sulfur, and Petroleum, under which latter definition we duly find our *tar*, *plastic*, and *diesel*. Under "Microbiological" we find *baker's yeast*, *sauerkraut*, and the startling *sweaty*, not to mention the even more startling *horsey* and *mousy*.

"The purpose of the wine aroma wheel initially," Ann Noble has written, "was to facilitate communication about wine flavor by providing a standard terminology. The requirements of words included in the wheel were very simply that the terms had to be specific and analytical and not be hedonic or the result of an integrated or judgmental response."

What I love in this passage is the word "hedonic," which of course we have already met. So it is hedonic studies again! And what, I wonder, is an "integrated response"?

The wheel proudly claims to be nonjudgmental, just as enlightened Americans are proud of being both hedonic *and* nonjudgmental. One cannot help feeling that all along wine professionals have been convinced that wine needn't be mired in emotion or taste at all; it can be resolved analytically.

Of course, the aroma wheel needs to speak directly and plainly: a pear smells like a pear, usually. The aim is to train the nasal reflex of the accidental connoisseur to separate out different elements and thus break them down so that they are comprehensible. Noting that novices often complain that they can't smell anything in a wine or can't think of a way to describe what they do smell, Noble adds that "fortunately, it is very easy to train our noses and brains to connect and quickly link terms with odors."

Some garish instructions then follow for the intrepid novice wine taster. Go down to the grocery, Noble suggests, and buy some canned asparagus, some butter, some vanilla extract, a few bell peppers, some cloves, a bit of soy sauce, a bag of frozen berries, and a pot of strawberry jam: these will be your smelling and tasting guides for most red wines. For the much trickier Riesling, Muscat, and Gewürztraminer wines, however, she suggests a box of Handi Wipes. Handi Wipes contain a citrusy, floral chemical called linalool that has exactly the aroma of these wines. Put the Handi Wipe in a wineglass, or else a few Froot Loops, and you have the perfect linalool scent.

To acquaint yourself with the aromas of sparkling wines, Noble suggests putting dollops (gobs?) of vegemite, hazelnuts, and malt syrup in glasses and breathing in. Rose's lime juice and sour cream complete the arsenal. There is even a sparkling wine aroma wheel. Defects, meanwhile, show up as things like ethyl mercaptan (like a gas leak), brettanomyces, which smells like a barnyard or a moldy Band-Aid, and sulfur dioxide, with its characteristic whiff of dried apricots. Oxidization often results in an aroma akin to nail polish remover.

Noble tells us that while the word "floral" is analytically descriptive, and therefore useful, other terms such as "fragrant," "elegant," and "harmonious" are not and are therefore "imprecise . . . hedonic and judgmental." But elegance and harmony are exactly what even the wine ignoramus can tell set wines apart. "Elegance": what a derided, misunderstood, vast word! In wine, elegance is everything. But elegance is impossible to describe; it is a word into which we pour complex feelings.

Elegant things definitely suggest each other. Could you say that a wine makes you think of an Egyptian face, austerely carved, with hard, chiseled lines and monumental purity? Why not? Or—this gets a little cheesy—a Mozart opera?

Whether one can or not without ending up in *Private Eye*'s Pseud's Corner, it's clear that the cheery jargon of aromas and tastes, the blackberries, tannins, phenol contents, flowers, tars, and so on, is little more than an airport-novel language that tells you nothing about wine, and it is refreshing to recall that in the nineteenth century, long before today's fads for boysenberry notes and boudoir metaphors, connoisseurs lustily referred to the structure and breeding of wines—in a word, to their elegance, finesse, and distinction. They thought that wine had the qualities of architecture and sculpture—of Parisian bridges!—not those of Pierre Cardin wallpaper and Bonne Maman jam.

How, then, does France fare in this braver newish world of psychedelic taste sensations? My own earliest memories of that country are precisely of that protocol-driven sobriety which makes for profound wines on the one hand and the sinister gloom of the Restaurant Vérot-Dodat on the other. I have always thought of it as a place inimical to the aroma wheel, to organized happiness, to cheap chocolate, and to infantile hysterias all around. But its depth is also its Achilles' heel, the fount of its mournful scorn.

And what about Parker, the man who has remade the image of

France for legions of accidentally inclined bibulists? For many, the ultimate proof of Parker's democratizing credentials is his championing of the *garagistes*, the small-time grassroots wine makers of Bordeaux who are now making fortunes for themselves by going over the heads of the haughty Medoc châteaux, their uneasy and reluctant neighbors. Nothing gives the Jeffersonian Parker more satisfaction than the thought of the châteaux getting their comeuppance from lone iconoclasts working out of their own garages. For Parker, this is the hopeful new France.

Garage wines are typically made by wealthy individuals who imitate artisanal wines—as a public personal hobby. They're described as being intense, dark, small-production wines made with an artisanal attention to detail. Being dark and dramatic, of course, they appeal to Parker's "overendowed" palate.

The apostle of the garage style is Jean-Luc Thunevin, an Algerian pied noir and ex–bank clerk who bought his first parcel of vines in Saint-Émilion only in 1991. Since then, with his ex-nurse wife, Murielle, he has learned to make a highly profitable wine called Valandraud, which in the 1995 vintage Parker scored at a staggering 95 points.

Indeed, all of the vintages from '93 to '99 scored high marks, the '94 reaching a majestic 94 points. Overall, their charms were (as Parker puts it) a "tell-tale thickness of color," "high class toasty oak," "a gorgeous nose of black cherries," as well as a string of nasal qualities beginning with iodine and ending with *pain grillé*. The '95 was seamlessly constructed with layers of fruit and glycerin, and overall contained "the stuff of greatness," this being contained in generous scads of various berries—blackberries, currants, cherries, the usual suspects. "The finish," Parker added breathlessly, "lasts for over 30 seconds."

Bordeaux responds by pointing out that Parker's nose is still an American organ, and that it drifts by nature toward what they like to call robustly obvious flavors. Nor are the *garagistes* the plucky

Davy Crocketts they are so disingenuously made out to be. They are sly operators who have glommed onto the Parker system by carefully crafting "hedonic" wines which the Master is bound to love.

Moreover, in Bordeaux it is often pointed out that most of the *garagistes* have bought land at the edges of the Saint-Émilion appellation, where land is relatively cheap because it has always been considered undesirable. In this, it is the wisdom of generations which speaks, for by common consent the best lands in Saint-Émilion are places like the plain of Figeac. *Garagiste* wine is mediocre, they say, because it comes from mediocre land. Hundreds of years of trial and error do not lie.

By his own account, on the other hand, Parker is incapable of making such mistakes himself. To *Paris Match* he confessed that he had indeed been wrong, once. It was back in 1983, he wistfully recalled, with the Burgundy vintage. "Keeping in mind," he added, "that I have been tasting professionally for twenty-one years, this is the only major error in vintage judgment I have made."

The Nose, then, sails on down the vast river of wine, imperturbable, decisive, as majestic as a galleon of Her Majesty's Royal Navy navigating seas and rivers populated by wine ignoramuses and shelling the natives when they dare to give themselves airs. But has Parker transformed Bordeaux in the ways that he claims to have done? What of the confrontation between *garagistes* and châteaux which admirers of the organoleptic critic have declared to be the sign of his liberating influence? Can a critic possibly change the world with such innocent truths?

Is Bordeaux, at the very heart of the idea of France, about to be turned upside down by a second American Revolution, this one enacted not in the forests of Virginia but around the low, miserable, and silty estuaries of the Garonne? I thought, a little desultorily, that it might be time to find out.

An Afternoon in Bordeaux

Most of our customers frankly wouldn't know the difference between a Bordeaux and a claret.   —Basil Fawlty in *Fawlty Towers*

The Garonne at ebb tide flows past Pauillac so slowly that at first sight it seems to be a sea unaffected by the gravity of the moon. The grassy waterfront is scuffed and beaten up, mostly deserted in winter, its piers creaking and tinkling in relentless winds. Its upscale hotels are the peeling France et Angleterre and the dreadful Le Yachting, but these too are moribund in the winter months; only a little Shell station contains signs of human life. The pumps for boat gas—*carburants sous douane*—suggest a nautical tourism which must materialize only with heat. The glow of Bordeaux, that rich and easy city thirty miles upriver, is nowhere to be seen.

Considering the tonnage of journalistic ink expended on Pauillac, the world capital of wine, and the string of small towns surrounding it, its winter solitude comes as a surprise. Between the villages dark forests widen and deepen the sky; the famous vines stand like sinister upended lobsters waving their claws over rows of pebbly-white gravel soil. Pale blue silos offer the only man-made color. You pass through villages of a consummate, spine-chilling weirdness, places Walt Disney might have sketched on his trips through France in the 1930s as he searched for skylines with which to populate his demented tales, places like Cos d'Estournel with its mad little *chai* perched on a hill and its plethora of stone elephants and miniature bells hanging from the eaves of octagonal towers. A perfect example of that coquettish architectural style named for its exponent, Bourguet, and which was apparently designed to lure the British Indian market. The château as marketing gimmick. You pass through Blanquet, and pale yellow farms with conical roofs lost amid isolated palm trees. In the middle of the vines, more towers rise up, as queer as the place-names nearby: Château Plantier-Rose, Haut Marbuzet. You pass through the hamlet of Leyssac, through Saint-Estèphe with its dark-honey church, through Arcins in a bend of the road, through Margaux with its sorbet-yellow château brooding at the end of a sweeping alley of trees. And a short way down the road, there is Issan and the Château Palmer, as unreal as anything invented in Los Angeles, its points jutting skyward like a Thai temple. It is impossible not to be reminded of the straining eclecticism of Napa—but which came first?

On my way to Pauillac I went for lunch at the Lion d'Or in Arcins. The Lion d'Or is one of the famous restaurants of the Medoc and an inevitable destination for restless wine buyers. Cases of wine line its walls, boxes of Château Meyre, Talbot, and Moulin de la Rose, and what seems like miles of bright modern wainscoting of a particularly funereal and depressing kind. There are mirrors aplenty, gold plates with wine names, shelves of slim glass decanters, chandeliers with small glass grape clusters hanging down from them. Everywhere one turns one is confronted by grape motifs, grape metaphors, grape symbols, grape devices, grape vignettes. It was a cold weekend lunchtime and one of the large round tables was filled with raucous American merchants swapping stories about their secretaries. I was suddenly thankful they were there—a burst of life at least! I sat alone and listened to their bold innuendos, which they assumed that no one could understand. The rest of the long room was empty. As I drank my glass of the house Medoc the Lion d'Or took on a rosier, more elastic form.

A plate of rabbit appeared, *râble de lapin comme autrefois.* A simple undisguised cross section of a rabbit, with thinly shaved potatoes, as beautiful as an anatomical illustration and tasting of wet grass, woods, bracken, and earth: a hunter's dish, bare and austere. I sat back. I was filling up with the *geist* of rabbit, while the room began to look emptier and emptier. The Americans paid their bill and left. I moved on to a plate of warm *canelettes*, crunchy little cakes doused with iced sugar, lightly burned on the outside and stuffed with cream.

As I was slipping the second *canelette* into my mouth I noticed that I was not, as I had thought, the last diner left in the main room of the Lion d'Or. At the far end, huddled alone at a table by the window, sat another rumpled, thickset American eating garrulously alone. How did I know he was a fellow citizen? For one thing, Europeans rarely eat with their mouths open, smacking their lips. For another, there was a solitary intensity about him. I have rarely seen a Frenchman eat or drink with solitary intensity, and my fellow diner seemed to be focusing all his inner energy on *his* plate of *canelettes*. It had to be a compatriot. I felt like going up to him and starting one of those annoying conversations compatriots are always foisting upon each other in foreign parts.

But something held me back. I had written to Robert Parker hoping for an interview, but my perhaps offhandish missive had gone unanswered. Sitting thus in the Lion d'Or, I thought that I recognized the man himself at the far end of the dining room. He was about fifty-five, thickset, unsmiling, in Hush Puppies. The Hush Puppies, I thought irrationally, must have some dark significance. *Hush Puppies.* Isn't that exactly what a famous wine critic would be wearing? Didn't this unknown man eating *canelettes* at the far end of an empty dining room look a little like the pictures I had seen of Robert Parker? And wouldn't Robert Parker—if this *was* Robert Parker—typically be wearing Hush Puppies at lunch?

After some time spent fuming in this way, I realized it was not Robert Parker at all, or at least he could not be proved to be so. He was probably just another American merchant or salesman doing the rounds of the Bordeaux wine houses. Or perhaps he wasn't in wine at all. He could equally have been a carpet salesman or a sewage disposal expert. There was no way of telling. Nevertheless, out of sheer shame and impotence I waited until this unjustly maligned gentleman had left before paying my bill and departing myself. I had a solemn appointment at Château Lafite and I was already wondering if my mood was the correct one in which to taste one of the world's most intimidating wines. I had to steady myself and my tongue as well.

The waiting room of Château Lafite is one of the smallest I have ever come across in a lifetime largely spent in waiting rooms. The room is about six feet by six feet, which is to say little bigger than a vertical coffin. There are two ornate Louis XV–style armchairs and a moodily unnerving full-length portrait of Baron James de Rothschild, who seems to eye you wherever you stand in the cubicle, never letting you out of his inscrutable gaze. Who was the Baron, you wonder to yourself as you click your heels in this suffocating, silent, bathospherelike chamber? What malice did he bear in his heart? What joys did he hide there? Who and what is more mysteriously unknowable than a Rothschild? Through the door I could see the noble architectural planes and angles of Lafite itself. Serene and reposed, open to the sky but horizontally self-contained, it looked like the palace court of a minor Swabian prince. And it was silent; only an occasional crunching of galoshed feet on the immaculate gravel made me peer out to see who was there; and there was nobody.

Deep inside the building a bell rang and the door to the waiting room opened. Charles Chevalier, Lafite's wine maker, stood there, mildly curious as to who I was. He was short, a little red-faced, in comfortable and expensive tweeds. Behind him was his office, which could easily have been that of a police bureaucrat in the aforementioned Swabian court: prints, scattered books, file boxes, certificates. The room was fairly drowning in magazines. Chevalier is a merry soul who seems more than a little incongruous in his cool surroundings. I quickly ascertained that his favorite motto is *"Hors du vin, pas de salut!"* (Without wine, no health). Chevalier had that *let's go get a drink* glint in his eye and we didn't waste much time in the bureaucratical office. He brushed his nose—which seemed as jovial and red as the rest of him once the initial *froideur* had been brushed off.

We went into the tasting room. I suppose it must be counted one of the most awesome tasting rooms in the wine world, but in the physical sense it was more like a typically functional steel and ceramic laboratory. A blue heater glowed in one corner; I spied a Bunsen burner, glass phials, test tubes. The tasting glasses were spaced out on a sheet of paper printed with numbered circles. We would taste the 1998, 1999, and 2000 Château Lafite alongside the same vintages of Duhart-Milon, one of the lesser Lafite properties, which lies a stone's throw from the château. It would be an interesting contrast: the ultrafeminine Lafites alongside the more stiffly masculine Duhart-Milons.

As we turned the Duhart-Milon in our glasses, Chevalier explained that his father had been a vigneron, that he had always wanted to be a vigneron, that he could not imagine being anything else. A question of blood. But, I said, a vigneron was an individual, wasn't he? How did an individual impose his own style on such a gigantic reputation as Lafite, a wine which surely had to preserve a commercially viable continuity, not to mention a tradition going back more than a century.

"I always like to think that if I ever went to Margaux I would still make a Chevalier wine at Margaux."

"A Chevalier-Margaux?"

"I would hope so. I'd like to think so. Naturally, a Lafite is a Lafite. You have to be able to tell that it's a Lafite, or why would you pay for a Lafite?"

So a Lafite was personal and impersonal at the same time?

"I want to make a Lafite above all."

We started with a 1998, which was still far too young to really gauge. A good-year Lafite can easily last for fifty years.

We tried the '98, and I felt it best to keep my peace. What can one say about so great a wine when one is not in possession of a hyper-refined taste? Could one prattle about the pencil-lead nose and the "powdered minerals"? It seemed best not to.

The great enologist Émile Peynaud revolutionized Bordeaux in the 1960s by insisting on maturer fruit picked later in the harvest and more rigorous methods. He had created a new style of Bordeaux, bigger, brighter (in Mondavi's sense), and bolder. Peynaud had been a consultant at Lafite between 1983 and 1986 and his ghost was everywhere in the Medoc, as it was in California.

"Simplification," Chevalier said, lifting the first 2000 Lafite. "Peynaud took the view that everything was explicable, and easily explicable at that. He urged greater vigilance and regularity, greater hygiene, better control of fermentation and bacteria. Things like that. It was a total transformation. He showed how the grape itself is the basis of everything. So now we've evened out the differences between good and bad years. We don't have bad years anymore."

The tasting of the wine had taken over; we stopped talking for a bit. The Duhart-Milon was gaining depth as we went back in time. The '98 was *costaud*, powerfully built, Chevalier said, "like an adolescent boy, obstreperous, a little ungainly. But, you know, just like a wild boy, *timide et sauvage*." He smiled with a queer tenderness, as if the Duhart-Milon actually was his teenage son. There is a difference, I have found, between wine-speak, that awful ersatz poetry, and the way a wine maker talks about his wines. The wine maker's talk may sound fanciful when written down like this, but in the mouth the language is simple and straightforward. The vigneron rarely parades. He just wants to say *what it is*. We moved on to the Lafites. It was quite clear to their maker that here we had the female side of the coin: *plus raffiné, charmant, séduisant, feminine,* etc. The suppressed language of Alexis Lichine! Chevalier actually rolled his eyes at the thought of young girls, *des jeunes filles en fleur,* like that other Chevalier, Maurice. His cheeks suddenly glowed pink, and so did his nose.

"This is a female wine, a *woman*. No, it's not nonsense to talk like this. Listen to the wine."

I closed my eyes: Watteau? It seemed like an arbor wine, a medium of frivolous seduction, eighteenth-century in its mixture of steely sophistication and glancing sex.

It was strange, he said, that the Lafite should differ so markedly from the Duhart-Milon. That they should have, so to speak, different genders. The soils of the two wines were the same, right next door to each other. And yet they were completely different, were they not?

They were.

"There's no secret for making great wine," he said. "All wine makers know the same techniques. But tiny details in the terroir make for huge details in the wine."

I said that Parker had given a score of 100 to the 1996. Did that mean that it was the world's most perfect wine?

"Ah," said Chevalier without missing a beat and with a quick twinkle. "*That* I don't know."

I then asked him about the 2000. According to Parker, it was the greatest vintage of Bordeaux in history. Greater even than that "classic, long-lived" 1996. Parker's remarks generated a feeding frenzy for the 2000, pushing its prices into the stratosphere. Virtually the whole crop had been presold as a "future," making the vintage a watershed in the long history of wine and capitalism. Parker had also added, however, that he saw no reason why Bordeaux prices should not tumble downward, given the worldwide recession. It was just that the 2000 was such a monumental vintage, unparalleled in living memory. Bordeaux, Parker went on, was now living up to its status as "the world's reference point for wines of richness, longevity and complexity." *Enormously rich, incredibly potent, and concentrated.* Bordeaux was now at the top of its game, greater than ever in its history, and the competition from the *garagistes* had only made things better.

Chevalier was silent, nursing his own glass of stratospherically priced 2000 Lafite. At the mention of Parker's name he seemed to twitch. With amusement, with deep recognition?

"All of what he says is true," he conceded finally. "As for prices, it's a psychological question, isn't it? We're in the luxury product range, so it's difficult for us to compare ourselves with other wines." A gentle shrug, a winsome smile. "Myself, I love this wine, I truly love it." And he added breathlessly, "*Hors du vin, pas de salut!*"

He was becoming a little more sphinxlike, though still smiling from ear to ear. It was clear that he *did* love the 2000 Lafite, which bore some delicate trace of his own personality. But Lafite is Lafite, and belonging to Lafite is a little like belonging to Microsoft, whose technicians often exude a quiet but genuine passion for their work.

I thought I heard a bell ring somewhere in the depths of Château Lafite, and a secretary came pattering to the door. There was a knock. Someone was here to see Monsieur Chevalier.

Chevalier half bowed and apologized, glancing at his watch.

"Duty calls," he said. "It's two and I have an appointment."

Passing back through the office, I felt that everything was a little more tense. The secretaries fussed about with small pecking motions; Chevalier seemed a tad *tuned up*. We said our au revoirs and I was escorted quite swiftly back to the waiting room. When the door opened I saw that the room was already occupied. A tall, thickset American in Hush Puppies was standing there like a statue, looking at the moribund painting of James Rothschild. As I squeezed past him, Chevalier said as if absentmindedly, "*Voilà Monsieur Osborne, un autre américain!*" But the new guest looked past me, his face frozen, and I made only the briefest note of the bulldog face before tumbling out onto the gravel and wondering if this pair of Hush Puppies might indeed mean what I thought they might mean. I turned around, but the guest had already slipped into Chevalier's office. I could almost feel the cogs of Château Lafite churning as he entered.

Perhaps it wasn't the great critic at all; it might have been a carpet salesman, a fermentation tank expert, a journalist from Idaho. But I had a frisson. Yes: most definitely, I had a frisson! Moreover, as I walked out it began to rain, and on the road to nearby Vertheuil, as I was careening smoothly in my rented car around the undulating vineyards of Lafite, I nearly struck a tipsy field worker also careening about in a Renault 5. We got out and screamed insults at each other. It began to rain harder and harder, and the fields were now cloaked in drifting plumes of smoke reminiscent of an artillery barrage.

This went on for some time, until I realized that my rage was in reality being directed at the pair of Hush Puppies. Calmly apologizing, I drove on cathartically to Vertheuil, through one of the gloomiest landscapes on earth, and stopped at the church in the center of the near-deserted village. I was on my way to a *garagiste*.

The Vertheuil church dates from the eleventh century. Visigothic faces stare out of the capitals like Easter Island heads. The chapels of the apse are still faintly colored, ghost colors depicting the vanished rural life of the dark ages. The Christmas lights were on, draped around a manger, though the church itself was stone cold and empty, as if it had been abandoned for seven hundred years.

I walked around a Sainte Thérèse de l'Enfant Jesus, past figures of bears, oxen, starlings, and humans laboring with bushels of wheat. And then, looking down, I saw that the floor was made of a pattern of grape leaves. It must have been what the peasants of the eleventh century recognized most instinctively, what reassured them most deeply.

Only in these primitive temples physically close to barbarism and passionate death do I feel moved by Christianity. The supernatural forms writhing on the capitals are not false spiritualism: they are believed in with a desperation that keeps them alive. It cannot help occurring to you that perhaps you are always looking for this primitive quality in all things in the modern world, where you never find it. And in wine, too.

Which brings us to the *garagistes*.

Aren't the *garagistes* the avatars of this primitivism? Aren't they the missing link between high and low, past and present?

If we are talking about the *garagistes* beloved of Parker, the answer is that no, they are not. How much one yearns for Medoc wines which are not the equivalent of Rolls-Royces and Bentleys! The luxury Bordeaux is, after all, a relatively recent invention going back some three hundred years. Somewhere under this suburban carpet of commercial flim-flam, underneath the endless signs for *Conseils Oenologiques* and Châteaux Parking Lots, the endless *caves de dégustations* and preposterous Disney mansions, there had to be a land of mud, oysters, and raw tastes. Something equivalent to the broad, yearning faces carved into the columns of the church at Vertheuil.

And so, as a result of this no doubt naive premise, I came to the tiny domain of Iris du Gayon. If there really are *garagistes*, then Domaine Iris du Gayon is certainly a garage and its owner Pierre Siri is certainly a *garagiste*. For the "winery" is actually just a self-built house and its garage, and Siri himself—like Parker's beloved Thunevin—bought his land when it was cheap in the 1960s, which is to say when Bordeaux was in the doldrums. Before that, he had been a nuclear engineer.

The curious thing about Iris du Gayon, however, is its geographic position. As if to lend credence to Parker's otherwise far-fetched notion of a *garagiste* peasants' revolt against the seigneurial châteaux, Iris du Gayon shares its vineyards with none other than Château Mouton-Rothschild itself. There was nothing sensational about Siri's purchase of this gold mine back in 1966. He had been looking for a house, not a winery. But a strange coincidence had landed him on Mouton-Rothschild's doorsteps, and *inside* their vines. I was curious to see if he was another canny fraud or if he was something else—a genuine loner.

Siri certainly looks like one of the Visigothic heads of Vertheuil. His face is ruddy, sturdily carved by the years, positively gnomic. He has ceased looking like a nuclear engineer, although to be fair I am not at all sure what nuclear engineers do look like. But he had worked on the first French nuclear submarine, the *Rhapsodie*. (What other nation could name a nuclear submarine thus?) Siri traveled the world and met his wife in Senegal, though she is not African. Arriving in Pauillac, he decided to start up a vineyard equipment company: handmade scissors, knives, adzes. Meanwhile, he bought the parcel of vines behind his house. Mouton was desperate to get its hands on it now, but with a few other old-timers Siri had held on and made a sly calculation. If the château made wine from these plots of gravelly soil, why shouldn't he? If terroir was a great reality, why should his own production be so very different from that of Mouton-Rothschild? He shared the same soil with them, the same subsoil, and the same hydraulic system, which is to say the same natural ebb and flow of water. Like Mouton, Siri's ground has a thin topsoil filled with white pebbles which reflect the sun and heat the grapes. At night, they give back calories to the vines.

The Siri house looks like a wooden hobbit cottage from *Lord of the Rings*. Iron vineyard tools hang like talismans from the eaves of the porch. Inside, little statues of medieval saints stand in niches, there is a log fire, a bookish intensity, an American frontier feel: like the cabin of a trapper with intellectual inclinations.

I tried to imagine him tinkering with the complexities of nuclear devices. But his whole body seemed now to have been transformed according to the demands of the land. And yet the house is actually set back from a suburban street, because nearly all of the land around Pauillac is blandly suburban. The vines sweep down between the Siri garage and a row of condo-style new houses in the finest Alphaville French style. Siri therefore seemed to be a suburban avatar of something *buried*. He was fond of talking about the ancientness of things. The Medoc had been making wine for two thousand years, he declared with some magnificence of effect.

Siri sat at the head of the table before a massive oval plate of carved roast beef, his nails still black with soil, his hands as massive as the plate. What seemed to motivate him was an indignant but charmingly self-serving conspiracy theory. The essence of this theory was, I suppose, the essence of all such theories, namely that greed and the imperatives of big business were dominating the practices of the great châteaux. Siri held up some slabs of purple roast beef and his eyes went into a jolly fit of truth telling. You should *see* what these people get up to!

Siri launched into complaints which I had been hearing all over France: France was a *nation des assistes*, a bureaucrats' welfare state geared almost entirely to the needs and fantasies of sinecured *fonctionnaires*. It was almost impossible to run a small business without sinking into penury. The state, in fact, was nothing more than a dysfunctional contraption which sucked the life out of everything. The *garagiste*, like any other small businessman, was therefore in an inherently contradictory position. France wanted her small wine makers, but at the same time she did everything to make their lives hell by taxing them into oblivion. Hence, Monsieur, the direct appeal of the Americans. Yes, the Americans.

"We are not anti-Americans!" M. and Mme. Siri said almost at the same time, as if this was a revolutionary declaration.

And I was indeed struck by the fact that Siri had expressed no anti-American sentiments. At some point in any conversation with a French wine maker, one could expect an anti-American jab or two. But not Siri. No, he remembered the war. His wife agreed. They both remembered the war, which their compatriots so loved to quietly forget. The Americans were not the bad guys, when push came to shove. The bad guys were *other Europeans.*

After lunch we went out to the little field next door. Siri wanted to show me the exact difference between his viticulture and that of Mouton. We crept into the Mouton vines and stooped. Six grapes were bunched together along the shoots in close formation. So close, in fact, that the grapes actually touched each other.

"Too bunched," he whispered, as if the Mouton Gestapo were listening through hidden microphones in the leaves. "So the sun can't heat them all equally."

Two grapes, he said, must never touch each other. And he demonstrated what the ideal space should be with his fist. The Mouton practice was simply quicker and cheaper to use on a large scale. Siri's vines, on the other hand, were all cut obsessively by hand, that is, by his own and by his wife's hands, with a little help from a friend at Lafite. Returning to his own plants, he stooped again to show the distance with his fist. The Gironde slang word for a bunch of grapes is *crougne*, and Siri used it with relish. This was what a *crougne* should look like, this is how a *crougne* should be spaced, this is a true *crougne*! Meanwhile, I asked why tiny bouquets of human hair were tied to the vines. Oh that: that was to repel rabbits.

"Rabbits hate the smell of human hair. They hate human hair more than they love grapes." Then he turned to the wretched Mouton plants a few yards away and shrugged.

"What they do is too rushed. They can't work at a proper pace. And it's all to make more money. You can see it in their wines, too. But people will carry on paying for them."

The cellar, winery, and tasting room of Iris du Gayon is the garage, which is warmed with American aerospace insulation. The barrels are marked with the names of Siri's grandchildren: Juliette, Jean Antoine, and Lea. The walls sport recommendations from *Le Guide Hachette* and a host of medals from wine competitions, a Grand Prix d'Excellence here, a Gold Medal Paris 2001 there. Siri wasn't struggling in the eyes of the press and the wine committees. To the contrary, they loved his wines. All except Parker, that is. In 1996 Siri sent Parker one of his offerings and in return received, as he put it, "one of the worst reviews Parker has ever written. Ah, Monsieur, Parker is not for lovers of delicacy!"

Siri poured out a few glasses of this and that and then declared, in a very friendly way, that wine writers were largely full of crap, that they nattered on and on and spoiled it for everyone else, that wine in general tasted of grapes and that was about it, that he much preferred it when people just shut up during tastings and enjoyed themselves (well, I thought, that's a relief!).

But criticism, I asked, was it necessary or not?

"Naturally it's necessary. But let silence prevail while drinking. You can't really describe wine; you can only remember it. Wine is animal, solitary. In my view, anyway."

The wines were good, though I no longer much felt like comparing them with Mouton's. What would be the point? What mattered was the mental chasm separating that waiting room at Lafite and the musty smell of the primitive weaponlike tools hanging from the rafters of Siri's crazy garage. Neurotically and obscurely, of course, they were connected. Siri, like Chevalier, loved to use the word *raisonné*, reasoned, reasonable, but also rational. His wine making was the result of *une traîtement raisonnée, une production raisonnée*.

There are many angles to such words in French, but above all I think they denote a vision of harmonious smoothness, of an ordered orchestration of different elements according to laws which can be claimed to be natural. Ironically, it is also a vision which fuels the idea of the French state that Siri himself finds so absurd when it comes to tax time.

Before I left, Siri went to a grotty upright tank in a corner equipped with a spigot and poured out two plastic cups of his private liqueur, a thick, amber-colored nectar which he makes for himself in his spare time.

We drank it in silence, as Siri prefers. But as we did so I felt his eyes becoming mercurial, cunning, and noticeably more Dionysian. It began to rain, and drops drummed loudly on the flimsy roof of the garage. Surrounded by his ferocious implements, Siri took on a slightly goblin air, an air that corresponded well, however, with the gentle and honeyed fire of his after-hours liqueur. We drank glass after glass, standing there in the garage, and when it was time for me to drive back to Bordeaux, Siri merely smiled and lifted his hand in a mute farewell. He was mildly curious, however, as to where I would be going next. I said it would be Languedoc—I was tiring of the gloom of the Gironde.

"Yes, yes, quite," was all he said. "It's never a bad idea to go south."

He asked if I would like to take a bottle of the liqueur with him. I could drink it in my hotel room, in perfect solitude.

"And that way," he added, "you will remember my *crougnes!*"

In Bordeaux that night, I drank the whole bottle after a dismal meal at Didier Gelineau, another "famous bistro," and a long drive along the embankments swarming with beautiful prostitutes. I staggered through the cold, cleanly serene streets of gray stone. Somewhere near the frosty spires of Saint-Pierre, in the deserted heat of the city, an African mendicant followed me with boxes of Camels crying *Cigarettes, Cigarettes!* as if cigarettes also had their crazed devotees. At 10 p.m. we were the only people up and walking in Bordeaux. I gave him the last of the Siri bottle and took a damp packet of bartered Camels back to my hotel. It seemed, all in all, a perfectly reasonable exchange.

The Colossi of Gaussac

❧

Taste is tiring like good company.   —Francis Picabia

A month later I was in the southern city of Béziers. I was staying there idly, for no particular reason, and during the days I would walk about looking at Roman fragments and churches, enjoying the pale-toned and elegant dullness of its streets.

There is nothing I like more than dull provincial French towns, because their very dullness (which is no different from the dullness of any other country's provincial towns) seems to be the outward expression of a touching, fragile sense of respectability. But one day as I was out walking I found myself in a sudden whirlwind of violence, an eruption of irrational fury which I at first mistook for a soccer riot. Cars burned, sirens wailed, enraged men in heavy beards lunged about with bricks and pipes in their hands. Stones flew everywhere, ricocheting off walls and posts, cracking windows wide open and bouncing off cars. The streets were soon thick with smoke. Down them charged the usual suspects of French riots: activists with bleeding noses, CRS riot police with truncheons and tear-gas guns. Were these activists the usual mob? Enraged schoolteachers, unionized garbage men, administrators demanding an increase in pensions? Or perhaps a few soldiers of the trade unions demanding a timely end to global capitalism? A cheese strike gone sour could not be ruled out.

Then I saw a revolutionary pennant hanging from a lamppost. It read: *Au debout, les viticulteurs!* (Stand up, wine makers!) I asked a cop. Yes, he confirmed, it's a wine riot. A wine riot?

This area of southern France is militant country where farmers inspired by Jose Bove regularly torch McDonald's branches and loot supermarkets. Farmers on the warpath against globalization, hamburgers, and canned fruit, and for Europe's, if not the world's, most extravagant farm subsidies. The French farmer, who is largely subsidized by the urban taxpayers of all the other countries in the European Union, can smell the end of his golden age. The Germans and the British, for one thing, are tired of paying for him. He is therefore indignant. He cries that it's the end of the French countryside, the end of everything decent. But the butter lakes and the milk lakes have been joined by the wine lakes, and the Union's lumbering bureaucrats are now trying with all their might to convert mass-production, low-end vineyards to other purposes. The wine proletariat is not amused.

Had the protest organizers set up a free bar somewhere, somewhere for the tired wine rioter to slake his thirst? But all the bars were closed and the riot was becoming numbingly pointless. An hour or two later, I was in the silent town of Pézenas drinking Muscat de Lunel in the fantastical Hôtel Molière and the riot already seemed like an improbable artifice. Do men really practice violence for the sake of their wine?

Lost in the flat fields of Nizas a few kilometers outside of Pézenas, the Prieuré de Saint-Jean-de-Bebian began to make a famous wine in the 1970s under Alain Roux, whose father Marcel had bought the place in 1952. Roux turned to the noble varietals of the Rhône:

Syrah stock imported from Chave at Hermitage, Mourvèdre from Domaine Tempier at Bandol, and the many obscure whites of Châteauneuf-du-Pape: Roussane, Marsanne, Clairette, Counoise, Bourboulenc, Grenache gris.

Saint-Jean-de-Bebian became the aristocrat wine of Languedoc—something which would have been a contradiction in terms a few decades earlier. For Languedoc has long been France's own little third world, and her wine the unwitting symbol of her backwardness and surly underdevelopment.

This last fact must have appealed to Jean-Claude Le Brun when he bought the estate with his wife, Françoise Lecouty, in 1994. Le Brun and Lecouty were the editors of the prestigious wine magazine *Revue de Vin de France*, but Le Brun is also a wealthy sometime Trotskyist whom I met through a mutual friend. Boyish in salt-and-pepper curls and green galoshes, Le Brun gave off a fierce energy which seemed stabilized by his orderly surroundings: the beautiful house, the strangely distant wife who shook my hand and disappeared, the vineyards themselves, which stretched down to the lonely road. A few laborers milled around the courtyard. There was a tension even between Le Brun and them.

"These people in Languedoc," he said. "Hopeless. It's like working with savages." He held up his hands. No, he wasn't being serious.

"Do you still read Trotsky?"

"Sure. But I hate being called the red millionaire. I can't have political views because I made good?"

This was fair enough.

We walked around the edges of the vines while Le Brun told me impishly how he had once thrown the influential New York wine importer Michael Skurnik out of the house. He wasn't going to take any shit from Americans; but he loved Americans all the same. New York? The most fantastic of cities.

"Now I want to sail around the world. I'm getting ready to do it. That's the most important thing right now for me: sailing around the world. That's the dream."

"More important than making wine?"

"There's nothing like sailing round the world."

We drove into Pézenas for lunch in his SUV, listening to the soundtrack for the Cohen brothers' film *Oh Brother, Where Art Thou?* The mournful Louisiana riffs and Baptist dirges got Le Brun going. "Listen to that—fantastic! What a country!" We barreled along country roads at top speed with Harry McClintock booming out his "Big Rock Candy Mountain." Pézenas is one of the South's most architecturally noble towns, with its blond lemon stones and airiness, but within such rational constraints Le Brun seemed to overflow, if a man can be said to overflow. We found a restaurant and drank our way through his Saint-Jean-de-Bebians—from the '96 to the '99—while Le Brun subjected them to his own glancing criticisms. The wines were different from the only Roux-era Saint-Jean-de-Bebians I had tasted before: they seemed fruitier, a little heavier but also smoother. I asked Le Brun what his thinking behind them was. Languedoc was in a period of upheaval. It was a wine backwater now trying to launch itself like so many backwaters on the proverbial "glittering international career." Had Bebian had to retool itself to be the flagship of a region on the move?

"But that wasn't my thinking at all. You can only make the wine you have latent in your bones. It's an animal feeling . . ."

But, I persisted, he and Lecouty were intellectual wine aristocrats, former wine editors far more aware of the outside world than most in Languedoc.

"Ah yes. But as I said, I threw Michael out of my house because I have my principles. This idea that there's an international market to which we inevitably conform—"

"What would Trotsky say?"

He laughed. "I'm still *rouge*, you know."

"Isn't everyone in Languedoc?"

"I don't know. I suppose in some ways it's the most Communist region in Europe. I wouldn't know. I'm not into activism anymore. Maybe it's a shame."

I found it hard to imagine him as an activist in the first place. Too gay, too charming; an aura of poetic impatience. Very often the most severe of wine activists and moralists are not those who actually toil on the land. I asked him about the wine riot in Béziers. Was this the farming proletariat rising up against the disappearance of their world?

"The powerhouse wineries in Languedoc now are all the creations of outsiders. If you look at Mas Jullien, Mas de Daumas Gaussac, or even a corporation like Fortant de France, they're all run by outsiders. Mas Jullien belongs to an old family, but it's the son Olivier who came back from Paris to create the new wines. Aimé Guibert at Daumas Gaussac used to be in the glove business elsewhere. Fortant is run by Robert Skalli, who's an Algerian Jew. Then there's me—I don't exactly look local."

This all gave rise to an awkward question. If the best wines in Languedoc were being made by people who were not really Languedoc wine makers, then what was authentic and inauthentic in Languedoc? One might object that continually fretting about authenticity is a bit adolescent. The Béziers rioters were surely the authentic growers of the region, but the wine they made was still execrable. And Languedoc was first discovered for the wider world by the American Kermit Lynch, not by a local luminary.

The growers were interested in cash, new roofs, dresses for their wives, a bit of capital, and not much else. They made subsidized wine lakes. Was a subsidized mass commodity "authentic"?

I offered the view that French farming in general was a bit of a swindle, paid for by the taxpayers of other countries, who then quite rightly treated it as a tourist park. I think Le Brun winced a little at that. Every Frenchman will defend the honor of his countryside and its golden produce. But wine, the ultimate farm produce, was clearly not made by the same men who turned out cabbages and onions. Languedoc wine as we now know it was in reality invented thirty years ago out of nothing. The varietals were there, but no one was doing anything with them.

In *Adventures on the Wine Route*, Lynch describes the pioneers in Languedoc as they were in the 1970s, and one of them was Alain Roux at Saint-Jean-de-Bebian:

> I am the first to admit that there are better wines than Alain's Domaine de Saint-Jean-de-Bebian. If he had vines at Chambertin or Hermitage, one would take his success for granted because the quality of those sites has been proven over the centuries and from them we expect extraordinary wines. But Alain's *domaine* is in the Languedoc. That is what gives his struggle a touch of the heroic.

Roux, in fact, had noticed the similarities between Saint-Jean-de-Bebian's soils and those of Châteauneuf-du-Pape. He therefore decided to uproot all the high-quantity vines traditionally grown in Languedoc to make cheap wine and planted the thirteen different varietals grown to make great Châteauneuf-du-Papes. He also resolved to plow phosphates into his soils to imitate the soil conditions at Hermitage, the great domain of the Northern Rhône.

According to Lynch, the previous Saint-Jean-de-Bebians had been fun to drink—*désaltérant*, as the French say—but lacked the length and depth of distinguished wines. They were slight. After Roux's curious experiment to create terroir artificially, Lynch thought he saw a new wine emerging:

> And one can see from the 1984 Saint-Jean-de-Bebian that his gamble of yanking out his vineyards has paid off, that the *terroir* of the Languedoc possesses an unexpected nobility. . . . The brilliant splash of purple in the glass is the first sign that

you have something extraordinary. The aroma suggests thyme, fennel, black cherry, and black pepper . . . it has the warmth and generosity of a wine from the sunny south, but it is not too heavy, too alcoholic, nor is it mean with tannin.

This suggested that terroir might not be so mystical as some believed. Roux's 1981 Saint-Jean-de-Bebian, Lynch claimed, even tasted exactly like a top Châteauneuf-du-Pape, with its "stony *goût de terroir*." "It is not," he concluded, "a little wine."

"Those were strong words," Le Brun agreed. "A Languedoc wine suddenly comparable to Châteauneuf-du-Pape or a Hermitage—which, you know, many consider the greatest wine of southern France? It was very improbable. It sent a shock wave through the wine world."

I leaned into my glass and searched for the thyme and fennel, the scents of the garrigue, the arid scrubland of the Midi, which many Languedoc wines are supposed to exude, and which Lynch claimed to have found in the older Bebians. But it was difficult to connect the wines before me to the Roux wine, to say whether Le Brun had continued Roux's experiment to some logical conclusion or not. I told him that I seemed to be following precisely in Kermit Lynch's footsteps. I was going to Faugères later in the day, a village which Lynch had depicted as being "always deserted" in the shade of its plane trees, and I was going to the Abbaye de Valmagne, the Gaussac Valley, and Mas de Daumas Gaussac, which Lynch had called "one of the most remarkable new wineries in the world."

"Is that intentional?" Le Brun asked.

"Perhaps I'm curious to see how things have changed."

"But then, there's one thing that's not in his book which you should investigate before you go to the Gaussac Valley. And that is Fortant de France. Alas, Fortant de France is the rising power here."

The name rang a bell. It's the wine of choice for Indian restaurants on Sixth Street in New York. Almost every curry house on Indian Restaurant Row has a choice of Fortant de France wines. Someone must have decided at some point that these industrial vintages like "Couleurs du Sud" went well with chicken korma and rogan gosht. If the rioters of Béziers, Le Brun suggested, were irate about anything, it was the growing power of efficient corporations like Fortant de France that were outgunning them in the pursuit of mass production.

For Le Brun, I thought, this must be the crux of a nagging doubt. Fortant de France represented a new form of capitalism which he must fear as well as loathe. Fortant planted whatever varietals it liked, a rare insolence in France, where native varietals in each region are dictated by law. It hired Australian experts, the famous "flying wine makers," who flew from site to site in small aircraft. And above all, it used financial models to map out its wines.

"But of course," Le Brun observed, "this is the new way of doing things—in publishing, in entertainment, everywhere. The accountant and the marketers are the creators. In France, we've only seen this kind of thing in the last ten years or so. In the States you've had it for thirty years. But where does that leave all of us?"

As we drove back, the black chain-gang songs from *Oh Brother* got Le Brun into a mood one could call "redder." America was great . . . but the condition of the blacks . . . On the other hand, didn't this racial melodrama sensed from afar make America that much more darkly glamorous? The local savages of Languedoc, after all, don't have any comparable songs. All they have is food.

At dusk the next day I reached Sète. Around the city, strung out along the flat and colorless beaches, lie huge Floridian resort suburbs. But the port itself is another world. It is like a miniature Marseilles, with docks, canal bridges, a white church on a hill. Its claim to fame is that the songwriter Georges Brassens is buried here in the Cimetière Marin overlooking the sea, as is the poet Paul Valéry. In the winter it is half-empty, uneasy. The most garish, if decayed, hotel is by the quays: L'Orgue Bleue, with the two words displayed in bright blue neon and flickering on and off due to some faulty wire. I stayed in an immense room with a balcony overlooking the fishing boats, and spent a day walking around the Cimetière Marin searching for the grave of Valéry. I could not find it. The cemetery was crammed with Italian immigrant fishermen who had all met unnatural deaths on the sardine-and-tuna boats or who had fed the cannons of empire. Names like Eugène Herber, *tué glorieusement à Pekin, 1900*, or bombastic Italian hyphenates like Imperator-Liguori, Apicella-Autori, and Avallone-Laude. Under the sad lighthouse you are reminded what a cruel sea this was before international nudism and the holiday business arrived.

It was into this immigrant mélange that Robert Skalli made his way from Algeria in the 1950s. It's an unlikely setting for a wine empire. The Fortant headquarters occupies several buildings nestled in the industrial port zone, amid endless avenues of bricks and cobbles. The vestibule is a forum for wine-inspired artworks of improbable dimensions, organized around a reception desk garlanded with wine bottles. The dominant color is aqua blue. One sees at once the Fortant wines: Couleurs du Sud laid in bright orange picnic boxes, Terra Vecchia, and "F" (inspired by Skalli's son François, who was killed in a plane accident). These are varietal wines on the Californian model, inspired by Robert Mondavi, and we learn that Fortant was one of the first companies in France to make them. The artwork is intended to match their spirit. Most overwhelming is a huge pop sculpture called *Figuration Libre*. Inspired by comics, it consists of garish clusters of grapes decorated with demonic and cartoony faces. Art and wine: usually a banal combination. But sandwiched between two of the buildings and visible through several windows stands a stranger installation, a boat in which sits a giant Muppetlike fisherman. *We're the New World of France*, the walls declare.

I was met by Jérôme Boutang, Fortant's boyish marketing director. The HQ was already beginning to feel like Willy Wonka's Chocolate Factory, with men in white lab coats speeding along corridors as brightly decorated as those of a primary school. Jérôme too was bright and amiable—impossible to dislike. We went on a whirlwind tour. "Like the art?" he said as we climbed stairs sheathed in glass. "It's to show our new and modern style. We're very connected to California. I often say *franglais spoken here*!" We passed into the bottling plant, which has been deliberately constructed to accommodate visitors, with a windowed gallery looking out over enormous automated conveyor belts. Thirty million bottles a year, seventeen thousand an hour. Overhead, little vine gardens planted on the roof fluttered in the rain while Boutang regaled me with well-rehearsed statistics.

France, he said, farmed 59,650 hectoliters of wine in 1996, but consumption inside France was falling and had been falling for decades. The crisis began to bite in the 1980s. The problem was the stubborn and old-fashioned French consumer, who could not think outside of the AOC system. He or she was unable to imagine, let alone drink, any foreign wines or wines that were made untraditionally, like Fortant's. Foreign wines made up about 3 percent of the French market. Pitiful xenophobia. It's true that French wine stores are generally provincial: no Italian or Spanish wines, no great German whites, almost nothing from the New World. The French know nothing about global wine. Even practiced French drinkers are woefully parochial compared to their American counterparts, for the world's most eclectic wine stores are in New York, not Paris.

"Well," Boutang said, as if forlornly, "the French don't want brands and varietals. The very notion of the brand is completely alien here."

Of course, that might not be a bad thing?

"Not if it means becoming fossilized."

We walked to the labs, with lab coats still swirling efficiently around us. If only Fortant, Boutang went on, could explain to French consumers—those hopeless mules!—the principles of brands, varietals, and open markets, they would understand. The French might even start tasting other people's wines. Naturally, there was a small minority of cosmopolitan people in France, people who spoke English, who were looking for new things. Speaking of which, he suddenly wondered aloud why it was that British journalists hadn't taken the lead from Robert Parker. They were so much better than he was. But they didn't have chutzpah. That was a shame. It would be better if the British had chutzpah.

"Numerical scoring," he scowled. "Ridiculous!"

But then, he clarified, it was in the American character to be expansionist, to dominate, to lead moral crusades. To have moral passions. That was what made Parker distasteful to the French: moral passion!

"And his incorruptibility?" I asked.

"No. The *undue* influence."

In the labs, we met two highly energetic and articulate enologists, Philippe Tolleret and the superbly named Pierre Gouttenoire. Tolleret walked calmly to a blackboard and began sketching curves. There were, he explained, 275 million hectares in Languedoc. It was an enormous growing area, as large as California's wine regions. And extremely diverse. It had once been underwater, like parts of the Sahara, a fertile sea which had deposited vast arrays of marine organisms into its soils. There were chalk cliffs as in the Minervois, cold highlands around Limoux and the hills around Montpeyroux, and hot plains. If traditions could be "mutated" into a new way of generic wine growing, Languedoc could be a wine superpower all by itself. Fortant alone worked with five hundred growers. The idea was that if they culled fruit from a wide smattering of parcels, they could create a wine that didn't vary from year to year. It would be the wine equivalent of a Honda Civic.

Skalli had to start at the bottom of the market, making cheap brand wines—Sunny Wines for Sunny Dishes, as one wall ad had it. But now they were buying new vineyards, plots of poorer soil in colder altitudes, which were going to yield more complex wines. And chief of these was going to be a premium Coteaux de Languedoc called Silène des Peyrals, which was going to be launched in a few weeks' time. The plot was forty hectares in the middle of nowhere, up in the mountains, and planted with Grenache, Carignan, and Syrah. In Corsica, meanwhile, Fortant was turning out a wine called Terra Vecchia which had taken Scandinavia by storm.

"It's the top-selling wine in Norway!" Tolleret beamed.

I wanted to see a vineyard-in-progress, so I spent most of a day with Boutang in his little company car winding our way up to Silène des Peyrals and back. It was bitterly cold, not at all Kermit Lynch weather. We swept through the acres of Muscat de Frontignan, the rain beating their clipped vines. The lines were widely spaced for machine harvesting. The old days of North African manual labor, Boutang said, were over. Everything was by machine down here. California again.

Around Silène, the soil turned dark red as if suffused with iron. The land is scrawny with garrigue, sloped and luminous: Cézanne country. Mont-Saint-Clair loomed through the rain. Huge white pebbles littered the Martian mud while in the far distance, forming silvery gray lines on the horizon, oyster beds adjoined the sea.

The winery hadn't yet been built, but the vines were there, neatly trellised and widely spaced. Freshly cleared fields stood ready for replanting, the rocks broken up by heavy machines. We walked around the empty spaces where the winery would stand some day, a sleek affair using "gravity" as its main operational principle. So a kind of smaller Languedoc Opus One? The idea, Boutang said, would be not to stress the grapes. And the Silène would be their top wine: it would eventually retail at forty-five dollars a bottle.

We drove down to the Abbaye de Valmagne, where Kermit Lynch marveled at "the largest wine casks I have ever seen." In truth, it was these Rabelaisian casks which I wanted to see. Lynch had also written that the Abbaye's own wines, made then under the direction of François Serre (a friend of Roux) were promising. Boutang had not tasted them, but he was curious.

There are only five monks living at Valmagne now and none of them was in the cloisters, which are green with bamboo. It used to be a Roman villa: Gallo-Roman columns of smoothly fluted marble lay around like gigantic crumbs. The monks' old fish pool still stood bubbling in the rain, though empty of carp. And in the bare nave of the church, surrounded by corroded stone, stood the monumental casks like something out of a fairy tale (a wine-making giant?). They had been used to make wine until the 1950s. What kind of wine, though, could it have been? The Abbaye now makes its wines using strange varietals that I had never heard of—and Boutang, who should know, had never heard of them either. Grapes like Morrastel, which makes a wine called Morrastel de Frères Nonenque. Alone in the chilled tasting room, we sipped from the current offerings, Les 10 Arpentes, a Colline de la Moure, a 1999 Cuvée de Turenne made from Syrah and Mourvèdre. Unsurprisingly, the Morrastel was the oddest, with its flavors of cinnamon, orange rind, and caramel.

We then sat by the cloister fountain, under sprawling vines. I asked Boutang if he felt the force of any wine history in a place like this. I'm not sure the question really made any sense to him. He was an intelligent young man with great internal energy directed toward his job, which of course was wine. But I also had the sense that wine for him, as for me, was a sort of open book which we had not read from beginning to end. In sum: was the world of tradition, in Languedoc, in fatal opposition to everything Fortant de France stood for?

"I don't think so," he said confidently. "Because what tradition would that be? There was very little here before. I think we're filling a vacuum more than anything. You saw Silène des Peyrals. We're not *replacing* anything. We're developing a wilderness."

I drove on alone toward Bedarieux. The rain stopped and the

road fell between lonely Hérault mountains. I came to a place called Prieuré Royal de Notre-Dame de Cassa, lost among its own vines, with two towers—one square, one round—set like huge chess pieces among the leaves. The sun came out unexpectedly, giving me a moment to sit under the priory walls with a bottle of Domaine d'Aupilhac, a Montpeyroux which I love and which I had bought in Pézenas before leaving. It seemed to refute Jérôme's remarks quite squarely—thus it was a shame that we hadn't opened it together. Its earthy subtlety might have made him reconsider. I drank half of the bottle alone, letting its chocolate softness slide into my mouth and listening to sluggish crickets come awake one by one around the field of Our Lady of Cassa.

When Kermit Lynch visited Mas de Daumas Gaussac in the early 1980s, its wine was a startling novelty, but already the darling of the wine press on both sides of the Atlantic. *Gault Millau* had cried that it was "the Lafite of Languedoc." The London *Times* had made its own pronouncement after the very first vintage in 1978: Daumas Gaussacs, it sighed, were "more like Latour than Lafite . . . with their enormous color and immense, hefty, tannic character." Enormous color? Lynch snorted. "Can color have size, bulging perhaps beyond the boundaries imposed by its vessel, in this case evidently a wine glass?"

Whatever the dubious metaphors, Daumas Gaussac had arrived as a serious wine and Lynch found its creator, Aimé Guibert, to be a remarkable man. His sensational debut, he noted, had been a bit like the entry of California's Cabernets and Chardonnays onto the world stage in 1976. "Clearly," Émile Peynaud wrote of this new Grand Cru, "quality has emerged where it was not expected." And the man? Lynch wrote that he was "brimming with capitalist energy" and that he had astonishing aquamarine blue eyes that said, "Let's go, let's not tarry." Guibert sounded a bit like D'Artagnan.

The Mas is in fact an old flour mill built on the dark and winding Gaussac River. Once upon a time, Guibert was the rather patrician boss of one of the world's top leather glove makers, a business in the nearby town of Millau which once upon a time had sold to luxury stores on Fifth Avenue and the rue Saint-Honoré. He went to New York during the Marshall Plan and enjoyed a kind of leather glove golden age. He was given the red carpet treatment by Saks and Bergdorf Goodman; he was a glove millionaire, probably a fun thing to be in the 1950s. Indeed, he told me, it was a glorious age, an era of taste, especially when it came to leather gloves. And Guibert Frères had been one of the biggest. Ah, *les gens de cuir*. The leather aristocracy. All lost! For globalization and the rise of the Asian industry had smashed the French leather business in the 1980s. Guibert left the glove trade all but broke.

We sat in his study in the heart of the mill, the seventy-eight-year-old ex–glove king still chic in a crisp dark blue shirt and plum sweater, his shock of white hair and craggy face lit up by an orange table lamp which made the whole room—with its vellum books, prints, and antiques—look submerged. Guibert has the dainty formality of the very age whose passing he appears to regret: the modern world, in any case, is not his cup of tea. On that we immediately agreed. I was still curious about his previous life and *les gens de cuir*.

"Ah, I knew everyone. I remember when Gloversville, New York, was the center of the world. Gloves were a wonderful line of work."

"Gloversville?"

"I see you've never heard of it. And you live in New York. It's all vanished. The vile multinationals wiped it all out. Au revoir, Gloversville. They destroyed the glove business, you know. And now they're trying to destroy the wine world!"

After Guibert went bust with gloves his thoughts turned to the land. The forgotten flour mill in the forgotten Gaussac Valley appealed. But he had no thoughts about wine. He thought he'd go into the corn business. The place looked perfect for corn. So he signed a contract with one of France's largest corn conglomerates and bought Mas de Daumas Gaussac. At the age of forty-five he was starting all over again.

Before long the Mas was visited by the famed enologist Henri Engelbert. Engelbert told Guibert that corn was a waste of time; he could make this iron-rich soil into a southern Margaux. Émile Peynaud came next.

"He had more papillae in his mouth than anyone alive," Guibert proclaimed, lifting up an apostolic index finger. Peynaud pronounced the same judgment as Engelbert.

Guibert sighed and leaned back in his chair as he paid Peynaud (who is slowly dying in Paris from Parkinson's disease) the ultimate French compliment: "A monument. The man is a monument. The immensity of his culture is astounding. He is a *savant sage.*" He looked me in the eye and I heard the cold waters of the Gaussac swirling almost silently below the window. "He is a great artist—almost superhuman! A monument. I compare him to Michelangelo. And only I have been loyal to him! He's advised me all along. Our wines are Peynaud wines."

"Michelangelo?"

"Certainly. Michelangelo."

"And what was his method?"

"You do analyses, you read 'em, you stick 'em in a drawer and then you use your mouth." Laughter. He paused with emphatic drama and raised his eyebrows. "You know, he wrote us a magnificent letter after our first 1978 vintage came out. I'll publish it after his death. He told me, never ask me about money, and I never did. I love him. It's an *amour d'homme.*"

Guibert shrugged before the ineffable.

"We have a motto here," he half whispered. He looked at me gravely before pronouncing it.

"*Ne pas posséder, être.*"

Not to possess, to be: an ancient proverb. Peynaud, Guibert said, had the exactly same philosophy.

"He is like Michael Broadbent," Guibert said, referring to the legendary British connoisseur. "A gentleman. A dying breed. Yes, I love those old-style English gentlemen, too. Broadbent, Johnson . . . they are amazing men. Their culture is extraordinary. You know, the English made us. When the English lords had to sell their cellars after the war, Christie's and Sotheby's were flooded with the greatest wine, and men like Broadbent were able to develop their palates unlike anyone else. The old English—marvelous, generous. Like Americans used to be!"

And suddenly Guibert became ferociously animated at the thought of Americans. Not the good old Americans, but the nasty modern ones. The modern American political class: it was cruel, hard, villainous. Especially President George W. Bush. *Votre président, excusez-moi, mais c'est pas Tony Blair!* I nodded meekly; what can one say? In a way, I was surprised that I had not heard this most popular of rants more often. Nor the equally popular observation, and far more dubious assertion, that the political class of Americans was "villainous" but that the amiable American people were on a different planet.

But George Bush was just the beginning.

The malaise, Guibert said, had spread everywhere. Even into supermarkets. Yes: even supermarkets expressed this Twilight of the Idols! There, I put in quickly, I agreed with him. Supermarkets were demonic.

"Auchan, Carrefour, Tesco," he cried, listing the French and British supermarket giants. ". . . *Hitler!*"

Guibert slammed his palm onto the table and we laughed—or sort of. The growers of Bordeaux, he said, used to sell to English lords who valued their wines' complexity. Now they sold to supermarket thugs.

"We are in the world of Dr. Strangeglove, Monsieur Osborne.

Science perverted by money! We have become dominators of nature. We observe or we dominate—a basic choice. So there are two types of wine maker, observers and dominators. You know, money is humanity's curse. Brands are our curse too. Look at the Greeks—fine, elegant. Then they were steamrollered by the Roman juggernaut—"

"So we are the Greeks and the Americans are the Romans?"

"I am not the first to say it! *Ne pas posséder, être!*"

(Am I Greek or Roman? I pondered.)

I wondered then if Guibert had understood the subtle irony embedded for him in the word "Strangeglove"? *Strange glove.* I peered down at his hands and wondered what they would look like in a pair of his own luxury calfskin gloves. Come to think of it, he would have made a brilliant Strangeglove himself, much better than Peter Sellers. That categorical edge in the voice, that piercing gaze. Those hands. Naturally, though, we would have to talk about that real Strangelove of the wine world, Monsieur Robert Parker. The pope, Guibert quipped (and I gathered this was a much-used term for the Sage of Monkton).

"He is a corsair!" Guibert thundered. "A pirate! A wily pirate—but one can't blame him, after all. He has a strategic intelligence."

Like President Bush, all in all?

"Ah, one could say that."

Was he a typical Roman, too? But naturally he was.

Guibert's face grew genuinely sorrowful, astonished, dismayed; even a little tortured. Was there a cry of "Let's not tarry!" in the eyes? I couldn't say. One grows older—and Guibert had made his name in the world, he was probably less restless than he had been earlier. He was also calm in the certainty that with his wine, as with his gloves, he had made a "work of art."

That afternoon I drove around the estate with his son, Samuel. Samuel did his apprenticeship in New Zealand. It's a surprising fact that there are strong links between Australasia and Languedoc. The region is crawling with Australian wine makers, and not just the "flying doctors." Most Australians do their apprenticeships in France. Australian viticulture is accordingly far more French than its Californian equivalent. And the sons of Languedoc repay the compliment. Samuel put in six years in New Zealand. It was "eye-opening," and for dismaying reasons.

For one thing, the French business environment was stifling. "We are not," he said, "even in the same century as Australia. I mean, the thirty-five-hour week in France: it's stupidity on a grandiose scale." Therefore the Australasians were conquering. It was like competition between a capitalist country and a Communist one. But France had the right elements, the small terroirs, the habit of working close to the ground.

The Mas is high up, close to the La Seranne mountains, with the vines planted on its northern slopes. Nights are cold; there is no humidity in the soil. For every hectare of vines, the Guiberts have left intact a hectare of wild garrigue, a tumult of lavender and scrub oak. No chemical fertilizer, only sheep dung. Everything is done manually. Even the grapes are crushed through gravity. Moreover, the six thousand plants of the estate are "all different." Why, Samuel asked rhetorically, were there no Grand Crus in Languedoc? Because Grand Crus were the product of a microclimate and carefully appreciated soils—Daumas Gaussac was one of the rare places which had both.

We looked across the valley, toward the Mont St.-Baudille. Samuel explained that Mondavi had recently tried to buy his way into the valley. His father had been outraged (or merely threatened?) and the local politicians had got involved. Uproar ensued, and the American predators were beaten back, for the time being anyway. Mondavi, of course, had realized how valuable this earth was, what its potential might be. On the far side of the valley, for example, the Jullien family was making the other great wines of the region. It had to be a question of soil.

We got out of the Jeep and went about plowing fingers into this gold-dust soil. It was powdery-fine, dark red, iron-rich. Next to this red dust, the fields yielded a browner chalk soil. Around the fields, banks of wild herbs reared up—the garrigue that subtly flavors the wine.

Why, I asked, had there been such a fuss about Mondavi?

"A question of sensibility. It didn't seem right to my father."

"Wasn't it a bit of a storm in a teacup?"

"Not at all. Mondavi might have overshadowed everyone else. And what kind of wine would he have made? Not a Languedoc wine."

But, I persisted, Mas de Daumas Gaussac wasn't exactly a traditional Languedoc wine either. Cabernet wasn't a traditional varietal in the South.

"There's always been a Daumas Gaussac wine," Samuel countered. "Even if it wasn't a Cabernet. Even when it was just peasants buying and selling it. We think Charlemagne probably drank Daumas Gaussac in the eighth century: his foreign minister Saint Benoît lived in Aniane down the road."

It was difficult to know what to make of this. From Charlemagne to Émile Peynaud? That had been a long, dark interval between the two. I pondered the connection in the tasting room as the light began to wane, sipping from the Moulin de Gaussac Cabernet Sauvignon as I went over a copy of Michael Broadbent's tasting notes for the Daumas Gaussac reds. By this point in my peregrinations, my palate was beginning to learn some tricks, to know some of the ins and outs. But Broadbent's notes were nevertheless satisfyingly simple and easy to grasp. Some of the wines had "rich legs," others had a "muffled nose" and a color of "youthful purple," while most were described as evolved, austere, suave, or developed. His language was restrained and sensible. I thought I could detect even the "crystallized violets" somewhere in this wine, if not the all-imposing terroir which Peynaud and Guibert thought was its heart. The test, I simply supposed, would be the aroma of garrigue. But try as I might, thyme, lavender, and laurel did not come bursting out of the glass. I went to the window and breathed in the cold air of the river below. Was there something I was missing? Broadbent talked of "a pleasant, easy style," which I could understand, as well as a sweetness combined with a whiff of pepper on the nose. But beyond that, I was lost. Being very honest with myself, I found the wines a little indistinct. Could I ever have picked them blind out of a lineup? *Une note de charme*, Peynaud would write of the 1987 in *his* tasting notes, and that pretty much summed it up for me. There were many of these notes of charm, but no central axis I could relish. Perhaps, then, my palate had not yet caught up with other sensual sympathies?

As the moon came out I wandered outside into the shade of the cypresses where Aimé was waiting for me to say good-bye. As if suddenly, a spectacular beauty overwhelmed the place, cold stars bursting out of the sky, the cypresses stabbing into dark blue air. We shook hands and stood for a moment saying nothing, looking at the silhouettes of umbrella pines along the hills. Guibert's wife, Véronique Guibert de la Vassière, is one of the world's leading authorities on Celtic rites, and I now understood why she loved Daumas Gaussac. I said there were moments when this land was very Roman. Guibert thought about this for a few seconds, then huffed and puffed.

"Yes, but that Julius Caesar," he said. "What a bastard! Just like Louis XIV and *Hitler*!"

Leaving the Mas, I drove up the valley to the monastery of Saint-Guilhem-le-Desert. Driving through a windswept Aniane, I couldn't help thinking how oddly America intrudes into even the most remote medieval backwaters. Not only had there been this recent scandal with Robert Mondavi, but Saint-Guilhem-le-Desert itself was one of the monasteries from which New York City constructed its famous landmark, the Cloisters, which had been transported stone by stone across the Atlantic. I wondered if the French would ever want it back, Elgin Marble style. Or whether they'd spent all the money and would leave it at that. In any case, Saint-Guilhem is usually a tourist trap, but on a dark night in winter it was anything but. The road turning through gorges was empty. It really was a desert, a narrow sliver of Judea in southern France.

In the main square of the village, a druidic tree stood in a net of fairy lights. And in the courtyard of the Abbaye de Gellone a hunting party loitered with exhausted dogs under the trees, guns laid against the walls. There is a sound of trickling water everywhere, as if the hermitage were a huge clepsydra lost in the mountains. I wandered into the church, primitive and gauntly cold. Three or four monks in white robes singing to themselves, a bareness in balance with the severe cypresses around the cemetery outside and a sky of cruel stars. And the water tumbling down from the mountain above, fanning out through gutters, crevices, and cracks. There is an eremetic remoteness to such places in the Southwest, like the Cathar castles at Peyrepertuse or Quiribus. The spirit of place here is, deep down, otherworldly, dry, and reclusive. It is Christian-primitive, *cathare*: pure.

The following morning I went to visit Jean-Pierre Jullien at Mas de Cal Demoura. Mas de Cal Demoura is one of the intriguing success stories of modern Languedoc wine. The Julliens have been farming wine for generations around the sleepy villages of Jonquières and Saint-Felix-de-Lodes. But in the 1950s the wine business slumped and there was an exodus from the seemingly worthless vineyards. The broke growers who remained played it safe and went into cooperatives churning out blending wine. Following the trend, Jean-Pierre made cooperative wine for years and dabbled in olive oil on the side. It was his son Olivier who decided in 1985 to start a new winery called Mas Jullien based on completely different principles: it would make a terroir wine, not a cooperative one. In 1993 Jean-Pierre thought it might be amusing to imitate his son and start a winery of his own next door, the Mas de Cal Demoura. Father and son today make wines side by side, each clinging to his own style. Olivier is one of the young stars of southern French wine, while Jean-Pierre has patiently built up his own reputation somewhat in his shadow. "A peasant is an individual," he says. "We couldn't make wine together."

Olivier was away that day, and in a sense I was glad. It's often said that wine is about fathers and sons, but within that equation the fathers are often more interesting than the sons. Jean-Pierre Jullien lives in a simple house on the winery, which looks like nothing at all from the outside. A garage, a garden, a small warehouse. He came to the gate, his voice booming over the roses, ruddy and quickly alert, filled with a physical electricity which brimmed over into his hands, which moved about like a pair of purposeful scissors. Inside the house was the same. It was filled with handsome hunting guns, a Christmas manger in models, old oil lamps; and by a fire stood a table of fresh oysters. An old man suddenly rose and came toward us. At first I thought it was an optical illusion, for Jean-Pierre's ninety-year-old father Alipe was dressed in stand-fall collar, ancient black suit, and a pair of pumps which seemed to have been worn continuously since 1930. Alipe was a prewar wine maker, a peasant vigneron straight out of the pages of Jules Renard's *Nos frères les paysans*. He had a glass of Picpoul de Pinet in a wobbling hand. And suddenly I realized that they were all singing together— Alipe, Jean-Pierre, and his equally jolly wife, and a young man named Virgile, who has just opened his own *domaine* down the road. They were singing and downing glass after glass of this Picpoul de Pinet, a local white:

> *Je suis de Midi*
> *Je me rajouis!*

So I joined in. At least I could sing the refrain.

We sat down and dug into the oysters—floppy oysters with a

sharply briney taste. Jean-Pierre brought out another bottle: a Clairette de Die, a bubbly from Saint-Romans-en-Diois near Lyons made by a man named Didier Cornillon.

"Ah, Didier Cornillon," sighed our host, raising an oyster to his mouth and tipping it in. "How I love Didier Cornillon. Who can say that Didier Cornillon doesn't make the best of all Clairette de Die?"

The family sighed along and shook their heads with pleasure— the memory of many a Clairette de Die from Didier Cornillon? Who indeed could deny that Didier Cornillon was the best producer of Clairette de Die?

A toast, and the Didier Cornillon. It had a sweet, voluptuous taste of Muscat. On the bottle I read the words *méthode ancestrale dioise*.

"It's just one of those wines you love," Jean-Pierre said. "It's simple, but you love drinking it and that's all."

Alipe turned to me with eyes that perfectly matched the oysters all around us.

"Monsieur," he said, "did you know that we had a wine riot here back in 1907? My father was there. We threw our harvest in the ditches." His eyes lit up. "After all, they were trying to *assassiner la république!*"

"Who were?"

"The landlords. The bosses. They sent in troops."

Madame Jullien promptly got up and came back with an old photograph of the 1907 wine riot in Béziers. It showed a band of vignerons with pitchforks sporting handlebar mustaches and cocky straw boaters. They looked a pretty fearsome lot, like a band of Pancho Villa's revolutionaries. She pointed to a jolly face in the crowd that looked exactly like her. "That's my great-grandmother. As you can see, everyone was there."

The leader of the 1907 Wine Insurrection, as it was sometimes known, was a farmer named Albert Marcellin. The movement commanded large demonstrations across the South—half a million in

Montpellier—and later forced Prime Minister Clemenceau to send in the troops, killing five. The immediate cause was the fall of the price of wine from thirty francs a hectoliter in the 1880s to ten by 1900. But as always, perhaps, the rioters had misunderstood the root of this malaise. They blamed manufacturers of "fake wine" for creating the huge wine lakes of the early twentieth century. In reality, the problem was simply overproduction. Algeria, Spain, Sicily, and all the French regions were flooding the French market. But it was also true that in the north of the country winegrowers had found a sneaky way of competing with Languedoc: chaptalization, or the adding of sugar and water to intensify the wine. The Languedoc riots were therefore, in a sense, antichaptalization riots replete with cries of "*Vive le vin naturel!*"

Thus wine riots, like other kinds of riots, have a way of returning us to conflicts which are not as resolved as we like to think. Clemenceau eventually relented and set up the nation's first census to determine how much wine was being made: a first step in the integration of wine into the national economy in a rational way. Historians like Hugh Johnson have argued that the 1907 riots were the pangs of modern wine's painful birth, a birth which occurred over a half century of crises beginning with the roaring 1890s and ending with the Second World War. During this period, slumps, war, overproduction, and the phylloxera epidemic forced wine into a reckoning with itself. Extensive fraud, with merchants inventing phony wines left and right, had undermined the authenticity of almost every region, forcing the state to intervene to reestablish legitimate definitions of regions and their wines. In the general crisis of the early 1900s, however, the fake wines had collapsed even faster than the real ones, something which the Béziers rioters had not grasped. But then again, revolts are mythic events, and are intended to be. Their songs are more important than their rationales.

And now a new round of songs erupted, this time worker songs. There was the refrain *assassiner la république* and Jean-Pierre gave

me a nudge in the ribs. He liked nudging, and he nudged in a delicate, friendly way that was actually enjoyable. He nudged and said,
"I hate Paris. Back in 1907 we weren't yet subjected to Paris. I'd
rather have Arabs making their *mechoui* here than Parisians." He
added that as a result of his participation in the wine riot Alipe's father had been placed on the front line in 1914. It was a punishment.
But now it was time for a house rosé.

The rosé was called *Qu'es a quo?* In Oc, the ancient language of
Languedoc, this is *Qu'est-ce que c'est?*

"It's a shame, Laurent, that you don't speak Oc. We could talk
much more subtly about this and that if you spoke Oc. It's a fantastic language for talking wine."

We drank one of Jean-Pierre's softly earthy wines, a Coteaux du
Languedoc L'Infidèle 2001, and then a pure Cinsault, one of the five
Southern varietals with which the Julliens work, blending their
wines from all five. Terroir, again? It was rustic and gay, I decided,
and here (unlike Daumas) I could taste something from the earth.
Garrigue, perhaps, though to find garrigue in a Languedoc wine is
the smoothest of clichés. More to the point was that there was
something of Jean-Pierre in Jean-Pierre's L'Infidèle. Something
booming, warm, square-shouldered. But how could I *not* think this
since he was gesticulating right in front of me?

Carignan, Grenache, Syrah, Mourvèdre, and Cinsault are the
five elementary colors of the Languedoc wine maker. And while
Syrah alone can produce the pedigree reds of the northern Rhône
and Mourvèdre alone can make the chocolaty elite wines of Bandol,
Cinsault and Carignan are the traditionally humble grapes of the
peasant trying to make a living. Which is why Jullien has a fondness
for them, especially for the Carignan, which he calls *la femme irre-*
placeable, the irreplaceable woman of the house. But all five varietals are "women" for him. Syrah above all is *la femme enfardée*,
the sensually exotic woman who is the very opposite of *la femme ir-*
replaceable. When we moved on to the 2000 Mourvèdre, however,

we noted at once its greater austerity, and Jullien explained that the old name for Mourvèdre was *le spar*, or bishop's cross, because of the vine's natural hooped shape. But the chocolate richness remained. What kind of woman would that make it? He didn't say.

I asked him about Guibert on the other side of the valley.

"Guibert and Olivier were the two trailblazers. But why did Guibert have to go and plant non-Languedoc varietals like Chardonnay and Cabernet? For me, this means he has gone astray. But of course he's not from Languedoc."

This was meant to be self-explanatory.

And what about all the Australians crisscrossing the region?

"I've nothing against New World wines. The two systems are complimentary. I've worked with a man called Virgile Joly in Chile. It's just a philosophy which is not ours. For example, they abhor oxygen. But we are not afraid of oxygen. Ah, not a bit of it! We let the oxygen in. Why not? That's why an Australian wine, say, is dead beat by the end of the meal—wiped out, dead. But ours are still feisty and alive." He paused, then erupted again with a fantastical question: "What do they have against oxygen?"

So on to the 1997 Mas de Cal Demoura. I had drunk these wines before, of all places at the tasting bar inside Legrand et Fils in Paris. They are simple and unpretentious, but also warmly rich, with an aftertaste of dried flowers. It feels like something Jean-Pierre has molded gently with his massive hands—something round, full, as moist as clay. *Une femme irreplaceable?* I asked him instead about its dark purple color. Consumers love dark colors, but I was sure he hadn't emphasized it on purpose.

"Ah, not at all!"

Could I taste licorice?

Yes, a *bright* licorice.

The five women, he implied, had merged into one. The Liquorice Woman!

Afterward we drank some *eau de vie de marc* Mas Jullien. Jean-

Pierre was proud of his son's wine. It expressed something intangible which they had shared during their life together, but at the same time it was Olivier's wine and not his. The two styles were apart. Jean-Pierre plucked a sugar cube from the coffee table, doused it in the eau de vie, then put it on a teaspoon to eat. "I'm a big child, as you can see." Then again, Jean-Pierre can find his own roots in his own father, and even makes a wine called Pierre d'Alipe. So the wines have spiraled down from Alipe to Jean-Pierre to Olivier—from the beginning of the twentieth century to its end.

We went outside. Jean-Pierre was in a high mood and he wanted to drive me around this Sleepy Hollow of Languedoc. After all, wine equals land and you can't understand the one without "tasting" the other. And it was his land. It had to be shown. Half tipsy, therefore, we clambered into a tiny tinny car and set off into the empty streets of Jonquières at surprisingly high speed. Jean-Pierre was laughing and rolling his body, rolling so forcefully as he laughed and shouted that the car seemed to roll from side to side with him. He slipped a cassette into the player. Deafening bagpipe music suddenly exploded into life. The bagpipe music of Oc, the old music of Oc. Jean-Pierre began to sing along to these demented, wiry tunes set to pipes and old men chanting alongside, like the folk music of the Kybile or the valleys of Crete. "It's such a shame, Laurent, that you don't speak Oc." He nudged me. "We could really have a conversation in Oc, let me tell you. Listen to this bagpipe music. What music is there in the world like this?" I had to agree that there was nothing quite like it. "But Oc is even better."

I had no idea where we were, but we were driving across a plain. One of those rare plains which isn't monotonous, a great quilt of irrigation canals studded with small stone *mas*. Jean-Pierre had a name for every ruck in the land, every hill and peak, even if it was almost invisible on the horizon. There was the Col du Vin; there was the Rocher des Vierges, the Pic Bourdil. We dipped through endless tracks. Lines of Mourvèdre stood on their rusted metal rods, sometimes underneath electricity pylons, sometimes below cherry trees. These were his grandfather's lands, spread out around the crumbling chapel of Saint-Genies, a near ruin among vines. For a while we could see the suburbs of Aniane, the usual red-tiled French suburbs of generic villas for which Jean-Pierre had a ready word: *merde*. Then smaller tracks wound through the vineyards of Cal Demoura and Mas Jullien, wide-open fields of royal dimensions. Here and there we stopped by stone shacks belonging to the family, renovated hovels by the sides of the vineyards where the peasants bunkered down a hundred years ago with their scythes and cooking pots. It must have been a grim existence, no?

"Not at all. Primitive doesn't always mean grim. I can just remember that old French peasant life when I was a kid. You'd be surprised how happy people were then. You'd be truly surprised."

To make his point, he took me to the house where he had spent much of that childhood. It was a big *mas* built on a river, lost in the woods. The river was still, covered with leaves; a small chapel stood next to the boarded-up house, and we wandered around it for a while listening to shotguns popping in the distance while smoke drifted across sun-bright hills. We went from tree to tree: he could remember when each one was planted—in particular, a pine his father had planted in 1927. There were also trees he had planted himself as a boy. The place had once been a silk farm, there had been mulberry trees everywhere. Four hundred years the *mas* had been there, generations eking a living out of mulberry trees and washing in the river. Every child had carved his initials into the walls. Every beautiful day, his grandfather used to draw a little umbrella in the corner of his ledger book.

"That nineteenth-century life is unimaginable now. What they had most was *loisir*, leisure. You can't imagine how lovely our afternoons were—nothing to do, completely free, everyone on horseback. The work was over by one o'clock! Can you imagine today work being over by one o'clock? And now, I feel the ancestors here, my family—"

And suddenly tears began streaming down his face, even though the face beneath remained completely still. It struck me how completely that near-medieval world has been repackaged in films like *Manon des Sources*, Pagnol for the TV age, without ever suggesting that it was once real or desirable to live in. It survives as cliché, of course. As a background for the impressionists, for example, or the country life celebrated by the two Renoirs.

But it's also a country life I dimly remembered from England. Much ridiculed, naturally, as if its very existence was a threat: the house, the extended family, the settled rhythm. I said to Jean-Pierre that the two things that I remembered most from my own childhood in the country were the endless making of jams and then the curious fact that my grandparents were always with us instead of being sequestered away in their own house. As it happened, we were just then driving past Jean-Pierre's grandparents' house in Saint-Jean-de-Fos, and he had to agree. It was as if a house by itself can be a magnet which draws all living things into it. And now— excuse the sentimentality—he tried to make his wines into similar life-drawing magnets which expressed the same things. Hearth, home, family, the love of family.

At the end of the day, Jean-Pierre announced that he wanted to take me somewhere special—the remote chapel of Saint-Sylvestre. It was a fair drive, the land now Mediterranean, full of white stones and mulberry trees. The Romanesque church is locked but you can peer through the cracked windows into the cobwebs and stone chevrons. It has a wooden roof; and what is it doing here in the middle of this nowhereness?

Lying on the grass and smoking, it struck me that Aimé Guibert and Jean-Pierre Jullien both expounded the truths of terroir. They spoke a similar language on the surface. And they worked the same land. But how different their mental universes were. How different, too, was their conception of place. Really, it was not that surprising that Guibert had planted varietals from the outside: his was an international winery with an eye on the glamour of *other* places. He had not quite left behind him the allure of selling the world's best gloves at Sak's Fifth Avenue. Jean-Pierre, on the other hand, was like Zorba. He existed within a magnetic force field of ancestors which he could not rationalize or leave. His wine, too, could not really be other than what it was. It was fated to be itself. I suppose that his point in showing me the house was to suggest how a certain kind of human being could also exist: people fated to be themselves.

Of Corks and Screws

❧

Men lose their tempers in defending their taste.

—Ralph Waldo Emerson

Jean-Luc Godard lives in a dour little condo in Rolle, a stuffy lakeside town half an hour outside Geneva. To the door came a familiar-looking man of seventy chewing on an equally familiar cigar. I quickly ascertained that Godard also did not care much for the modern world. In fact, his new film *Éloge de l'Amour* (the reason for my visit: newspaper interview) was really a testy growl of disillusionment with what could be called "mod cons," or rather the underlying system of which mod cons are the expression. Of course, there were the Americans. Unsurprisingly, he hated Spielberg—but then again, Americans had a certain genius, didn't they? They did what they did well. The popularity of their culture could hardly be considered the freakish outcome of a conspiracy. Where was the energy these days?

"It depends on what you call energy," I said.

"Well, where would you rather *work*? Paris or New York? New York, alas."

So in France—in Switzerland, God help us—the problem wasn't the Americans. It was the French and the Swiss?

"*They* are the ones who make America alluring. There's something there that they want."

What was that?

Difficult to say. An escape, a dream life . . .

"In your film, you seem to dislike Americans."

"As I see it, the great power of the Americans comes from their having no relation to their own land. No relation to anything. They float in a void. Globalization, so called, is just an irrational spurning of history. It's like the modernization of the post office here in Rolle."

Godard suddenly looked far more animated. The modernization of the post office in Rolle, *there* was a scandal! The modernizing and therefore downsizing Swiss postal service had closed the second post office in Rolle. It was not a joking matter to those in their seventies who now had to walk the extra distance. And it was a perfect example of dehumanization. Modernity and dehumanization. Godard slapped his hand angrily on the table.

"Why can't the damn post office in Rolle operate democratically?" he cried.

In his film we see the detritus of economic change: the unemployed young sleeping on park benches in the rain, the decline of cities. We revisit Paris, not the post card panoramas of *Breathless* basking in the 1950s, but the bombed-out waterfront factories of today's suburbs. But this also results from the changed perspective of growing old. One looks at things differently. The center of Paris today probably looks far more prosperous than the exhausted city of the postwar era. But then again, I wasn't there, I wasn't young inside it.

Did he nostalgize the past?

"Don't we all? I'm very aware of it."

And at the same time, perhaps thinking your youth was better than your old age did have some truth to it after all?

"I look back, and I think I only made two good films, *Le Mépris* and *Pierrot le fou*. Both in the early sixties. And I'm sure I'm right. Sometimes the past *is* superior to the present."

All the way back to Geneva, slipping through the steep hillsides of vines, I kept wondering if the whole premise of Switzerland as a country was that the past was in some respects superior to the present, except when it came to the postal system. It was therefore a good country to be old in, or from which to decry the depredations of mod cons. In any case, every jeremiad against the vices of an age must surely rest on a belief that the past was in some ways superior to the present. But how could you tell one way or another? A single lifetime is too short to know.

The oldest bottle of wine ever drunk, a sweet German Steinwein bottled in the year 1540, was drunk in London in 1961 when it was 421 years old. But such cases are rare. It is possible to taste back about a hundred years, though most usually it's not more than half a century. But then again, the world changes dramatically in half a century. That was Godard's point. On the long drive down to the northern Rhône, where I had agreed to meet the famous New York wine importer Neal Rosenthal, I wondered how realistically I could measure the changes even in myself from decade to decade. Surely it was a hall of mirrors.

The northern Rhône is not a gay river. It meanders past sloped vineyards and rocky peaks with a sluggish gravity. The towns—like Valence—seem equally serious. And the wine here is serious as well. For just beyond Valence on the western side of the river, shadowed by forbidding crests of bare rocks and a ruined castle, lies the hard little village of Cornas. Cornas is a great name in Rhône wine, but the place itself is unprepossessing. Vines swamp it, bustling down all the way to the main road which runs through the village. But the great Cornas wines come from the vineyards high up near the crests. There sits the vineyard known as La Geynale, where Robert Michel, Neal Rosenthal's man in Cornas, makes his best wine.

Standing in the street outside Michel's farmhouse, Rosenthal looked like the very model of the New York city slicker. A slim fifty-six-year-old marathon runner, Rosenthal was in shades and jeans, trim and hale but not in the rural way. Of the same generation as Robert Parker, he was also trained as a lawyer. After dropping out of the law—"a horrible profession"—he eventually took over his father's pharmacy on the Upper East Side, launching it into one of the city's premier wine outlets. His importing firm, Mad Rose, also deals with honey and olive oil: all creations of the earth.

For American wine lovers, Mad Rose is a reference point. Rosenthal has made of himself an *arbiter elegantiarum* of what could be called America's alternative wine scene. The distinctively tall gold-edged labels on the backs of his bottles operate as compasses for accidental connoisseurs of all stripes as they leaf their way through the nation's confusing wine stores. Rosenthal is the fairy godfather of terroir.

With his cropped gray hair and highly emotional eyes, Rosenthal radiates a kind of rabbinical energy, at once erudite and pedagogically emphatic. He is a moralist, a charmer, an educator, a left-wing activist, a toughly sentimental New York City salesman, and a bon vivant all at once. Despite being one of the nation's preeminent wine importers, and a longtime supplier to some of the country's greatest restaurants, he is also the American wine world's fiercest and most articulate iconoclast. It quickly becomes apparent why. Rosenthal is not a man to mince words. Indeed, he slips into frequent well-mannered rages, his eyes nevertheless twinkling relentlessly:

"When I see the kind of wine that is going down these days around the world, even in so-called top places, it makes me want to scream." He smiles crookedly. "It's a *scandal* what's going on now. The wine media, the prices—it's a farce."

He took me by the arm and guided me through a gloomy doorway.

"Robert Michel," he half whispered, "is without question an example of what we purists are looking for. There's no nonsense here. Listen, my wines may not be pretty-pretty, but they tell the truth. Michel tells the truth."

It was late afternoon and the crags behind the village were turning an ominous purple. Cornas was silent, nobody abroad in its streets.

Madame Michel came rather officiously to the door and ushered us into a courtyard. *Le maître* was downstairs in the cellar. We found him among his barrels, an archetype of the French vigneron—cap, overalls, bright pink flush, black currant eyes. Now about sixty, he is one of those wine makers who have trodden very carefully in their father's steps. He left school almost immediately after learning to read; wine was already his passion by the time he was fourteen.

We bobbed under the bare bulks, among unusually large barrels. For Rosenthal this was not a social visit. He was on his annual tasting and buying tour, which takes him across the Loire, Burgundy, the Rhône, and northern Italy, with an occasional diversion into Tuscany to visit his producers there. The importer-producer relation is at the core of the wine world, a symbiotic relationship similar to that between agents and writers. The importer has to encourage, criticize, flatter, haggle, cajole. It is, moreover, sometimes fraught with tension. In France in particular, American importers are often accused of bending their producers toward styles that are more congenial to American consumers. Rosenthal would be the first to admit that this is often the case, but not, he insists, when it comes to his own work. To the contrary, Rosenthal makes an artful effort never to place an obstacle in the way of his producers' own creative bent. He wants them to say what they have to say, not what he has to say. The wines are then presented to his clients in an uncompromising way, as expressions of both terroir and the producers' personalities. Robert Michel is a case in point.

Cornas is a powerful, firm, often tightly closed wine that requires time to evolve in bottle. There would be no point trying to make it pretty or endearing too soon: its profundity would suffer.

As we tasted from barrel, however, Rosenthal offered his criticisms freely. As it happened, the 2000 "first fruit" from La Geynale was already fragrant despite its raw youth; and the more finished 1999 was already a potent but sleek beauty. That, said Michel, was unusual. A top Cornas normally needs to age. And that made them difficult to market.

"We live," said the chthonically sturdy Michel, "in an age of impatience. I am all for patience. We are all so very impatient, when in fact we should be patient and nothing but patient. If we are impatient we will not wait for wines to age." He shrugged and shifted from one foot to the other. "We drink them as soon as we buy them."

Patience, impatience: Rosenthal agreed. It was hard these days, and even in France, to find restaurants that are patient with their cellars. But ordinary consumers find it an uphill struggle. People want to drink what they've bought straightaway.

"How many people now own a wine cellar? It's an impossible demand that they wait for five years before actually drinking their prized acquisitions. I try to persuade my clients to be patient with their Cornas."

It struck me watching Michel and Rosenthal together that this was the other side of America's supposedly deleterious influence on the rest of the world. American importers and drinkers are often the ones who keep many a small French artisan in business. For although French wine makers, like Michel, can often sell to a handful of Parisian restaurants, the French themselves are not necessarily liberal with their wine budgets. Americans have more disposable cash to spend.

But Rosenthal would see himself as an anomaly. A sixties contrarian who has poured his beliefs into the wine trade, Rosenthal would say that he is a counterweight against the momentum of American monotony, and a contradictory entity: a preservatory agent of radical change.

Why preservatory?

"Because everywhere in the world globalization has created the same dilemma. How do we preserve a tradition without betraying it? How do we not betray it while pushing it forward? It's a very intricate dialectic. On the one hand, one has all the baggage of the sixties, which is obviously sort of against capitalism in many ways—"

"Globalization is just a buzzword for capitalism?"

"—right. And then you have the profoundly *conservative* impulse to preserve traditions. Actually, more than traditions. Diversity—life's inherent richness."

But wasn't wine culture, I asked, the creation of capitalism? The beginning of modern wine, the 1855 Bordeaux classification, coincided with the railway age, though admittedly that didn't in itself prove anything.

"I'm not sure. That's true in some ways. But it's older too. The monasteries—"

The Hungarian-American historian John Lukacs once remarked that the world is now divided not between Left and Right, but between those who choose to live as creatures and those who choose to live as machines. It's a statement which Rosenthal would surely understand.

We wandered outside, to the edge of the vines. Under incoming darkness, the crests above us looked even more Wagnerian. Michel escorted us out and cast an unsentimental eye not at these but at the clouds above them—the vigneron always sniffing out his meteorology.

"Rain?" he grumbled.

Rosenthal and I agreed to meet the next day in Châteauneuf-du-Pape, where he does business with an estate called Domaine de Monpertuis. As we left, Michel patted our shoulders and told us to drive carefully. He peered again at the sky. "See you in the spring," he said to Rosenthal. Then he disappeared back into his walled house and the rain began.

Next to the ruined Châteauneuf-du-Pape itself, I had lunch at Le Verger des Papes and ordered my fateful bottle of Beaucastel. As I sat there with an aperitif of red wine mixed with *crème de pêches* I thought of Rosenthal's honey-buying trips to Morocco. By a strange coincidence, we are both addicted travelers to Morocco. We have both visited the waterfalls of Immouzer des Ida Outanne near Agadir, with its appropriately named Café du Miel. Rosenthal's quest for honey is part and parcel of his quest for wines. I remember driving through the Atlas, through the fossil town of Midelt, and into the Gorges du Ziz. Ginger-haired Berber girls run down the hillsides at the sound of the approaching motor with trays of ammonites and wooden spools of lavender honey to sell. The honey tastes unlike any other, dark and raw, with a smell of crushed herbs. Was that "tradition"? The rawness of the spools of honey belongs to the same world as the little girls' naked feet, their filthy hands, and the look of crazed hunger in their eyes. Only honey made in the poverty of empty mountains could taste as good as that, because it is gathered from the hives almost unconsciously, without too much concern for the taste buds of passing tourists. It is as raw as the fossils dug out of the same hillsides.

France plays an artful game with her peasant roots, a game which the honey gatherers of the Atlas would not understand for a moment. And as I looked at my bill, I noticed the following sentence printed along its bottom: *L'abus de l'aioli est recommendé par l'académie des amoureux de l'aioli.* Very cute. And we cannot forget that everything in France has its ironic "academy" and its *amoureux.* There probably *is* an Academy of Aioli somewhere, and an Academy of Honey as well. When I met Paul Jeune, the owner of Domaine de Montpertuis, later in the afternoon, I also thought of an academician, for Jeune bears a passing resemblance to Michel Foucault, though no doubt he is considerably more sympathetic than the dismal sage and has a more convincing mastery of his disciplines.

The winery stands among eucalyptus trees just below the château, on the Chemin des Garrigues. It is therefore poised between the shiny new houses of the village and open countryside. Jeune's property has more of an urban feel, and he himself, lean and dome-headed, seems more an intellectual than a farmer. He recently bought some plots in nearby Ventoux, at Château Valcombe, where he makes a wine that has revolutionized Ventoux's somewhat musty reputation. But Châteauneuf-du-Pape is the apple of his eye, the wine he always wanted to make.

Rosenthal and Jeune were emphatically in agreement on most things.

"I don't ask wine makers to make things," Rosenthal said. "I impose nothing. Not my tastes—nothing. Wine changes every day. It's not for me to say, it's for Paul to say."

We were now drinking Jeune's Châteauneuf-du-Pape Cuvée Tradition 1999, a Grenache-dominated wine only made in great years and from vines more than sixty years old. Jeune held up a glass. Grenache doesn't give the lush, inky color characteristic of the Syrahs consumers love. But adding Syrah just for the color was really "too silly" for Jeune. Grenache had its own charm. Similarly, if he had filtered it the wine would surely be more brilliant, more shiny, but it would have lost something too. It would have real Montpertuis character only after three to four years. Only then could you begin to separate a Monpertuis from a Vieux Télégraphe, or any other top Châteauneuf-du-Pape. Young, they all tasted good, but similar. All you could taste was the grape.

I asked him what he thought of Châteauneuf-du-Pape in general, given that it was one of the handful of French wines which almost everyone can recognize.

"Too much color," he said without hesitation. "I think most Châteauneuf now is phony. They're piling on the Syrah to make it overcolored. The huge quantities are a problem too—but a wine that's only 70 percent Grenache is never going to be the real thing."

Clos des Papes did good work, he said, and Bosquet des Papes and Beaucastel. But Beaucastel was always sui generis; it was commercial, but good. Rosenthal agreed. It was akin to the depressing situation in Bordeaux, where it was now increasingly difficult to tell the wines apart. More and more Merlot was being planted there to add deeper color and richness to the wines, which were therefore beginning to become homogenized. They were tasting "samey," in the same way that Châteauneufs were tasting samey.

"Ah." Jeune shook his head. "It's exhausting. Exhausting trying to keep up with such stupidity. I sometimes just want to pack it all in. The pressure—"

His eyes suddenly went sad and moonlike, but only for a moment. I looked around at his slick furniture: he was doing all right. What he hated, in the end, was not being left alone to be *small*. They were being forced to expand, to sell more. It was exhausting, surely, but also profitable?

"Acceleration," Rosenthal concluded. "Everything is acceleration. We're in an age where people are like mad children. Is complexity too difficult now? Or are we all children?"

We drank in silence for a while. I wondered if it was true that modern taste—our taste—is essentially the taste of children. Such was surely increasingly dominant back home in America, where everything had the energy and instantaneous relish of childhood. Childish sex, childish relationships, childish entertainments—and now, at last, childish wine. Perhaps childish wine was inevitable. And for a moment I pondered the horrible nightmare scenes of enforced childhood in Witold Gombrowicz's prophetic novel *Ferdydurke*. For nothing is more nightmarish than childhood, when all is said and done, and nothing is more oppressive than the tastes of children when they are forced upon you. The only consolation of being adult, in fact, is in not having to be childish.

Not being childish is a liberation. And relishing things that children hate has always been the escapism of adults. Or so I thought drinking Jeune's Cuvée Tradition, which no child could ever like. It had none of that opulent sweetness that children love. I tried to imagine what a child would think of it, and I was sure that to a ten-year-old it would taste menacing, sinister.

It then occurred to me that perhaps what I was searching for in my own quest for taste was some sort of adulthood. It was a startling idea. The quest for taste might be nothing other than a voyage *out of childhood*. In the case of wine, it was surely a pilgrimage away from the sweetness of mother's milk and toward the "unnatural" tastes of perverted (but sublime) old age! From sweetness to dryness; from simplicity to complexity; from certainty to ambiguity.

One cannot fail to notice the contemporary marketing of wines by means of fun-and-funky labels, with their fractal curves, tropical fruit juice colors, and animals designed to appeal to the inner child, that cretinous monster who lurks inside us all. There is an undeniable increase in animals, for example, on wine labels, a trend which is bound to grow. All one can do to protest this development is to point out that the quality of a wine is probably in inverse proportion to the ferocity of the animal on its label. Beware, therefore, of labels with eagles, tigers, or bears (though I have not yet seen sharks, leopard seals, or velociraptors, it is only a matter of time).

Then there is the screw top, now replacing the traditional cork. Even more ominously than feral labels, this latest device taking the wine business by storm is intended to make wine more appealingly infantile. Wine is becoming more kiddy-friendly as it comes to resemble bottled soda. I suggested to Rosenthal and Jeune that what was most appealing about corks was that they were difficult to extract, and therefore beyond the ken of children. There was effort, the risk of failure—a little ritual, in other words. It was as if wine was divided into two camps, the corks and the screws. The corks represented the tastes of adults, the imagination of the past; the screws, on the other hand, served the needs of childish taste, the gratifications of the present moment.

For Rosenthal the struggle between technology and tradition is not a simple one. Technology has undoubtedly improved the average quality of wine all over the world in the last thirty years. But now the baby is being thrown out with the bath water.

"When these tools," he says, "are used to exaggerate qualities or to transform the structure of a wine to meet some perceived market demand, or what some journalist thinks a wine should be—then we're in trouble. An overwhelming amount of wine today refers not to where it comes from, but only to where it wants to be. Do you see the difference?"

That night, as I was driving to the Italian border (for Rosenthal and I had selected Barolo for our next rendezvous) I wondered how childish I was myself. What was certain was that children do not enjoy the wine I had with me in the car, and which I had brought all the way from the Rhône—the Robert Michel La Geynale, which knew exactly where it was from, and seemed indifferent to where it was going.

Barolo sits within the Langhe Hills, an open land of wide valleys and gentle slopes of fine gray soil. The great red wines made from the Nebbiolo grape come from a cluster of secretive villages: La Morra, Castiglione Falletto, Serralunga d'Alba, Monforte, and the touristy Barolo itself, which houses a municipal enoteca permanently filled with curious Germans. Rosenthal comes here every year to taste the new vintages of his Barolo producers, the Brovia family.

The most atmospheric of the hillside wine villages is La Morra. Tourists love Barolo, but there is always a quizzical look on the faces of those who come to La Morra, as if they are not quite sure why they are here. They are here because of the wine; but it is almost as if this is not quite enough as reasons go, that there must be something more. But what? There is nothing in La Morra. Just a cafe and a line of tractors sitting in the street. A magpie flops across the same street; the snow of the Alps glitters far off on the horizon. There's the tang of mountain air, and on a large wall there is a burlesque painting on a wine theme from the Mussolini era (1939) by one Davide Savio, with the ringing words of Julius Caesar, *Et de murra optima romae metropolitim usque ad nostram perduximus vina*. The tourists look at this approvingly, perhaps because it's Julius Caesar. But what does it actually mean?

The most internationally famous producer of the Langhe is Angelo Gaja, whose three-hundred-dollar bottles of Barbaresco d'Alba adorn the windows of countless gastronomic boutiques from Paris to San Francisco. But Gaja does not make a true Barolo in the technical sense, because he was recently disbarred from the appellation, or AOC, by its vigilant guardians. The dark gossip of the villages is damningly clear: Gaja had tried to mix his Nebbiolo with *other grape varieties*. This is expressly forbidden by the Barolo AOC laws which govern its production. If a wine is not 100 percent Nebbiolo, say the laws, then it is not a Barolo. The scandal had shaken up the wine makers. Were they being reactionary or was Gaja a perfidious operator who richly deserved what he got?

Whatever the intricate details of this scandal, what interested me more was what Rosenthal wanted to find here, and how he went about finding it. Rosenthal is indeed a kind of evangelist against the Gajas of the world, for there is in him a yearning for purity, for what could be called the gentle sternness of unsullied tradition. Rosenthal has said that he decries the so-called new-wave wineries in Piedmont which increasingly use new French oak barrels and cut Nebbiolo with fashionable additives like Cabernet and Merlot. It's not that Rosenthal necessarily dislikes all of Gaja's wines; it's that the worldview underlying them is, to his mind, not conducive to the democratic aristocracy of a palate attuned with maximal alertness to the spirit of place. But here in Barolo, what exactly is the spirit of place?

I met Rosenthal in the Azienda Fratelli Brovia farm courtyard. He already had a glass in his hand, and the family was assembled around him. He looked considerably more relaxed than he had in France. There was a commotion as I appeared: tables and chairs scraped together, bottles, saucers of *grana cunese*, the granular cheese eaten at wine tastings. If wine commercials are now sold through Italian imagery instead of French imagery, then the root of such imagery is precisely these family commotions which are the center of Italian life.

The Brovias are not a stiff-collared wine dynasty. They strike you immediately as a family which has indeed been here since 1863. As with most Italian wineries, there was a hiatus in the mid-twentieth century as the *azienda* fell into disuse, a prey to phylloxera and economic slump. Thus the "classic tradition," as it is well to remember, it not a continuous one but one that has been reinvented recently. The family patriarch, Giacinto, began buying his plots in 1953, choosing sites from the best "cru" of the Barolo, such as Rocche, Villero, and Garblet Sue. These varied sites gave him a wide palette of soils and minerals to work with, from heavy clay to lighter limestone. The wines themselves, accordingly, vary from site to site. What Rosenthal esteems in the Brovias, therefore, is their time-acquired awareness of the qualities of each vineyard, and the spin which each one gives to the four varietals they use—Dolcetto, Barbera, Nebbiolo, and the white Arneis. This small *azienda* makes ten wines which display more diversity than most regions, and therein lies its mastery of terroir.

Giacinto's two daughters, Elena and Cristina, who now run much of the winery, wanted to show me the vineyards *before* we drank anything.

The first property was Rocche, high up on a road that gave views of Serralunga. On the way, we passed the large and famous estate of Fontanafredda. Fontanafredda provoked sarcastic whistles from the Brovia women: not "true" Barolos, as they explained. But Fontanafredda is nevertheless a majestic name in the history of

Italian wine, and ironically it is where Barolo itself was more or less born. Fontanafredda was once a hunting lodge belonging to King Vittorio Emanuele II, and in the 1860s the monarch had loaned it to Barolo's Marchese Falletti for wine-making experiments which would have momentous results.

Falletti was the inventor of modern Barolo, and his principal technician was a Frenchman named Louis Oudart, who set to applying French methods to Italian materials. Before the 1860s, however, the dry, long-lasting, and stable red wine which we now know as Barolo did not exist. Although Nebbiolo has been grown here since the thirteenth century and Dolcetto since the sixteenth, as recently as the 1840s they were known mostly for producing a mediocre sweet wine. In the seventeenth century Nebbiolo had spawned a popular light wine appropriately christened Chiaretto, but the court of the kingdom of Sardinia, based in Turin, of which this region was a part, imported its serious wines from France. A serious Barolo of any kind would have been unimaginable to them.

At Fontanafredda, Oudart and Falletti set about engineering a new wine. Oudart theorized that the reason Barolos were not dry was that their fermentation was incompetently conducted. In other words, the fermentation was allowed to fizzle out before burning up all the residual sugar, thus inevitably creating an effervescent and sweet drink. Italians have always liked fizzy and sweet reds, and these early nineteenth-century Barolos were probably merry thirst quenchers and little more. Falletti and Oudart changed all that overnight: were they not yet another example of nineteenth-century science's impact on wine?

On the way up toward Serralunga Rosenthal explained to me that there was a line running through Barolo. North of it, the wines were easier to drink younger, while south of it (in places like Serralunga and Rocche) they were deeper, more structured, and aged better. Rocche therefore yielded what could be called a classical Barolo. Perhaps the soil could explain why.

We got out and scrambled down from the road and into steep slopes of vines like a party of jolly geologists. Rosenthal had a certain glint in his eye. There was nothing he'd rather be doing than walking among vines. He pointed to the dust clinging to the skins of the Dolcetto grapes, saying that it was a dust that you could taste later in the wine. We poked about in the soil, which is fine and pale gray, as dry as sand. It's a soil that gives a light, heady wine, unlike the nearby plot called Villero, which has chalky, slaty soils which in turn yield up a darker wine with a more licorice nose. So here were two soils with distinctive wines. A living exhibition of terroir?

"I suppose," Rosenthal said, "that you've been told this time and time again. Because everyone in the wine world is always chattering inanely about terroir. But I dare to say that here it's irrefutable. It's a beautiful example of how wine is rooted in geology."

Nearer to Serralunga, the Brovias have a house with several sites around it. The house, plainly enough, is called Ca'Mia and the wine from there carries the same name. There is also a rarer adjacent plot of forty-year-old vines called La Brea, from which they make Barbera of great power and depth. If Rocche was like the high end of the piano keyboard, Rosenthal mused, then Ca'Mia and La Brea were like the bass keys.

The place itself reminded me of Jean-Pierre Jullien's house, the windows boarded up, the mulberry trees around beginning to turn color. The Brovia women ran their hands along the walls, peered into the long-familiar but half-empty rooms. Down from the house, meanwhile, Rosenthal also ran his hands through the vine leaves and invited me to get into the spirit of touch-and-feel vineyard visitations. Rosenthal's sensory immersion in a vineyard is complete; he smells, touches, sifts, brings earth to the tip of the tongue. The importer, perhaps, is as animal as the vigneron when he is not dressed in a three-piece suit at the Waldorf Astoria. It was a quality the Brovia women clearly respected because it put him on a mental *and physical* plane akin to their own.

"His palate is refined," Elena said in the car driving back. "Because his senses are refined."

I said that the place seemed to bring out an innocent enjoyment in him, infectious and light in spirit.

"He seems very gay, doesn't he?" she said.

"He does."

She leaned forward and tapped his shoulder. "Neal, are you gay today?"

"I'm very gay," he said.

"There, I thought so!"

How far away these fields seemed from the gloomy enoteca in Barolo. They reminded me of Mexico: the same tender light, the same shrines by the road with their sky-blue Virgins, the same pruners among their vines like Indians treading silently through milpas.

Back in the kitchen, the whole family assembled for a drink and some more *grana*. We started with the Barberas from Sori' del Drago and La Brea—of a dark, intense purple which seemed to be almost foaming at the edges—and then a Dolcetto from another site called Solatio. The latter was surprisingly concentrated and complex for a Dolcetto, more like a Barolo, with an alcohol level of 15 percent.

Dolcetto, Rosenthal went on, is a very "modern," even "international" grape with huge fruit which could potentially make it popular globally. And if it were to become popular, he said, it would be a better bet than the drearily ubiquitous Cabernet Sauvignon. This one was still young, and raw, but it would age well. There was a ferocity about it too which got into my head at once. Giacinto was now winking himself, and at me, unless I was hallucinating.

From these wines we drifted on to the Villero, Ca'Mia, and Rocche Barolos. Rosenthal showed me the color: Nebbiolo wines have a characteristic pale brick edge to them and with age comes a slight taste of dust. And as we dipped into these fabulous, noble wines with their ample acidity, the Brovias began to talk more openly about their Barolo. I asked them about the famous names of the region, Elio Altare, Gaja, Fontanafredda. Giacinto made a superb gesture of exasperated disdain, rather like a Roman governor dismissing a room full of oriental rabble.

"*E tutto quello*—" he burst out, evidently referring to the aforementioned Elio Altare, Gaja, and Fontanafredda, "—*è business!*"

Business: the English word provoked sarcastic jollity all around. But if these famed producers were not like their beloved Neal, I asked, why did the outside world take them so seriously and pay so much money for their wines?

Giacinto now said something curious while describing his own wines. He did not, he said, want to make *un vino ruffiano*. The word *ruffiano* is a tricky word to translate. It's related to our word "ruffian" but usually refers to a pimp. When speaking of wines it means something like "overly seductive," or "facile." A *ruffiano* wine is one that makes too much of an effort to seduce you—to open its legs, as it were, too easily. Naturally, the market—*il business*—was all about *ruffiano* wine. But a true Barolo never exhibited that odious quality. It was supposed to be regal, a little haughty even, a "difficult" and testy wine which revealed its profundity only with time. A Barolo wasn't supposed to be too likable on the first encounter. It was not a flirt. It required exploration, a little effort . . . it was not a casual acquaintance. And this, Giacinto exclaimed, was precisely the quality which Neal could grasp without any effort.

Rosenthal turned to me and said in English, "It's their work, not mine. I'm just a sort of metal detector looking for the precious stuff in the ground."

"So, Neal, you are the patron saint of biodiversity?"

"It *is* like the environment. The more species you have the *better*. Did you know there are wines that are now totally extinct, like extinct birds? Think about that. Let us have thousands of unique wines, not a few dozen that all taste the same."

It sounded like a moral crusade; but then again, why not a moral crusade? Wouldn't a moral crusade have kept the dodo breeding?

Over their protests, I declined dinner with the Brovias that night. I had a hotel waiting in Turin and if I stayed I would be leaving on all fours. We tumbled out into the wide farmyard and Giacinto and Rosenthal disappeared into the cellars, returning with copious armloads of bottles. For a moment they stopped under stars, which had appeared out of nowhere, and tried to persuade me not to go to Turin. But I wanted to leave Rosenthal with them for a while, for no doubt they had much to discuss. Rosenthal gave me a bottle of Dolcetto and then told me to meet him the next day in the town of Ivrea north of Turin.

"What day is it?" he asked.

"September 10."

"Then it's tomorrow, *ragazzo*. We're going to meet the great Luigi Ferrando!"

I wasn't sure who Luigi Ferrando was, but I had drunk the wine known as Carema, which he makes. I drove off and an hour later was in bed near the Stazione Centrale in Turin. Strangely enough, I had a violent dream about a cork forest in Portugal. I got up at dawn.

Turin is the city of Nietzsche, and walking around it even at night you understand why he loved this Baroque metropolis of geometry and Alpine cool. "But what a dignified and serious city it is!" he wrote to his friend Koselitz. "It has nothing of the capital city and nothing modern, as I feared: it is rather a residence from the seventeenth century, which had the court and the nobility, and a single prevailing taste in everything." This is still true today. "Aristocratic tranquillity" was what Nietzsche most admired in Turin, along with a "unity of taste." Not to mention clean sidewalks, beautiful trams, and cafes. This classical harmony and precision dazzled him; why were other cities not as humane as Turin? That is, why were they *modern*?

As you walk around Piazza San Carlo and Santa Cristina, through the airy arcades and the dark boulevards, you feel what Nietzsche felt a hundred years ago. It's a crystallization of something uniquely European. At night, it's like an emptied salon. No so-called nightlife whatsoever. I thought to myself how much the average teenager would hate Turin. Nothing to do! Aristocratic tranquillity . . . even the words mean nothing to most people now. Who is looking for either aristocracy or tranquillity, let alone the two things heaped together? But in a sense, of course, Neal Rosenthal is. I wondered if he thought, like Nietzsche, that modern taste was a contradiction in terms?

The next morning I drove up to Ivrea. It's a sparkling mountain town built on two sides of a fast-flowing river full of rocks. Unsurprisingly, it is almost Swiss in feel. Its walls are colored like melons, with prim iron balconies. A fresh taste of snow pricks the tongue. Luigi Ferrando has his wine store here a few steps down from the Piazza Nazionale and the Corso Cavour, and here he is often to be found with his two sons, looking a little like Federico Fellini, a warmly curious expression always on his handsome face. Although Ferrando's wines were among the first top Italians to be imported into the United States back in the 1960s, along with Antinori and Gaja, his vineyards are so tiny—and his production so small—that you have to search out his red Caremas and his refined white Erbaluce di Caluso.

Rosenthal puts both into several noted New York wine stores, but it would be a fair bet that most wine drinkers are aware of them only through repute. Carema is known as one of the most rarefied of all appellations, with only sixteen hectares to its name, though its Nebbiolo wines are considered worthy cousins to the more famous Barolos. The vineyards lie north of Ivrea in the Alpine foothills of the Valle d'Aosta, on terraces painstakingly harvested by hand. I had the feeling, when I met Rosenthal in the Ferrando enoteca, that he had a special fondness for both the Ferrandos and for Carema, and that these vineyards meant far more to him than all the others.

Months later, Rosenthal would invite me to his upstate New York house for dinner, for an evening of wines drawn from one of the finest private cellars on the East Coast. The house is high-timbered, with a custom-built basement tasting room resembling the inner sanctum of a synagogue. Rosenthal went down and up the cellar stairs for hours. I remember a 1985 Corton-Charlemagne, a 1971 Château d'Yquem, a 1985 Clos de la Roche from Hubert Lignier, a 1983 Meursault "Les Charmes" from Bitouzet, and then, like a comet out of nowhere, a wine I had never heard of: a 1961 Chambave from the same region of the Valle d'Aosta and from a producer named Ezio Voyat.

The Chambave was the star of the evening, zesty, incredibly fresh for a wine as old as I am, and with a startling aroma of strawberries. I could tell, I think, that this wine was a personal love of Rosenthal's and that he cherished it because of its geographical provenance. It was a mountain wine, and a border one which could almost be said to straddle two cultures. It resembled nothing but itself.

At lunch in Ivrea with Ferrando and his sons, Luigi asked me how I had liked Turin.

"It is not," he said, "to the taste of everyone."

"It was to Nietzsche's taste. I like it very much."

The Ferrandos shrugged.

"You know," Luigi said, moving along, "the wines we make here you can see in Turin—in a way. It's aristocratic, orderly. Calm and reserved. Those are its qualities. Those are our qualities as Piedmontese."

Did that, I asked, apply to everyone else in the world?

Luigi was breezy. "Certainly. Take Australians. They're simple, brawny, two-dimensional. Their wines are the same."

But then again, he hadn't been to Australia. I couldn't resist saying that I personally loved Australia, and that I found Australians to be subtle, intellectually curious, and perfectly three-dimensional. Unlike their wines, perhaps.

"Ah," he admitted, "then perhaps it is an anomaly."

And I added: "They have the best food in the world, too. Outside of Italy."

This provoked outright astonishment.

"Is it true?" they cried, turning to Rosenthal.

But Neal had never been to Australia either. He had tasted many of the top Australian wines in the course of his professional duties, but he found them "steroidal," square, and . . . two-dimensional.

"Let's just say they're not my thing. It's the kind of wine the English like. Heavy, massive—"

"Brawny," Luigi said.

"Not aristocratic?"

"They're like American football players. I like female tennis players."

"But their food is extraordinary," I persisted. "And those wines taste quite logical when you drink them there. In the tropics, with parrots on the lampposts, when you're actually sweating."

So what, they wanted to know, had I drunk in Australia?

I described a business trip to Sydney, an article for a magazine, and my several nights in Pott's Point plundering the MacLeay Street Wine Store—a Vasse Felix from Margaret River had been my constant companion and I had carried it around in my coat pocket almost everywhere I went. That and a Penfolds Bin 407, modestly good with racks of lamb. They nodded uncertainly. Vasse Felix. So that was a bird? Like a roadrunner? They had them in Western Australia. And what did the wine taste like?

Perfumed and thick: the way I imagine (I thought for a moment) a wine of Omar Khayyám's would taste.

"*Que strano,*" they chuckled.

"But logical in the place," I insisted.

"Perhaps they are." Rosenthal smiled. "But for me they have no tenderness or idiosyncrasy. After half a glass my mouth is already tired, bored. You couldn't drink them with *this*."

We were eating in the courtyard of a converted stable. Stuffed onions with almond filling, stuffed cabbage, a little *salignan* or herbed cheese, bowls of fine egg pasta called *tajarin*. With its sour-sweet accents and odd combinations, Piedmontese food bears little relation to the rest of Italian cuisine, and it dovetails perfectly with the Carema 1991 Etichetta Nera, or Black Label, which we drank with it (Ferrando makes two Caremas, the Black Label and a lesser wine called White Label). I was curious to know where Rosenthal might place these wines on his internal scale of excellence, but in fact there was a weightier question which I thought better to ask him in English. What, I asked, was the *summa* of wine for him—the highest of the high peaks which populated the parallel universe of wine? There was no hesitation in his reply: Burgundy.

"Of all the world's wine regions, Burgundy is the most fascinating. The most complex, the most variable. You can walk across a single vineyard and watch the soil change under your feet. Burgundies are the greatest wines to drink, there's absolutely no question of that. They blow Bordeaux away these days. California is a joke by comparison. But here's the tragedy of Burgundy—"

The tragedy of Burgundy was that a few prima donna domains, most famously Romanée Conti had become so outlandishly expensive that the prices of many wines had become skewed. There was a great irony there because in fact Burgundies were the best-value wines on the market, if only drinkers knew it. They were better-value than Bordeaux, Napa, and many Spanish wines; they had more character, more integrity, more "flesh." There were twenty-dollar Burgundies that iced everything else at the same price. They were the most underrated *cheap wines* on planet earth.

"And what about Italian wines?"

Rosenthal's face went cloudy.

"Italy's a different kind of tragedy. The Italians have just Americanized themselves to death. They came late to the global market, but they came with a vengeance. They've massacred their own patrimony, in my opinion. Look at Chianti. *Are* there any great Chiantis anymore? There's Castell'in Villa, okay—but practically nothing else. Chianti today is a bad joke. And you know that I love Italy more than any other country."

Because we were so high up, I felt a little light-headed; when dessert came I began repetitively eating the small chocolate wafers with printed patterns known as *tegole*. The wine: the herbal, fragrant Erbaluce di Caluso made from that rare mountain grape whose name I tried ineptly to etymologize—*erba luce*, grass light? If that was right, it suited the wine. The more ordinary Erbaluces that one finds everywhere in freeway stores up to the Mont Blanc tunnel are usually named Canavese Bianco and have little of the flowery reticence of Ferrando's. I have since drunk Erbaluce di Calusos dozens of times and they have always filled me with a rarefied good humor which may simply be a psychological connection to my day in Ivrea with Rosenthal and Ferrando. Who knows? This is certainly strange, because that day was September 11, 2001, and when we arrived at the Ferrando *cantina* out in the countryside at three o'clock, Rosenthal received a call from his wife in New York.

We were all a little tipsy and in a bantering mood. Rosenthal walked away from the patio where we were tasting a headily perfumed wine from fifty-year-old vines called Castello di Loranze and stood stock-still in a field with his ear pressed to the cellphone. He then uttered a small cry, dropped the phone, and stood there like a puppet whose strings have suddenly been cut. The Italian field hands ambled to their car and turned on the radio. A hysterical announcement was being broadcast. We put down our glasses and tried to think of something to say. Rosenthal came back to the communal spittoon and his hands were trembling. A brilliant, playful sunlight, the deep yellow Castello di Loranze . . . and catastrophe.

From then on, the day took a decidedly surreal turn. I felt at once the chasm of difference that separated the reaction of Europeans—grave and appalled though it was—from the visceral sense of rapine which anyone living in New York had to feel. We said our farewells to Luigi and drove up to Carema with his son, Roberto. A thick muteness had descended. And at the same time the vineyard terraces of Carema, as Rosenthal said, are the most sublime in the world. Clinging to the edge of massive cliffs, dominated by the first towers of the Alps, they form a tiny shell or theater one thousand feet above sea level, like the remnants of an ingenious prehistoric horticulture. The track through them climbs steeply until the green onion dome of the Carema church looks impressively distant.

The lowest vineyard is Donnaz, from where one passes along the Via Francigona up to the more rarefied plot of Siei, and finally the eagle's aerie of Silanc. The terraces are covered by lines of squat concrete pillars with the vines spread out on trellises known as *tipiun*. It is one of the most northerly vineyards in Italy and its production is so concentrated, so artisanal, that its output of fifteen hectoliters per hectare is comparable to Sauternes. That's a mere eight hundred cases of Carema a year, most of it either consumed in Italy or exported to the United States. And there are only two producers of what is widely considered one of the five or six greatest wines in Italy: Ferrando and the Cooperativa.

We wandered around with Roberto and a loose bottle of Erbaluce spumante, dipping in and out of these terraces where no machine is small enough to pass. Rosenthal confessed that, in many ways, this was the center of his world, insofar as that world was constituted by wine. It was the core of his vision. Was it not easy, he said, to imagine the Romans cultivating these same terraces? The vineyard was like a microcosmic ship sailing all by itself through a vulgar and despotic world in a spirit of the most imperturbable calm. When Roberto kissed our cheeks good-bye there was a warm smell of sun and grapes on his cheek, a sexual smell which had no homosexual overtones to either of us, just an affectionate physicality. Rosenthal and I walked down the hill back toward Donnaz, blinded by the sun and the burnished air. We were both thinking about New York, the clash of civilizations, the road checks on the tunnels into Switzerland. And yet there we were in Carema, in the heat of the most sensually immaculate day of the year, buried among terraces of Erbaluce leaves. Rosenthal asked me where I was going; I was no longer sure. I had been planning to drive back to Geneva but now I was having doubts. Perhaps I would turn south instead, away from the inevitable storm. Perhaps I could get a plane back to New York from Rome. He, with foreboding, was returning to Burgundy.

"Well," he said, "I hope I managed to show you something despite all that's happening now. It feels like a blissful moment here, doesn't it? So calm, as if nothing were happening. And you know—that *isn't* deceptive. In a strange way I'm glad I was here with you today. This is the place closest to my heart. Everything I believe about wine is around you right here." Then he added, pursing his lips: "But I think it's going to be a hallucinatory couple of weeks."

And so we parted ways at the little intersection just outside Carema, he bound for the north and I for the south and Tuscany. The rest of the day I listened to the radio in a state of stupefaction. Several months later I saw Rosenthal again at a dinner party. He had brought a bottle which he considered the epitome of *veritas in vino*: a Volnay Taillepieds from Bitouzet-Prieur. While drinking it we compared our memories of the afternoon in Carema. They corresponded quite remarkably.

"But what," he said, turning back to the wine, "is there to say about this Volnay Taillepieds? We could say that it's perfectly structured, firm, equilibrious . . . I don't know . . . but ultimately you know what you're tasting. It's as perfect a wine as you can drink. It's a dazzling expression of place."

But what, he added, about Tuscany?

"It was something of a homecoming," I said.

"Well, you know what I think about Tuscany."

Nevertheless, I had secretly hoped that he would be wrong.

Mondo Antinori

Taste may change, but inclination never.   —La Rochefoucald

The Palazzo Antinori sits in a slight bulge of the Via Tuornabuoni near the Via de' Corsi. Tuornabuoni is one of Florence's most chic streets, its rusticated palace walls housing the odd Hermès, Les Copains, and Loretta Caponi clothing stores, as well as the opulent House of Florence hotel. The piazza is a delicate crescent of dark, dusty orange mansions with lofty eaves throttled with traffic. Although the Antinoris are one of the oldest families of the city and have been here since the fourteenth century, their fame today is based almost exclusively on wine. Indeed, in the outside world the name Antinori is virtually synonymous with modern Italian wine, with the Italian wine renaissance. And it is especially synonymous with Chianti, that uncrowned prince of the peninsula's nectars. Since the Marchese Piero Antinori is a real prince, he could be aptly named the Prince of Chianti, and it's a moot point whether he would object. To judge by the palace, he would not.

Inside, the ground-floor reception rooms are squirely and restrained. A huge neorealist painting by Ferroni dominates the main room: an ox, barefoot peasants brimming with garlands, a bright pale sky. Through French doors a garden appears, one of those dark little Florentine gardens with potted trees. The drawing room houses a serious collection of trophies, including a glass cube improbably designated the Wine Spectator Hall of Fame Award, a thing called the Côtes du Coeur, a 2000 Wine Spectator Wine of the Year for Solaia, a prize from the 2001 New York Wine Experience, and an unexpected salute from the American Heart Association, Dallas Division. The mood is High Victorian. The paintings here are also rural—scenes of hunting dogs by Coppola—and some strange bottles of wine accompany them: a Hungarian Aranyhars, a Tormaresca from Puglia, a venerable Prunotto. Are they for family drinking or just for show?

Since I had some free time, I scoured through the ample bookshelves. *Mysterium Wein*, *Les 100 Vins de Légende*, *L'Italia Agricola del XX Sècolo*, volumes of Hugh Johnson. I was served espresso in some exquisite Antinori teacups decorated with stenciled lemons while I paged through an album of sixteenth-century Florentine landscapes by forgotten artists like Cecco Braso, Baccio del Bianco, and Filippo Napoletano. How strange to see these views of the city and its suburbs of which almost nothing but the largest monuments have survived. The meadows of Braso, the rural inns, the souk-like medieval city—all gone. But there are the vineyards, seemingly eternal if in fact not at all so. The vineyard and the Duomo, the two threads that keep the past from looking alien.

The Marchese arrived in a sleek suit, a refined man in his late fifties with a full head of hair. He asked me very politely what language I would like to speak, it didn't matter much to him. His French, English, and Italian were interchangeable.

"But weren't you in school in Florence?" he asked.

"It's been a long time . . ."

"And the old lady has changed, hasn't she?"

I admitted that the center of Florence had horrified me. It was becoming like Pisa, a nightmarish tourist installation.

"It's the way of the world," I said.

"Some people don't like it. But I suppose you're right, it's indeed the way of the world."

Then again, the way of the world has been kind to the Antinoris. The family has prospered mightily in Tuscany's new wine commerce, which unsurprisingly is a vital part of the larger tourist enterprise.

We went in to the Cantinetta Antinori, the in-house palazzo restaurant, and the Marchese moved with a regal ease among his employees. The Cantinetta has become one of the chic eateries of Florence, and is filled with what could be called the Hermès crowd. We got a private table upstairs. In his dark blue suit and his tie decorated with silky airplanes, Antinori was a model of the Italian gentleman. I liked him at once; he had that quality which in sculpture is known as *morbidezza*, smoothness—the smoothness of old marble, which is quite unlike cold stone because it has been warmed by a kind of sculpting force. In his case, that force was social grace. Not snobbery or aristocratic privilege. Florentine aristocrats who don't make money soon fall by the wayside, and Antinori was not just a coat of arms: he had become an economic force unto himself.

He inherited the Antinori wine business from his father in 1966, the year of the catastrophic floods in Florence (floods, incidentally, which destroyed a priceless library of old wines in the Antinori cellars). The 1960s were a very bad decade for Chianti. Growers had undertaken the biggest replanting of the twentieth century as the old system of Italian sharecropping began to expire.

"That period," said the Marchese of the 1960s, "was complete madness. Huge investments were made in the vineyards but mostly with no clue as to what should be done. By the end of that decade, the picture was dismal. Quality falling—" He made a falling plane gesture with one hand. "—prices, prestige declining. Chianti was becoming the tacky cheap wine of Europe. You know, mandolins, pizza, the merry and cheap Italian image. We were selling to the United States and Germany very cheaply. They looked at us as a third-world country. Folkloric, you see, but no quality."

He laughed, but you could sense him bristling somewhere beneath the surface. Some kale bruschetta had arrived with a bottle of Vino Nobile di Montepulciano from a *fattoria* called La Braccesca. Antinori pointed out that tasting wine without food was "emotionally sterile" and that one shouldn't "judge wine intellectually." I confessed that I was pretty much incapable of judging wine intellectually anyway. Well, he said, that didn't much matter in the larger scheme of things. What mattered was enjoying the pleasures of the mouth.

"One sometimes forgets the pleasures of the mouth!"

"Does one?"

"Writers . . ." Antinori began, then politely gave up.

Not me, I thought. The Braccesca was good. And so was the kale.

"You know," Antinori said, "you always have to remain simple. I am a simple man."

"Are you?"

"Very much so."

His tone suggested that I take this profession seriously. It seemed to say: No, I *don't* have a private helicopter.

The narrative resumed. Antinori's problem circa 1970 was to reinterpret the differences between Chianti and Chianti Classico—the latter being the nobler version cultivated on a high plateau between Florence and Siena. Antinori and his star wine maker, Giacomo Tachis, traveled to Bordeaux to meet Émile Peynaud. They prevailed on the latter to come to Tuscany. And here we see how small the wine world often is, how its personalities are constantly crossing paths. It was Peynaud who first suggested removing white grapes from the Chianti recipe, which traditionally called for 20 percent of the mixture to be white. A practice dating back centuries was scrapped virtually overnight. Why had they done it in the first place? Because traditionally the grapes in Tuscany were fermented with the stems and skins intact, giving a very hard wine which constantly needed to be softened. Peynaud suggested other ways of softening, especially malolactic fermentation and gentler pumping methods. The effects were immediate, according to Antinori. At the vineyard of Tignanello, the Antinori team feverishly experimented with the Peynaud doctrine and eventually began fermenting in small oak barrels instead of the traditional huge ones. This experiment—which they had never intended to market—accidentally became a revolutionary wine which struck the palate of the wine writer Luigi Veronelli (the father of modern Italian wine writers) as an epiphany. He suggested to Antinori that he market it under the name of the vineyard, but not as a DOC wine classified and approved by the system. As it happens, the DOC system itself had not been introduced in Chianti until 1967.

"We wanted the DOC system," Antinori said, "but at the same time we had this Tignanello thing, and it was a mere *vino da tavola*. But it was better than most DOC Chiantis. A typical Italian contradiction. And thus, you see, the first Super-Tuscan was born!"

Tignanello was released in 1973 and immediately became one of the most successful Italian wines of the twentieth century. The Super-Tuscans had also arrived: modern, technically refined international wines on the Tignanello model whose high prices dragged Italy back onto the amateur connoisseur's radar screen. Americans in particular loved them, as they still do.

Another of this new breed of viticultural racehorses was Sassicaia, created equally by accident by Antinori's cousin Marchese Nicolo Incisa della Rochetta in Bolgheri, on the Tuscan coast. Sassicaia and Tignanello—along with Antinori's other creation, Solaia—transformed the image of Tuscan wine in the outside world. They created, at least according to their inventors, Chianti's current prestige. They also helped improve quality laws which now dictate that Chianti can be made with 100 percent Sangiovese grapes.

But there were also criticisms. The wine, some pointed out, tasted of oak and little else. It bore little relation to anything that up to then could have been called Italian wine. Sassicaia, indeed, was notoriously made from Cabernet, not even an Italian varietal. But Antinori defends the Super-Tuscans by simply pointing out that they did not displace any prior noble wine. Rather, they flew into a void in the 1970s much as Oudart's new Barolos had in the 1860s. Italian wine, it was implied, needs to be constantly reinvented by means of such radical breaks with the past.

Antinori laid his hands flat on the table and raised his eyebrows.

"Thus," he said, "the Super-Tuscan is not a freak. It's often the way we Italians operate. We go into a lull, then we revive."

He made a subtle gesture and a few seconds later a bottle of Tignanello appeared on the table.

Antinori poured.

"Well, you can tell me if you like it or not. But I suppose you've already drunk it in New York?"

I said that I hadn't, and that the wine itself surprised me. It had a slightly perfumed fruit-gum aroma and certainly didn't taste like an Italian wine. I wasn't sure what I thought. Being honest, I admitted it wasn't really my thing.

"Oh, I understand." Antinori smiled. "But when you go down to our estates at Badia a Passignano, you'll have some of them too."

Lunch over, we went down to the Via Tuornabuoni. A faint spring heat seemed to roll off the walls of rusticated stone, and the dazed tourist faces shone with sweat in the sun. I felt a sudden physical weariness at the thought of having to struggle through them, navigating around this small city which I knew like the back of my hand but which in the intervening years of our alienation had left me far behind.

"Are you going for a nostalgic walk, then?" Antinori asked.

He was a kind man, with a paternal inflection in his voice. Perhaps he was worried for my mental health as I prepared to visit the scenes of a disappeared adolescence.

"I think not," I said. "Just the Gates of Paradise and then straight to Badia a Passignano."

"Ah, the Gates of Paradise?" he sighed, shaking his head with some melancholy. "If you can see through the crowds, that is."

The Gates of Paradise are one thing the foreigner in Florence never seems able to avoid, and which always prove disappointing because of the crowds. And so, after I had taken my leave of the Palazzo Antinori, I decided not to pay my respects to the Gates of Paradise after all. Instead I drove straight out of Florence and south into Chianti, to the manicured village of Badia a Passignano, where the Antinori enterprise has its most treasured vineyards.

The abbey has been closed for years, but around it the Antinori wine business has spun a web of discreet glitz. The Bottega is like a bed-and-breakfast for honeymooners, its walls covered with prints of *The Cottage Breakfast* and *Bacchus and Ariadne*. Its shelves groan with the riches of the Antinori production lines: bottles of Aleatico, Guado al Tasso, Tignanello, Solaia, Peppoli, Castello della Sala. At the wine bar you can drink a Merlot Braccesca by the glass and chat with the Americans ebbing and flowing with an endless energy through the Antinori landscape. It's remarkable how successful the Marchese has been in the United States. Every tourist on the Tuscany circuit knows exactly who Antinori is, and what the difference in price is between a bottle of Solaia bought in Chicago and one bought here.

I wandered outside before my meeting with Barbara Luison, Antinori's public relations *responsabile*. The commune is little more than two intersecting streets overwhelmed by steep slopes of vines on all sides. A notice board set up by the local leftist town council, the Centro Sinistra per Tavernelle, declared itself hostile to *forze conservatrici*, as well as being *contro tutti terrorismi e per i dritti delle vecchie* (against all forms of terrorism and for the rights of old people). This seemed logical enough in the realm of pure rhetoric.

But where were the leftists? The place appeared emptied but for the trickle of elderly Americans buying wine in the Bottega. Perhaps it was their rights that were being defended?

At the bar there was a group from Illinois.

I asked them if they realized the commune was defending their rights.

"Senior citizens?" they cried.

"Free wine for all senior citizens."

"It's cheap enough as it is," the nearest one said. They all laughed. Yeah, it sure was cheaper than Grape Vine Liquors in Peoria.

The biddy nearest me, in the thickest glasses I have ever seen (her eyeballs nightmarishly magnified like two goldfish) then unfolded a filthy photocopy slipped from her raincoat pocket. I leaned over. Tasting notes?

"You bet. We go *armed*."

Sure enough, it was Parker on Guado al Tasso. She read out loud: "Thick, juicy, succulent personality—"

"It sounds like a steak," I said.

"That's what we like," ancient hubby chipped in, pulling Mrs. Biddy a little to one side so he could get a look at the photocopy: "Go on, Amy."

"—copious glycerin—"

Everyone nodded. They knew all about copious glycerin.

"Good for the arteries," I offered.

"Oh," they all screamed in unison, "red wine definitely makes you live longer!"

When Barbara arrived, we drank some Solaia together in the tasting room and then drove up to the restored *borgo* of Tignanello. Tignanello is actually a ghost village. It was abandoned by its peasants and then converted by the Antinori corporation into a kind of wine-oriented rural tourist spa. It's a common phenomenon in Tuscany these days. The family is renovating the old Santa Christina villa on the ground and recasting it as the home shrine of

Tignanello. They know that a famous wine brand needs a concomitant place to make it serviceable to the affluent traveler. All around, the vineyards are being recast as well. The lines are being rearranged, stones in the earth freshly pulverized. New cement fermentation tanks were being built as we watched: the whole place was a hive of construction, not at all the aristocratic idyll I had expected.

"The Antinori business is on the move," Barbara said breezily. "We're replanting all the time."

I wandered with Barbara onto the road and gazed down at the hillsides of vines, the campanile of the Badia presiding over its arc of photogenic Tuscan typicality. It seemed almost like the ancient version of the modern photo-op. At that moment, however, a battered car suddenly roared into view and came flying past us, a half dozen African men staring out with wild eyes. Barbara looked baffled for a moment, but then again this car full of immigrants was as sure a gauge of the wine economy as the restored houses of Tignanello or the campanile of Passignano. Tuscany is now international, and it isn't just because of the villa owners from London and Berlin. Wine is always the lightning conductor of an irrepressible and often iniquitous cosmopolitanism.

Tuscany may have the oldest continuous wine-making tradition in Europe, and wine dynasties like the Antinoris and the Frescobaldis are by far the most venerable of their ilk (both were trading in the fourteenth century), but Chianti is, like most wines, a relatively modern phenomenon. The Grand Duke of Tuscany created some of the first wine zones in Europe in 1716, and Chianti was among them. But it was a moody aristocrat named Bettino Ricasoli, Count of Brolio, who invented the modern wine now known under that name in the 1840s. Experimenting in relative isolation in his castle near Radda, Ricasoli devised a formula for Chianti which consisted of three parts—Sangiovese, Canaiolo, and the white Malvasia.

In the twentieth century, experimentation continued, sometimes almost accidentally. And one of its results has been the Super-Tuscans. Of these, none is more renowned than Sassicaia.

The story of Sassicaia, in fact, is one of the better known fairy tales of Italian wine. The father of the present owner, who is Nicolo Incisa della Rochetta, was originally from Piedmont, and like his nineteenth-century predecessors had become interested in importing French varietals to improve the quality of his estate's wine. In 1940 he moved to Bolgheri, a small town on the Tuscan coast, and planted some plots of Cabernet Sauvignon there in 1944. It was never his intention to make a commercial wine; the Cabernet was purely for his own private and Francophilic consumption. The provincial aristocracy of the impoverished Maremma drank imported Bordeaux, partly from social affectation, and partly, no doubt, because the local wines were so bad. The first private bottles of Sassicaia appeared in 1948, and were drunk by the Marchese Mario Incisa della Rochetta, and his guests on his estate. It was not until 1968 that the family decided to sell it using their cousin Antinori's distribution network.

The wine's rise to preeminence, however, was largely fortuitous. A London tasting in 1972 made its lofty international reputation, despite the fact that it was a relatively amateurish garage wine of which only six thousand cases were made a year. The Incisa clan was astounded. It was unheard of for an Italian wine to make such a commotion at an international tasting, let alone an Italian Cabernet. Sassicaia, an unknown dark horse, had overnight become virtually the most expensive Italian wine in history.

The Tenuta San Guido, where Sassicaia is made, stands a mile or so from Bolgheri at the end of Via Aurelia, a long Roman-style road walled on both sides by cypresses. Nicolo was waiting for me at the gates. He bore a startling resemblance to the tender old man with the deformed, cauliflower nose in Ghirlandaio's famous painting *Old Man with a Child*. A slightly baggy man in later middle age, he has a shy and intelligent face sympathetically deformed by the Ghirlandaio nose. A slight mole on his left eyelid completed this face's lovely asymmetry. I saw too that the doors of the winery bore the Masonic-looking star which is the emblem of Sassicaia. In his paisley tie and tweeds, Nicolo is every inch the country squire. I found him gentle and hesitant—the most likable of personal qualities in my humble book. We went for a casual stroll around the winery, but as we did so I said I'd seen enough fermentation vats and pumping equipment to last me a lifetime. They are all much the same after a while.

"Well, you have a point there," he laughed. "Much more fun to drink, don't you think? As long as you promise not to spit. I do loathe it when wine people gurgle and spit. I don't labor over my wine so that you can spit it out!"

He went off and returned with armfuls of bottles: an impromptu short vertical of recent Sassicaia, the '97, '98, and '99. As we opened the '97 and began drinking from it, Nicolo reminisced. The whole Italian wine culture, he said, was only about fifteen years old. Italians drank wine like Coke until the sixties, a half liter per person per day. Now it was about half that. And wine had suddenly become internationally competitive, like football, while charging toward homogeneity. "Quite funny, really."

"In Italy," he went on, "the wines are definitely becoming less elegant, more extracted and showy. I have seen how this business operates from day one, because as you know in 1985 we made a Sassicaia that is now considered mythical. Parker loved it, it became the darling of Sotheby's, and so forth. Parker, for one, has never given us a better source since. But all that has nothing to do with the wine itself. The '98, for example, is almost as good as the '85 . . . ."

The '98 was a soft, feminine wine, as they say. The *Wine Spectator* gave it a 95. We fell silent for a while, mulling it over and listening to the rhythmic hissing of the bottling machine at the far end of the cellars. You could say that Sassicaia is sui generis, an Italian wine made from a Bordeaux varietal and according to a unique sensibility. It was the only Super-Tuscan I had sampled so far that I actually liked, though as always it was not easy to say why. As it happens, the '98 was a tremendous success with the international press, but the '99 was perhaps less so because it's a somewhat tighter, harder wine of greater austerity. I said, however, that for these very reasons I enjoyed it more than the '98, which is a very obvious wine. It was also, I dare say, relaxing to drink it alone with Nicolo in his work environs, without psychological pressure, without the need to say anything especially clever. I said aloud that I thought official tastings with critics must be excruciating. Didn't the artificial tension in the air completely distort the whole undertaking?

"I agree," said Nicolo. "But you see, a critic takes only thirty seconds to taste something. I believe that's Parker's average. Thirty seconds! It's grotesque, really. That's how so-called global taste comes about. But all one can do is work and produce. The rest is . . . psychology."

He uttered the last word as if he did not approve of what it denoted.

"Personally," he added, "I'm in favor of doing what that restaurant in Brussels has decided to do, charge a maximum of thirty-five dollars for every bottle on its list."

We carried on drinking and not spitting, and I soon forgot all about the *Decanter* awards and prizes from the Italian Association of Sommeliers on the walls. The 2000 was the most fleshy and concentrated of the four, for it had been a hot year, and soon I was flushed and light-headed. This was not very "professional," but my host seemed indulgent and merely asked if I was tipsy.

"I am tipsy," I admitted.

"Such is wine."

It was the end of the afternoon and I had only to drive to my hotel in Bibbona down the road.

"Can you make four kilometers without hitting a tree?" he asked. "Tonight, by the way, you should eat at La Pineta in Lido di Bibbona. *That* is a restaurant."

He opened a cellphone and made the reservation for me. He gave me a few bottles of the '99 and we staggered out together into a stiff ocean wind. The Via Aurelia was flooded with pale sun.

"I think," said Nicolo by way of farewell, "that the food at La Pineta is roughly equivalent to my idea of wine. Will you send me an e-mail telling me what you thought of it?"

There are two great restaurants on the coast near Bibbona and Bolgheri, both of them no doubt nourished by the multimillion-dollar wine trade inland. The more renowned is Gambero Rosso, in the little tourist port of San Vincenzo, one of only two establishments in Italy to garner two Michelin stars; and the other is La Pineta, which has no Michelin stars at all (a slight which, given the Michelin's inability to understand Italian food, might be counted as a compliment) but which sits more beguilingly on a lonely beach amid the pine forests of the tacky German resort of Bibbona.

At the more flashy if starchy Gambero Rosso, I ate the food of Italy's gastronomic enfant terrible, Fulvio Pierangelini, who with his curly bangs and tremendous gut looks like a genial cross between Friar Tuck and Cupid. There was tuna marinated with figs, chickpea soup with prawns, monkfish with asparagus and white truffles, seafood ravioli, sea bass with artichokes, cheeses with chestnut honey—pecorino di fossa, chèvre with chestnut leaves—and then crepes with warmed *agrumi*, or citrus fruits. At the end of this wondrous menu came cold grapes covered with chocolate and with the leaves still attached.

Pierangelini came out and chatted about wine. I had made a secret and horrified note of the prices of their Sassicaia, which ranged from 320 euros for the 1981, 1,000 euros for the "mythical" '85, 400 euros for the '88, and a relatively modest 120 euros for the '99 (my free bottles were still lying satisfyingly in my car trunk outside in the parking lot). But this same list also yielded a 1995 Trebbiano d'Abruzzo from none other than the Old Man of the Mountain, Eduardo Valentini, as well as a Raveneau Chablis for under forty euros and a 1988 Moscato di Chambave which was equally reasonable.

I offered Fulvio a glass of the Valentini and he agreed that it was one of his favorite wines of all, perhaps one of the three or four greatest white wines of Italy. It was slightly clouded, dark yellow-green in color. Had I ever drunk it before?

"Our tourists rarely ask for it," he pointed out.

The room was mostly full of foreigners. A large German gentleman sat at the neighboring table with a much younger blond woman, putting the chocolate grapes in her mouth with two nimble fingers. *Ja, ja . . . so!* They drank a Sassicaia.

"I think," Fulvio whispered, "people go by the price."

In other words, a wine is cheap enough or not cheap enough.

I wanted to ask the lovers if the Sassicaia was making them horny. But such questions are of course off limits. The Valentini was not making me horny, but then it didn't have to. I was alone, and what I wanted was to be made contemplative. And so the Valentini duly made me contemplative. In other words, it made me happy to be alone.

The Chambave made me sorry that Neal was not there with me, though it went very well with the chocolate grapes. Then, setting it aside, I went back to the Valentini just to recover my composure. For me, there was something freshly monkish about this wine, something cool and cerebral. It made me *grateful* to be drinking it alone. But after ten minutes of asceticism I returned to the Chambave and felt once more the need for carnal company. It's true, in a sense, that one never drinks completely alone. Wine summons ghosts out of the cupboard.

Driving back inland, I found a few days' hospitality in the heart of Chianti at the tiny estate of Podere Pruneto near Castellina.

Podere Pruneto clings to the same mountainside as the more

renowned Castello di Volpaia. It is run by a quirky refugee from
Milan called Dr. Roberto Lanza, who lives here with his wife and
children in a smattering of stone houses given over to wine making,
chicken breeding, and the various philosophies of the Mohawk nation. Lanza was a shy and gangly man in spectacles, and their family kitchen was a robust retreat from the rigors of the international
scene. Lounging around the mountainside for a while, I felt like
a First World War soldier recovering from a small shrapnel wound
at a hospital mysteriously endowed with reservoirs of small-scale
organic Chianti. My room was equipped with a large quote from
one Lame Deer, which began "We, who know the meaning of the
pipe . . ." There was a poignant Curtis photograph of an Indian
from vanished eras, *The Rush Gatherer Arikara*, and elsewhere
stylish matador posters reflected another worldview entirely. But
nature can be a stern ideal. The family rooster lodged on my win-
dowsill erupted every morning at four and could only be dislodged
by a fierce reflection directed at its head with a shaving mirror. But
Lanza was against physical violence to roosters.

"He drives us all crazy as well," he admitted. "But it's all part of
knowing the meaning of the pipe!"

And he laughed with what can only be described as ecological
malice.

The Lanza family was that supposedly rare thing: a happy one.
Every night we tried different Pruneto vintages, about which Lanza
himself was unfailingly diffident. Back in 1988, the *Gambero Rosso*
(the guide, not the restaurant) had given him a rating of three
glasses, its highest accolade, and the little estate became briefly famous before the wine juggernaut moved on in its fickle way. Lanza
more or less shrugged at these developments. His wines have simply
gotten better and better regardless. Now, as he approached middle
age, they had found their equilibrium. They were a modest but polished balance between rustic heartiness and urban sophistication:
much, in other words, like the man who made them.

"But," he added mournfully, "it seems that today expensive wines sell more easily than normally priced ones. It's bizarre, to say the least. It's harder to sell a normal wine than a conspicuously expensive one."

We were now at table. He turned to his wife and made the Italian *beh* sound, which corresponds in written notation to a question of such futility that it cannot really be answered.

"Roberto," his wife said, "you're going to have a heart attack thinking about prices. It doesn't matter. It's the way of the world."

Rather than the way of the pipe, I thought.

At dusk I walked a few miles through gloomy woods and down the mountain to an *agriturismo* called Podere Terreno, where they have a restaurant for overnight guests. The Terreno is run by a forceful Frenchwoman named Sylvia Heniez, who also makes her own wines—like Lanza's, straightforward and uncomplicated Chiantis at a high level of competence. I noticed here the same Native American themes and exhortations that filled Roberto Lanza's house; on one wall Sylvia's rather playboyish husband, Roberto, had pinned his proud Ambassador of the Red Earth certificate. The Italian middle classes, it seems, are susceptible to anything Native American, though naturally they rarely meet any living examples. The idea is to have ecological paradigms with a human face, preferably an exotic one. Sylvia, on the other hand, was more down to earth. She had worked in the fashion textile business in Prato before buying this olive farm in 1980 with Roberto at a time when "Chianti was the worst wine imaginable." The invention of a wine became an emotional preoccupation.

"But," she said, "you used to live hereabouts, didn't you?"

I said I had run a small olive oil outfit in Panzano down the road while writing my first book as a college student in 1983.

"So you see how it's changed?"

She explained that Radda, the largest village of the region, had traditionally been the center of an iris industry. Chianti's main export, in fact, had been dried iris flowers for the perfume industry in

Grasse. But the wily *parfumiers* had eventually found an industrial replacement for fresh irises and the flower growers had gradually gone out of business. That left tourism and wine.

As it happened, there was a voluble French perfumer at the table with his wife. At mention of irises his ears pricked up. He looked like a perfumer, too, in his tidy tweed waistcoat, plum tie, and shiny hair tonic. Yes indeed, he chimed in: for a perfumer, the name of Radda was a faded legend.

"I regret to say," he added, "that nowadays all perfumes smell the same. Like Calvin Klein. They are all sweet, floral, or citrus. The most innocuous formula naturally will always appeal to the maximum number of people. The exercise today is how to make an industrial perfume. But then again"—he raised his fork, heaped with mushroom risotto—"national ideologies are collapsing in Europe! Who is 'Italian' these days? Who is 'French'?"

Who indeed? I wondered. But I said that I certainly felt "English." Or even English.

"That," said the perfumer with heavy finality, "is a luxury!"

But it was not clear whether his tone was scornful or simply deranged.

The next day, I paid a visit to the Castello di Volpaia at the very top of the mountain. Volpaia is one of the thirty-three original *aziendi* which formed the first officially designated Chianti Classico in 1929. It's a historic estate, in other words, rich in history and anecdote. Today it's run by Giovanella Stianti Mascheroni, the daughter of a famous Florentine printer and publisher who has presided over the renovation not only of the winery but of the *borgo* of Volpaia itself. With its primitive *pieve* church and helter-skelter flagged streets, Volpaia is like an enological stage set, a viticultural opera whose rarely seen inhabitants, who work for the estate, also seem like moving props designed to convince the tourists renting cottages in their midst that everything around them is traditional Tuscany. There's even a *cantina*, a village bar, and a grocery store. It's a canny three-dimensional illusion of village life—until, that is, you open a door by chance and find yourself staring not at the interior of a house or a barn full of hay but at walls of gleaming machinery and polished steel. For beneath its homey skin of stone and tile, Volpaia is actually a high-tech wine-making installation as artfully concealed as any villain's lair in a James Bond movie.

Giovanella is a tall blond woman of boundless energy: the elegant *fiorentina* incarnate. She wore a necklace of huge gold balls which made her look like a Babylonian priestess. Her father bought the property in 1966, at a time when the village was already dying. Volpaia used to have a population of about one hundred; phone lines connecting them to the outside world were set up only in 1992. The wine was peasant wine, hard and stringent. While Giovanella's brother took over the printing business, she was allocated the wine estate, it being felt that even a mere woman could handle so prosaic an enterprise. When she took over, she says, there was no marketing, no quality, no labels even on the bottles: it was a leftover business which her father had ignored while enjoying his hunting. In the early 1970s the family bought two-thirds of the whole village and gradually acquired forty-five hectares of land. Today, Castello di Volpaia makes the same quantity of wine from these forty-five hectares as the commune did in 1965 from just five hectares. Sixty clones of Sangiovese were brought in and planted; piece by piece the hard, impoverished village was transformed into a kind of landscaped factory.

Giovanella took me inside the twelfth-century church, whose lintels are adorned with a coat of arms bearing a wolf, a sword, and a serpent: the vanished Stiozzi family who once lorded over this domain of the *volpa*, or wolf. But of course the church is no longer a church. Inside the doors you are faced with huge steel fermentation tanks framed by the vaults of the nave. One crouches to the sacristy, and a crumbling tabernacle, through tiny wooden doors warped like autumn leaves, occasionally stopping to look at the crude rosettes cut into the stone walls. In another once-abandoned build-ing we went up to the attic to look at the rafters laden with long chains for drying Vin Santo grapes. The Stiantis even have a high-tech olive press in the same semisubterranean complex.

"I care about the *appearance* of Tuscany," Giovanella said sweetly. "Have you noticed these horrifying cranes everywhere above the villages?" She shivered with disgust. "They're building monstrous constructions all over Chianti just because people can't be bothered to commute to Poggibonsi, or a large town like that. The whole place is beginning to look like a suburb of Berlin."

"Perhaps," I offered, "it makes most of the population feel at home."

"They're not *all* foreigners, you know. We have the usual inter-national buffet. It's not their fault, though. It's the Communists on the local councils."

I wondered, as we strolled back to her villa at the edge of the vil-lage, if we shared the same vision of Tuscany. The Communist aes-thetic, if Communists can be said to have an aesthetic, would probably be dire enough: concrete and steel to defy the foreign *borghese* now buying up all their land. Yet my own nostalgia was itself a mishmash of British imagery whose authenticity could hardly be vouched for. If you had to make a list of its ingredients, it would probably look like this: E. M. Forster, the D. H. Lawrence of the let-ters, the Berenson villa in Fiesole, Ruskin, Gregor von Rezzori and Bruce Chatwin at home, Helena Bonham-Carter . . . and thereafter a swift descent into pseudo-cultural kitsch.

But the glamour of this conglomeration of clichés is nevertheless intense. For a while, perhaps a hundred years, Tuscany was the primary Continental incubator of the British intelligentsia—the "intelligentry," as it should more properly be called. Where South Americans went to Paris, the British went to places like Radda. In his film *Stealing Beauty*, Bernardo Bertolucci tried to impale this lit-tle world. But what is there to impale, in the end? Tuscany ceased being rustic, or even especially Tuscan, in the 1970s, and the intelligentry now flies to the Seychelles. Chianti struck me as essentially normalized and suburbanized. And the irritation in Giovanella's voice when she talked about construction cranes corresponded exactly to the little spurt of fury I felt looking at these same things. Didn't those cranes, I kept thinking, used to be brick campaniles?

The Stianti villa was full of bustling servants, whose birdlike voices came welling up from behind closed doors. The rooms were colored with amazing murals by the painter Luciano Guarnieri, in which photographically vivid beetles and cicadas crawled through vines. Naturally enough for the country retreat of a master printer, the library was superb, full of tooled volumes from the presses of Stianti Edittore. Racine, Flaubert, Rilke. The salon was luxurious, with views over a delicate garden and what can only be described as textbook Tuscan hills. "Just like one of those *Tuscany books*," Giovanella snapped as she tried to light a fire with what looked like an elongated hair dryer. The Italian impressionists on the wall and the frosted chandeliers looked on a little glumly as the hair dryer seemed to defeat the lady of the house. Eventually, a servant was called and the fire brought to life so that we were able to settle down to tea and cakes.

Giovanella wanted to tell me good things about her visiting enologist, the renowned Riccardo Cotarella, whose brother Stefano is also famous as a wine-making consultant working with the Antinoris.

"The thing is," she said, "I really didn't like the hardness of the older Volpaia wines. Now it's just my taste, but I like my wines softer. I like a *soft* wine. Riccardo knew just how to make our wines soft. The 2002 is going to be different because of his ideas—like heating the cellars during fermentation to induce malolactic. We've also put in some Merlot. When you're this high up, six hundred meters, Sangiovese can be a bit sharp. A bit nasty. But now we've got a velvety wine—"

"Is it a Cotarella wine, then?"

The Cotarellas consult all over Italy, and they put the stamp of their sensibility on every wine they help shape.

"Well, that's going a little far. But I suppose it's partially a Cotarella wine, yes."

I asked her about Antinori.

"Antinori, Mondavi, they're not top, but they're dependable. You have to understand how important dependability is to wine drinkers. People get tired of spending a lot of money and being disappointed. So Mondavi, for example, never lets you down. Nor does Antinori." She paused. "And nor, I might add, does Castello di Volpaia."

Oddly enough, no wine was offered for tasting. So I said that I had eaten at Il Torre restaurant in Castellina a few nights before and had ordered the most expensive Chianti on the list, a local Fonterutoli. The Japanese wedding party next to me had been drinking the same thing.

"And of course," I said, "Fonterutoli is really an American wine, isn't it?"

"Yes it is. But if people want Coke, give it to them. People want smooth wines."

"Soft ones?"

"Oh, we're not Fonterutoli. There, you taste the cellar more than the soil. But I admit that's true of an awful lot of Chianti these days."

Perhaps Castello di Volpaia's top wine is a Super-Tuscan called Balifico made with Cabernet. Did she think that was an American wine in some ways? She answered with a gorgeous smile.

"It's as Italian as I am!"

The phone rang. A maid tapped on the door. "Signora, the president of Tiffany . . ."

Giovanella went off to talk to him. When she returned she said: "Poor dear. He wants to play tennis, but it's cloudy and so he's bored. I couldn't help him out."

To round out our conversation I asked Giovanella what Chianti meant to her historically. Could you say that a Castell'in Villa was "true" and that a Fonterutoli was "false"? Was a contemporary Badia a Coltibuona better than one from the 1960s?

Giovanella didn't miss a beat.

"Who can say? Eleanora Stucchi at Badia a Coltibuona doesn't make the same wine her father did. But then again, why don't you go and see her? She'd be a much better person to answer that question than me."

The wine estate run by the vivaciously lovely Eleanora Stucchi was neither remote nor ascetic—in fact, it was not even remotely ascetic. Quite the contrary. The restaurant overlooking the wild ravines was filled with honeymooners from Brooklyn and a large luridly clad contingent of amateur cyclists on tour from Missouri. My ear also picked out dulcet tones of Polish, Urdu, and Chinese. It was rather like a scene in a Jacques Tati movie where six languages are being spoken all at once, all of them gibberish vaguely resembling real languages. Alarmed, I asked Eleanora if we could explore the old winery buildings attached to the medieval abbey instead. And so after lunch we set off across the terrace full of pendulous lavender and dove into the warren of Coltibuona.

The cellars are an archive going back to the beginning of the century. Each bottle cocooned in cobwebs is visible only by means of a metal tag which divulges its year. I quickly found the 1958, then 1959 . . . then a 1946, a 1937, a 1940. Wines from the Mussolini era. Had she ever drunk any of them?

"Not all, no. Some. I suppose we can't afford to actually drink them. The 1946 is great, I assure you."

The oldest Coltibuona I had ever drunk was a 1976. It must have been a wine made by her father, the late Piero Stucchi.

"Can you remember it?" she asked.

There was a note of anxiety (or filial tenderness?) in her question. Unsure, I said that I thought that I did. But at the same time I hoped that she wouldn't ask me for an analysis.

"Oh no," she smiled, "that would be rude. But it's interesting because we have a very long history here. We bought this estate in 1846 when Ricasoli was still doing his Chianti experiments up the road. So we've been with Chianti Classico since the beginning. But that doesn't mean that anything has remained fixed in stone."

"Didn't Ricasoli want to do just that, fix a formula for Chianti in stone?"

"Well, he didn't. Alas, tastes change. Frankly, the great old Chianti style with its high acidity is just too sour for international tastes. People associate greater concentration with greater value for money. So wines get sweeter and heavier all the time."

"Is that a shame?"

"One could say so. But how many people would know why?"

It could be said that Eleanora's wines are sweeter and more accessible than her father's, that they fall into exactly this curve. It would not be an offhand criticism to say this, because by her own admission the multilingual crowd upstairs in the restaurant heartily approved of this trend. Still, I was curious what relation had existed between father and daughter, what spirit of wine making had passed from one generation to the next. It was a question which kept recurring as I talked to wine makers who worked within family traditions. Yet it was not the right moment to do this, and I felt (perhaps wrongly) that it was a line of inquiry which could not be pursued in a brief visit. So we went upstairs into the monastic courtyards, where a mellow spring rain lashed the walls. I asked her instead if she had ever known anyone in Panzano. As it happened, she had. She knew Susan Rose, Michael Rose's wife, who had rented me a house there all those years ago. And a few other British people from those days. As a young girl she'd been invited to some of their fabulously drunken parties.

"It's funny," she said, "how you can remember someone's face from twenty years ago as if it were yesterday but not remember what they did for a living, or even sometimes their name."

Wine is like that for me. I can't remember wines as well as I'd like to, as well as I imagine wine writers do. And wines are a bit like people. You can remember a warm and magnetic personality from long ago, as if that person radiated an energy which had the power to touch even one's old age. Thus memory was a wondrous thing, as indeed it is often reputed to be. But also, of course, deceitful. And so I said that I was going back to Panzano in the afternoon to take a look around.

"Don't expect to see anyone you know. It's a whole new crowd down there. Then again, you might."

But when I got to Panzano, a place I thought I could remember perfectly, I found that I remembered nothing at all. True, the cemetery was still lit up with candles at night, the Pieve di San Leonardino still stood where it was supposed to stand. And along the road where I used to live, the Villa le Barone still stood among its cypresses along with a shrine to one Gerardo Maiella, *morto* 1916. But otherwise, it seemed like a place which had lost its precise correspondence to my memory. Everything seemed smaller, grayer.

Bewildered, I stopped short before knocking at the house where I had lived seventeen years earlier, turned away, and struggled back to the main road, where hideous new signs for tourist destinations were everywhere. Hotel Relais, Fattoria Vignale, Cantine Storiche, Old Worlde Honey. Some part of me had already decided that I had had enough of Tuscany and its polished sadness. Now I wanted something more primitive and more chaotic: the sun, a whiff of the hysterical Dionysus.

Walking with Dionysus

❧

Oh, this age! How tasteless and ill-bred it is!   —Catullus

A certain Dionysus
whoever he may be   —Euripides, *The Bacchae*

The Falesco factory lies on the outskirts of a town called Montefiascone, in a small industrial park. The region of Lazio, just north of Rome, is a wine nonplace as far as connoisseurs are concerned; but wineries are springing up all over it, places just like Falesco. My guide, an English sculptor named Johnny Madge who has lived in Lazio for years and who plans to open a wine bar in the nearby Sabine village of Casperia, looked around the little dust-white, nondescript parking lot of uncompromising antisepsis, and pulled a face. The boyish Madge is familiar with this particular brand of Italian entrepreneurial charm.

"Why, it's a palace, just like Reading!"

But Falesco is Falesco. The charmless factory makes one of the most ubiquitous Italian wines on earth. Indeed, almost every wine store in New York has a bottle of Falesco on its shelves, and one of their wines, Montiano, is a fifty-dollar three-glasses *Gambero Rosso* monster. The 1995 Montiano, 100 percent Merlot, scores a dazzling 95 with Parker. We must, in good conscience, give the

Parker note in full, for it shows just how and why Falesco has conquered the world of palates and tongues:

> This unfiltered, profoundly rich red wine is a knockout. The color is a saturated purple, and the nose offers up glorious aromas of smoked meats, cassis, chocolate and vanillin. Spectacular richness combined with beautifully integrated acidity, tannin and wood make for an opulently textured, multi-layered, stunningly proportioned wine of exceptional purity and richness.

It is, incidentally, a wine made by Riccardo Cotarella, of whom Parker writes: "He has gone against the flow of modern-day commercial winemaking."

Falesco started out in the 1960s making Est, Est, Est!, the generic Umbrian cheap white known around the world. Gradually, they came to revise the mediocre vineyards they had either bought or inherited, and in so doing came to create their lustrous portfolio: reds like Vitiano and Montiano, whites like Ferentano, a baseline Greccheto made from the ubiquitous Umbrian varietal, and the ever-happy Est, Est, Est di Montefiascone.

The winery, though, was as bare as a hotel in the Gaza Strip, full of functional rooms and offices. It was like the HQ of an import-export business dealing with aluminum siding. We waited in one of the bare rooms and wondered to ourselves how a winery could be so existentially inhospitable. An odd trellis stood in one corner draped with bunches of rubber grapes. Eventually, a man in a bright blue sweater and an expensive watch emerged. He was Pier Paul Chiasso, one of Falesco's wine makers. The word *chiasso* in Italian means "huge noise," but this Chiasso was the very opposite of a huge noise. He projected a very polite, measured voice which, I supposed, went well with Falesco's philosophy of precision and technical self-awareness.

The effervescent Johnny was searching for wines to add to his wine bar list, and he was wondering if Falesco might offer something profitable to slake the thirsts of confused wine tourists. They made, for example, a rose-scented Aleatico he had once drunk: a curiosity which might go down well.

"Wine bar?" Chiasso said. He sounded supremely unconvinced.

"Enoteca," Johnny reassured him. "You know, a place for visitors to explore the wines of Lazio."

"Interesting idea." Chiasso still didn't sound convinced. "And where is your bar to be?"

"In a converted butcher shop in Casperia."

Chiasso nodded. Who had ever heard of such a thing? "In a butcher store?"

"The tiles are superb."

Chiasso looked at his watch. Well, time to talk wine.

"We believe in local terroir," he began, and we nodded dutifully. "Here we use all local grapes. Well, except Merlot, that is. Merlot has its place here because it's been planted here for a long time. Montiano was created through a rigorous deduction from terroir and climate . . ."

I had the feeling that Chiasso was almost amazed at what a globally significant wine Montiano had become. After all, they released it in 1993 as a fairly cheap one: another homely Italian experiment, a rigorous deduction! "Easy to drink, easy price," he added. "And designed for the American market."

Restlessly, Johnny pressed Chiasso to see if he had any "peculiarities" under his belt, wines not geared to the mass market which might, primarily, give us momentary pleasure and might, secondarily, fit into his wine bar list. It should be stressed that, for an Englishman, Johnny speaks a subtle Italian (he is married to an Italian woman) and is able to charm and persuade in that language to a degree rarely seen in foreigners. "Aha," said Chiasso, visibly expanding inside his bright blue sweater, "I do indeed!"

And he disappeared, returning with a bottle.

"This," he said, "is a wine *molto particolare*."

It was an Aleatico di Gradoli, a sweet wine from an old DOC which was normally fortified but in this instance was not. They had wanted to make a Gradoli that was fresh, youthful, and, well, *molto particolare*.

So he poured it out and we drank it.

As expected, it was rose-perfumed. It was also undeniably fresh and youthful but not, to tell the truth, *molto particolare*.

"You drink it with fruit," Chiasso said firmly, swirling his glass. "We believe a lot in this product. It's a fantastic product."

"I would much appreciate it," said Johnny, "if I could take a bottle with me. I like it and I want to study it a bit."

"*Ma certo.*" Then he added, "This wine is a local tradition. A precious one which we're committed to preserving."

You certainly couldn't deny the cool professionalism of the Falesco ethos. For this ambitious young wine maker, Falesco was the perfect environment; for all the talk of terroir and tradition, the defining principle was "experimentation," a word which was much on his lips. Two other words were also much on his lips, and they were *politica* and *discorso*. I wasn't sure what the contexts of these two words were on every occasion—the talk was fast and elliptical—but I did figure out that *discorso*, discourse, was often applied to varietals.

"Ah, Cabernet," Chiasso said, growing suddenly earnest. "That's a completely different *discorso*."

In fact, they were launching a new Cabernet wine to be called Marciliano, made from an *experimental* estate where they were also growing plots of Aglianico, Malbec, Negro Amaro, and so on.

"So you see," Chiasso went on excitedly, "we're in continual revolution with our varietals." He paused. "And they're all reds."

This was not intended as a joke, but Johnny and I laughed. Chiasso cocked his head quizzically. There was another bottle *molto particolare* to taste, if we were interested, and of course we were. It was called a Roscetto, and it was indeed very rosy and odd. This was followed by another Aleatico, a sweeter one by the name of Pomele. Truth be told, we were not spitting out as we should have been and by now we were rolling along quite merrily. The Pomele was even stranger than the Roscetto, and I now saw what the Falesco technicians meant by experimentation. But on the other hand, it wasn't profoundly strange; just a mite unusual, in a Turkish delight, attar of roses kind of way.

"It's just another *discorso*!" Chiasso beamed triumphantly.

"Another *politica*!" I cried.

"The University of Viterbo," he put in, "is working with us on our experiments."

"Experimentation is necessary," we intoned. "Especially with the help of the universities."

"It's all the genius of Riccardo Cotarella. And now we have this Pomele. What do you think?"

"Pretty nice, pretty nice."

So much Aleatico had been poured by now that the room was beginning to smell like the shop of a florist or a perfumer specializing in dried rose petals. I looked over at the sad rubber grapes standing absurdly in the corner of the room: they seemed to be coming to life in some nightmarish way, like a mirage on the planet Solaris. It was time to move on.

Johnny loaded some crates of Falesco into the car like a scientist hauling off samples of rare metals to study back home at the lab. And then we drove off in a very rarified mood smelling like two rosebushes.

After eating *lardo alla colonnata*—lard marinated with herbs—at a slow-food restaurant in Bolsena over a bottle of Verde di Ca' Ruptae, we made our way to another winery called La Palazzola on the border with Umbria. La Palazzola is considered one of the region's best wineries by *Gambero Rosso*, which lauds its three-glasses Merlots and its experimental Rieslings.

But the place was little more than a construction site, smashed bricks, pipes, and planks lying in a chaotic ziggurat caked with hot white dust. A small army of workers laden with cement bags milled around. In the middle of this inferno stood a bald, handsome man with a black beard, the perfect simulacrum of an Arab pirate. Stefano Grilli was helping oversee the construction of some megalomaniacal windows in his new winery. The pale old red houses of the estate with their green shutters seemed to cower in the face of this cacophony and commotion, whose purpose appeared to be the achievement of scale, space, and pride. The swarthily energetic Grilli took us underground to view the new, grandiose cellars with their rows of concrete pillars. They looked like an underground parking lot of vast dimensions. Grilli laughed.

"*Ironico, no?*" His favorite phrase, we quickly discovered. Many things were *ironico* these days.

One irony was that within this emerging complex lay a lovely old family tasting room. And that's where we retreated to get away from the flying dust and debris. Stacks of familial paintings from centuries past leaned against the fireplace, and Grilli seemed to enjoy the topsy-turviness of his present temporary condition. It was *molto ironico*. He offered us some very ironic wines, too: a fizzy Chardonnay, a fizzy Riesling. The Palazzola Riesling spumante '97 was so startling that I think my eyes fairly popped out of my head. Grilli let loose an Arab pirate guffaw.

"Twenty years ago," he said, "I began my experiments with international varieties in Lazio. Lazio was—and is—a bit of a black hole. So why not? It's a bit American here. There's no iron tradition to hold you back. You can experiment in peace."

He looked at our glasses of bubbling Chardonnay and raised his eyebrows: no, he wasn't quite convinced by his own wine.

"We're too low down to make decent Chardonnay, I think. The Riesling, however, seems to work well. Look, experiments are sometimes shit. But then again, sometimes you come up with interesting things. This is not true terroir wine. But then again, we use local artists on the labels!"

Grilli reminded me of Randall Grahm. His good humor (and irony) smoothed everything out. He was a Cambridge engineering graduate, a man of the world. Pouring a truly bizarre Sauvignon/Riesling hybrid, he murmured that Italians were boringly provincial, they could never be induced to drink anything non-Italian.

"In reality," he said, "this provincialism is the curse of continental Europe. What European Union?"

But that wasn't all: "And yet America is where Italian wine is at now. Americans buy all our best wines, it is like a fabulous supermarket of Italian wines. The other Europeans know nothing. Not even the English—they only import rubbish. So there's an *irony*, no? I think it's symbolic of the wider picture, too."

Listening to Grilli, I understood why purists were sometimes wrong to sneer at men like him. As he said, Lazio was a "black hole." He wasn't spoiling anything. And his restless, slightly childish desire to mess around, to play, to experiment, was not such a bad thing. I wasn't sure what to make of the wines, of course, but Grilli's *impatience*—so inimical to the titanic patience needed to make real wines—was entirely understandable in the circumstances.

We moved on to a Sauvignon/Gewürztraminer sweet wine, or *tardiva*. Grilli watched me merrily, but also probingly. "So?"

"Strange," was all I could say. "Actually, it's quite good."

"Marijuana and tea," Johnny said, and he was dead on.

Grilli then asked me how I liked Greccheto. He said that he loved Greccheto, but it was a rare wine, it was so difficult to get really old Greccheto vines. Most Greccheto was phony. Well, here was his Greccheto 2000 offering, for better or worse. It was an unusual amberish color and tasted of honey and licorice, with a moldy nose. It provoked a comical dialogue unlike any I had ever had with a wine maker:

Grilli: "It's not good."

"Sure it is," we cried.

"No, it's not. It's not good at all."

"You have to be kidding," Johnny said. "It's the most wonderfully weird wine I've drunk in ages. And I've drunk a lot of weird wines."

"I'm afraid not," Grilli sighed. "Interesting, but not good."

He was perfectly genuine. Or rather, he was thinking of his customers, who probably would not like it.

"At least," I opined, "none of your wines are timid."

"Ah, like me!"

We moved on to a fizzy demi-sec Moscato which brought a demonic look to Grilli's face. He grinned as we tried to drink it.

"*Ironico, no?*"

Grilli's reds, like the well-known Rubino made from Cabernet and Merlot, were less intriguing to me, more like cerebral Californians, with their deliberate linear dryness. Like all intellectual wine makers, he had a passion for Pinot Noir, and as with all intellectual wine makers his Pinot Noir did not quite convince. His Vin Santo, however, was gloriously unironic. It smelled like an old church suffused with incense or your father's library nutty with old tobacco. I couldn't resist blurting this out.

Grilli cocked his head sideways as if considering the idea, then said, "Why not? Why not your father's library?"

"Your father's library?" Johnny looked at me. "Did your father *have* a library?"

It was a good question. He did not.

"No?" Grilli said. "Then how can it smell like your father's library?"

I said that I didn't know, but that it nevertheless smelled like my father's library, *if my father had had a library.*

"Ah," Grilli beamed, "*molto post-moderno!*"

Besides, I added, wasn't the whole principle of wine language to create images of things that didn't actually exist? I was getting increasingly used to doing just this. And if we could have melted asphalt and caramel-coated autumn leaves why couldn't we have "my father's library if he had had a library"?

Grilli found this perfectly convincing. *E anche bello.*

On our way back to Casperia, Il Madge and I stopped at the baroque theme park of Bomarzo, with its grotesqueries from the seventeenth century. Carved in blocks of tufa by order of the local Orsini family, it's a precursor of Disneyland with its leaning houses, elephants, and giant mocking pineapples. Fortunately, it was near closing time and utterly deserted. I was bound to thank him for such a delightful day; and as the light receded among the gymnastic goddesses and sea monsters of Bomarzo I wondered if sculpture was still more important to him than wine.

"That," he said, "is not really a question that means anything anymore. Am I a connoisseur of both? I hadn't thought about it."

"Perhaps being a connoisseur is the one consolation of growing old."

"But only because it's part of being a more complete human being. Wouldn't you say?"

And how could any accidental connoisseur disagree?

That night, Johnny and I went to a singular birthday party in the neighboring hilltop village of Roccantica. Count Luciano Robbio-Taci of Roccantica was celebrating with some friends in his declining restaurant, which is almost the last vestige of his once-extensive country estates. The aging Count is not the most energetic of restaurateurs, and the place is more like a family house than a business, a salon where friends drop by and pay you for food. Luciano is a member of the dwindling rural aristocracy which is gradually selling off its olive fields and vineyards in order to pay its debts. In his case, the family history is especially mad and tragic. Luciano is hopeless with money; he has "other interests," including collecting the remains of early Christian saints, many of whom are lodged (and cataloged) in the crumbling palazzo upstairs. I suspect that what he loves most in life are his lemon garden and his rose garden. So he is a connoisseur, if you like, of dead saints' bones and lemons. And so he "declines," as we like to put it. Alas, the walls of the restaurant are covered with images of his ravishing first wife, who died of cancer. And with his dainty potbelly, the fantastical curls at the back of his head, his thick yellow shirt and brown cardigan, and his fey lisping speech, he expressed to me the great gentleness of a lost soul.

He welcomed us graciously to a long table of what I took to be local Lazio aristos. More likely, they were the very nouveaux riches who were voraciously buying up his properties and leaving him on the brink of destitution. He served up a *locale*, a Roscetto wine which in its gay freshness reminded me of the lighthearted wines which were drunk everywhere in eighteenth-century Italy.

"Do you have any interest," he whispered in my ear, "in early Christian saints?"

I didn't want to be invited upstairs, so I said no.

"Ah. You'll excuse us for the humble wine. I'm sure with Signor Madge here you've gotten used to better."

"Not at all. It's much better than the usual Chardonnay del Lazio which all the restaurants seem to have here."

"I agree with you. In any case, it's what my father used to make on our farms. Before we sold them all off, that is."

There was sadness in his voice. Here, then, was the decline of the rural tradition of the *mezzadria*, of the landowners who were sometimes men of ineffectual refinement and precise feeling, like Luciano.

"It must be admitted," he smiled, "that business is not my forte."

During a quiet moment of this meal of tangy artichokes, livers, beef with caramelized fat, and pungent strawberries, Johnny asked me whom I planned to visit as I headed south. It was a good question. At first I had thought of the usual places: wineries, enotecas, vineyards. But now I realized that I was coming to the end of my little journey, and that the more wineries I visited the more they seemed part of a system whose elements I had now internalized. I said I just wanted to wander, to forget about the "wine business" just as Luciano had apparently forgotten all about the restaurant business! It seemed like a liberation, all in all.

"Well," he said, "then perhaps you should go down to the deep South, to Puglia. There's a person there whom I think you would enjoy meeting. Her name's Patience Gray. She's very ancient, but you'll get on with her, trust me. She wrote the most beautiful cookery book on Italy ever written. It's called *Honey from a Weed.* I think it was published in the 1950s. She's a living encyclopedia of Puglian lore, food, vegetation . . . and she makes a wine!"

And suddenly I was seized by an entirely unreasonable desire to visit Patience Gray at her crazy house in the heel of Italy's boot—a house, said Johnny, with no electricity and surrounded by the equally crazy sculptures of her husband, Norman Mommens, the surrealist artist. It was claimed that he had built a solar dish which channeled energy into their home-grown zucchini.

"There's no one like her in the South," he continued. "There's probably no one quite like her left in Europe!"

He gave me her number. Fortunately, her son and daughter-in-law had arrived from England to look after her and they had installed a telephone, as well as electricity.

"Patience, of course, is outraged. But at least you can call her now. And she'll tell you a lot about how the countryside has changed, how Italy has changed. We're too young to know."

I thanked him again and promised him that in the future I would try to be less of an accidental and more of a purposeful connoisseur. After which we toasted the birthday of Count Luciano with a *grappa marzemino,* a luscious blackberry grappa whose effects stayed with me as we strolled around the mystical streets of Roccantica, the yelp of dogs echoing in the valley and the lights of Casperia twinkling on the other side of the dark.

South of Sorrento, I stopped for a night at Castellabate. The old Castellabate is enclosed, deeply medieval, bristling with banana trees and sweating lemons. It's nothing less than an origami construction perched above the Mediterranean, which gives it a ghostly cobalt light. The following afternoon I went down to the sea and met Luigi Maffini, a small-scale wine maker who makes international wines with Greek names. Improbably, his white Kratos and his red Kleos have become enormously popular in New York where they can be found at Bar Veloce on Second Avenue. The petite friendly man in the Bennington College sweater seemed unaware of his far-off success. His winery appeared to consist of little more than a small farm, though like most Southerners he was restlessly dreaming of a "Bordeaux-style winery" with all mod cons.

"For years," he said, "our family made a wine which was, shall I say, *molto artigianale*. And many of us maintain traditional methods. I have decided to move on. And *ecco*—our biggest market now is not Naples, but Switzerland!"

We sat in his fields drinking some of his Fiano white, among bursting yellow cornflowers. I asked him about Puglia.

"Probably the same story as here. The South is out to make a buck. It's shoddy and ugly, but you can understand why people will grasp at any straw that helps them get out of poverty. *Molto artigianale* usually equals No Euros."

In the South, strip-mall-style development has spread out along the roads as far as the eye can see. Nothing is falsely picturesque, or *molto artigianale*; but nothing is handsome either. Moroccan migrants have taken over the abandoned old farmhouses by the roadsides which once harmonized with their surroundings. On the road which crosses the country to Puglia, passing through Avellino, even they vanish from sight. The farmland is like Nebraska, green and open, with a hard substratum. On the border of Puglia and Basilicata you pass the mystic mountain of Vulture, home to one of the greatest of all Aglianico reds, but a little farther on the land flattens out into the humbler region of Rosso di Cerignola and the earth becomes powdery and red. The change in atmosphere is not subtle. Puglia is a land apart, stony, withdrawn, and pale green from its seas of olive trees. The red earth and the endless stone walls are archaic, and deep in your nervous system you know that you have stepped into a space which is Greek.

The Greeks never strayed too far from the sea, their lifeblood. And everything in Puglia is a stone's throw from the sea. I stopped in Trani for a while, mournfully decayed on its Greek waters, and whiled away some alcoholic times in the Rondo wine bar by the ever-closed cathedral, wondering if Trani had been slumbering continuously since the Crusaders left it. If it had, no matter. Trani makes a famous sweet wine, Moscato di Trani, but in the Rondo all the old men drink Valdo Spumante with their dogs sitting in front of them at the bar. The Greek cities became Roman towns, then Norman ports for the Crusades, and then went into their long southern eclipse. All down the Adriatic coast you come across them, Barletta, Molfetta, the more grandiose Bari . . . the sea cities of Puglia with their sad milky harbors.

Another road shadows the autostrada away from the strips of subsidized industry. It passes through the Terra di Bari until you are among white *trulli*, the conical granaries of another age, and the gray ruins of Greek cities melting away on the edges of delicately miniature cliffs. Near Fasano and the "white city" of Ostuni, I stayed at an *agriturismo* called Il Frantoio, the Olive Mill, and every morning took a bicycle down to the sea, between fig gardens and mazes of white walls.

You see at once that olive oil occupies the psychological niche that fine wine occupies in other regions. The Pucklike owner of Il Frantoio, Armando Balestrazzi, is a virtuoso of the green oil. Although Il Frantoio is nowadays a famed gastronomic oasis, featured in all the best guide books, it could as well be a *masseria*, or Puglian farmhouse, out of the last century. Armando floats through his domain, obsessed with his homemade jams and his *olio dei pendici*—the luxurious oil tapped from the "boughs which hang down most." He also has a Puglian wine cellar, which sits amid the coconut-fiber oil-pressing baskets and the grappa casseroles in a perfumed basement. Here lie dusted bottles of Levenno Malvasia, sweet Primitivos from Pervini, wines called Archidamo, Erbaceo, and Ala Duke of Salaparuto, as well as the better-known Conti Zecca and Candido. Did I know the rarest wine he had there, something called Solaria Jonica made by a man called Antonio Ferrari? No? Not surprising—it was not especially well known outside of Puglia. It was made from sun-dried grapes in the old Greek style familiar in the North of Italy from wines like Amarone, which the Venetians had brought back from their trade in Crete and Cyprus.

"Well," he said, "I have a bottle of the 1959. And if you want to drink it, I'll bring it up to you in the courtyard. It is, as they say, *molto particolare.*"

The courtyard of Il Frantoio is Tunisian in its whiteness, in its effusions of lilies and tall palms. I sat in blinding sun, the peacocks cawing deep inside the tropical gardens, as Armando brought up a ceramic bucket bordered with intense almond biscuits, and in it the Solaria Jonica, the Ionian sun-wine fermented for forty years in darkened vats.

"Just as Del Monaco is the only artist of pottery," he said mysteriously, "so Antonio Ferrari is the only artist of Solaria!"

And who was Del Monaco?

The Solaria was a darkly inky nectar from one of the hottest, most sun-drenched years of the twentieth century. I tried to think what had happened in 1959. A dry heat rose out of the wine and I sank back in my wicker chair with my eyes closed, blocking out the dazzling whiteness of the walls around me. Armando's voice faded, but still I was able to hear him ask, "So, what have you learned on your journey? Are you a connoisseur now?"

Alas, I had to say that although I had enjoyed my journey to the maximum, I had not yet learned how to be a real connoisseur. If anything, I was even more ignorant than when I had started out. Or rather, I was more aware of my ignorance. As for my taste, I felt that all in all it had improved a little, had become a little more rounded, canny. Not by very much, but by an appreciable degree or two. I was no longer *always* in the dark when drinking the wines of the earth.

"None of us knows very much," Armando said, with a sadly philosophic shrug. "I myself know a bit about jam. But not much."

"I imagine jam is quite a complex subject," I said.

"Yes, no doubt. Like wine. But at least you got to drink a Lafite. I would love to drink a Lafite."

I said that I couldn't honestly remember that much about the Lafite. It had been good, but I couldn't go much further.

"So," he chuckled, "you would go so far as to say that Lafite is a good wine?"

"That's about it."

"So where are you going next? South again? There's not much farther south you can go . . ."

And I murmured, "I'm going to Spigolizzi."

He must have been bemused.

"Where is Spigolizzi? And what can there possibly be in Spigolizzi?"

I said it was practically at the end of the earth. The end of Europe, anyway.

"Spigolizzi," he sighed. "People find the damnedest places to go to, don't they? Personally, I wouldn't go to Spigolizzi. New York, perhaps. Bali would be nice. Paris, even. But Spigolizzi? No. It's a long drive down to the tip of our Italian heel. I think I'd give Spigolizzi a miss."

He brought out some sweetly caramelized onions, or *lampa-*

scioni, and an artichoke soufflé, a wild-onion paté, and a mint cake—the glowing food of Puglia.

"And who," he asked, "lives in this Spigolizzi? A famous wine maker? Winspeare? Cosimo Taurino?" For there are indeed reputable Puglian wine makers who bear those fantastical names.

I said I really wasn't sure. "Just an old English lady who lives alone," I replied, "and who used to write cookery books."

The endless roads of Puglia are a good place to think over the memories of a journey. I soon became lost. And being lost is the natural condition in this region which, if anything, is exactly like those landscapes which we invent when we read *The Tempest*: shimmering lemon gardens, a sea in the distance, flat and blunt faces of men in the fig trees like a lost Mediterranean race. Of all the landscapes I know, the walled fields of Puglia as it peters out toward nothingness—the pure blue of sea, but also somehow of the past which will never return—are the most smiling, the most benevolently easy.

Between San Vito Normanni and Brindisi I came to an abandoned shrine of Santo Biagio, where ancient terraces stand next to Byzantine grottoes shining with images of David and Ezekiel. Who remembers anything about the destroyed church with its vaults exposed to the sun, filled with storks? A green-painted inscription marked the year 1196, a year which means as little to us, perhaps, as 1959. We think of wine as memory, heritage . . . but how far back can we go? Do the tough men in leather jackets driving their goats on the road read Greek?

Surely, it's *The Tempest* without Caliban, unless you can call the Mafia Caliban, and it is almost amazing that you cannot hear bells and lutes on the winds that ripple ceaselessly through the vineyards glittering with poppies and flowered prickly pears.

This atmosphere intensifies between Gallipoli and Ceuta, in the Serre. The town of Pristicce stands between long cliffs, while above

it a road rises to a plateau on its way to the sea at Lido di Marina.
Spigolizzi lies at the heart of a maze of low stone walls and *pajaras*,
white rotundas built around an oven for drying figs. The house sits
at the end of a country track, surrounded by abandoned trulli and
masserie, its burnt-sienna fields littered with the forms of recumbent wide-eyed goddesses—the sculptures of Norman Mommens
placed like lares, or ancient Roman boundary gods, along "cosmic
lines" calculated by the mystical man himself. It's a white villa with
similarly foreign crenellations and sculptures, Minoan in feel.
Bizarrely, it briefly made me think of the Mondavi winery, the Mondavi winery as it might *aspire* to be in the ideal brochure. To the
door, however, came an English couple of bohemian middle age:
Nick and Maggie, Patience's son and daughter-in-law.

Married into the mighty Darwin clan (his brother-in-law was
Robert Darwin, the principal of the Royal College of Art), the
half-Belgian Mommens left his first wife and eloped with Patience
to Greece in 1959. They vagabonded around the Mediterranean in
the sixties, growing, I imagine, more mystical and unrepentant with
every year spent on the loose. But they were not hippies. They were
postwar intellectuals, a different generation altogether, and their
mysticism was always conducted with a verbal and plastic vigor,
not to mention a sense of irony. Inside, the house was painted with
Lawrentian frescoes, and I could sense at once a happy couple's
shared life in a place they had made in their own image. No light-
bulbs, no telephones, no heaters, no fans. For the suave Patience,
with her private-school education and her years writing the *Ob-
server*'s "Woman's Page" in the late fifties, it must have been a delicious shock—a "solar shock" as she would probably call it—to
find herself in this ancient world, in this stone house in which you
can almost taste the olive leaves pressing in from outside. While
Norman sculpted, she turned to pottery and bronze jewelry. They
led, as people say, the life. Patience's book *Work Adventures, Childhood Dreams* is full of insouciant glimpses into a long-vanished world

of international elegance straight out of the wildest affectations of Truman Capote. It contains scores of paragraphs like this, describing a lunch in Venice with the Countess Elsie Lee Gozzi:

> Luncheon for six at the Fortunay Palace, part of the Fortunay factory transformed into a yellow marble Claridges interior with Venetian marqueterie as "conversation pieces": the Count, a quiet elderly nobleman with poetic forebears, the Countess, voluble. . . . A sequence of dishes, sumptuously arrayed on silver platters, and served with dignity by the driver of the motorboat, now in white jacket and white gloves, brought us well into the stifling afternoon. . . .

Would one have wanted to be there? I suppose for Patience it was simply background decor of the best kind, an echo chamber for civilized conversation and a way of passing the time. I wondered, though, if she had ever brought her kids with her.

For Nick and Maggie were an odd couple. In fact, they were lifelong professional bargers, which meant that before coming down to Puglia they had spent years running a freight barge between Amsterdam and the South of France. *That* seemed about as far from luncheon at the Fortunay Palace as one could imagine. I noticed at once, too, that Maggie had a finger missing. Had she lost it in a barging accident? They reminded me of a sympathetically dotty couple out of a Mike Leigh film, Nick in his beard and work clothes, Maggie with her fresh, birdlike English manner, which in certain Englishwomen never seems to age. They seemed sore that they'd had to leave the freewheeling barging life in France. They showed me some pictures of leafy, idyllic canals in the Midi.

"That was the life," said Nick mournfully, plucking his beard and winking at Maggie. "Nothing better than barging, eh Maggie?"

"Barging is bliss," said Maggie. "I hope we can go back to a bit of barging some day."

"You don't," I ventured, "seem too happy to be in Puglia."

"Oh it's not that," said Nick. "We're happy enough to be in Puglia. But you can't barge in Puglia, can you? No canals. Living like this in a fixed way isn't the same as barging around France and being truly free. Plus, when we arrived here there wasn't any damned electricity!"

It was clear that it was Nick and Maggie who had drawn the line on that one. They'd insisted on the electricity as a condition for staying in Spigolizzi.

"Old Norman just didn't care," snorted Nick. "So we've had a bit of a war with Mum over that."

"We dropped the barging," Maggie explained, "and we could deal with that. But *no electricity* on top of that?"

She pulled a stricken expression. The wiring had been put in only two days before and Patience was fairly furious about it.

Patience herself was under the weather and in bed. The room was full of paintings, scrolled manuscripts, and hand-painted furniture; through her window you could see a field of magnificently tortured fig trees. Recumbent in superb pieces of jewelry of her own making, Patience was full of apologies for her immobility.

"It's so frightfully boring getting old," she crowed, glaring at her son as he brought in a tray of their homemade wine. "But to whom does one complain about one's arthritis? My son here seems to think I was in need of electricity to make my old age more comfortable." In a louder voice: "He is quite *spectacularly* mistaken."

It's strange how a people, a race, can change over the course of only two or three generations. Patience was rather like my great-aunts, splendid and fiery women of the imperial age, with their dowager accents and inner regality. She had, she explained, thought nothing of coming to Italy and learning to be a peasant. The peasants had adopted them and they had adopted the peasants. It had been a mutual exploration.

"And," she added, "we learned everything from the peasants. Everything about real life. Now, of course, like everything beautiful in the world, that peasant life is dying if not dead. From whom, my poor dear, are *you* going to learn anything?"

This was certainly a dumbfounding question. Was I really stranded and lost out there in *the world of electricity*?

"I have no idea," I said.

Patience smiled sadly and her bronze jewelry tinkled.

"Of course you don't. You poor dears. You don't even have real women anymore, do you? Let alone real peasants. The peasants here, you see, had a passion to show us the right way to do things. Because there *is* a right way and a wrong way to do things. Any peasant showing you how to grow artichokes can tell you that!"

Real women, real artichokes: were they connected? Perhaps they were. Or should we say real men, real women, real artichokes?

I asked her playfully if she liked Italy and Italians.

"They've always been a right-wing people, you know. That Berlusconi is just like Mussolini!"

The light was fading into the first golden moments of a dusk. I became aware that the room was dimming and that Patience's polished ornaments were beginning to glow brighter with a different light. And what about electricity? Patience made a great gesture with both hands and rolled her eyes. Electricity. The one thing that seemed stupidly inevitable in the modern world.

"You poor creatures," she moaned. "You have no idea even how beautiful night is. Have you ever seen and felt a real night without artificial light? Where in the world can you find it? When Norman was alive we savored every nightfall together. Real night— darkness, stars, nothing else. Now tell me, dear boy, is electricity really *worth* not having that?"

And so we moved on to the subject of wine. Patience's eyes lit up. Naturally, like true peasants committed to organic principles, they made their own wine. It was the milk of the earth, the expression of the land, of the peasant soul. Nothing was more beautiful than wine, or more profound.

"The flow of the old life is still here, you know," she said, leaning forward for a moment and pouring me a glass of the house brew. "The old Mediterranean. And nothing is older than the Mediterranean."

She then explained that her son had once been a wine merchant and that the current vintage—the one in our glasses—had been harvested somewhat too early.

"So it's not, alas, the true wine of Spigolizzi. The weather here's been very bad lately."

All through my journey I had made an attempt to link the geniality of a given individual and the geniality of the wine he or she makes. I admired Patience, admired her intelligence, grit, and sophisticated elegance. But when I drank her wine my vision went blank, I thought I was going cross-eyed, and a vile expletive floated into my consciousness, though it did not get past my internal censor. I half rose, stunned, then sank back again tempted to clutch my throat with my hand. It was, all in all, the vilest wine I have ever drunk. But Patience smiled beatifically and patted my hand.

"Don't look so upset, my boy. There are worse things. Look how beautifully dark it's getting outside! You know, I always said to Norman that this place was like an island in Shakespeare, a Shakespearean island full of whispering. As a matter of fact, there did indeed used to be water dividing Puglia from the rest of Italy. It used to be a real island. And it still feels that way, doesn't it?"

I laughed awkwardly and put down the glass of wine. And I thought, *Who cares about the wine? She's a beautiful woman.*

Bedridden and queenly, she was indeed exquisite. And I also thought to myself that perhaps she was right, perhaps I didn't know what real artichokes, real nights, or real women were like. I lived in New York, after all, where such things are rare—and who had I ever met like the octogenarian Patience?

So I kissed her hand, as men used to do, and took my leave in a state of unperplexed perplexity. Outside, Nick was lighting a parafin lamp. Far out in the fields the *pajara* glowed in the dark, the figs softly green as tropical fish, while a great velvet darkness seemed to pour down from the Milky Way. He had left the electricity off, and I was glad.

A book on wine should probably end with a glass of wine. But at the end of Puglia, there are few places where you could stumble on the equivalent of Gerald Asher's mystical discovery in the Simplon Pass. I drove in the dark back to Taranto, and on the far side of that terrifying city followed the built-up coast road toward the state of Basilicata. The Greeks were once thick on the ground here, but all trace of them is now concealed by the intense activities of the urban Italian vacationer determined to squeeze every drop of "leisure" from every square meter of tired sand. Even Metaponto, that famous city of philosophers, is now primarily a beach emporium. The tall cane sugar by the road barely hides a continuous strip of pizzerias, beachball outlets, and what can only be described as singles' gelaterias. The road is choked with miles of browsing cars: traffic circles, Stalinist hotel blocks, cinderblocks, cranes. The South at its worst. It is remarkable how unsentimental Italians are when they are not playing to foreign eyes. Here, you feel, they do what they want.

The day before, a gastronome of some experience had written down for me the address of a restaurant in the tourist village of Lido di Policoro. Should I be wandering along the Gulf of Taranto, he said rolling his eyes, I could at least stop in at the Hotel Poseidon and "have a great glass of wine." And so it was that, wandering along the Gulf of Taranto among the low-rent neons and the beaches packed with phalanxes of folded umbrellas, I came across the blue sign for the Hotel Poseidon which looked to be exactly what my contact had promised: an oasis of refinement in a sea of (as he had delicately put it) "proletarian trash."

I parked the car by the beach and walked over to the hotel. But as soon as I was in its neat, prudish garden and within sight of the gold-plated menus and the waiter in his awkward bow tie, my heart sank and I felt myself retreating, turning back to the proletarian trash of the beach. For there on the other side of the road was where everyone really ate—including the boy in the bow tie after hours. A wooden platform slung over the sand, a few Felliniesque bright lights, a sign for *Hambuerga e Cozze*, a foozball table and a satellite screen showing an AC Milan game, before which a small crowd sat rapt with bowls of mussels and marinated *alici*.

And quite by accident I knew that I had come to the end, and that there was nowhere better than this to arrive at that end. A violet light over the sea and the tuna boats, and on my table small dark shrimps, artichoke hearts, sardines and anchovies, mussels and fries, roasted peppers as livid as still-wet internal organs, and triangles of hot rosemary bread. The owner came out in his vest and slippers and asked me where I was from and what I was doing in Lido di Policoro. A small group gathered around me. Where had I learned Italian? Had I seen their hamburger-and-mussels joint in a guidebook? Did I intend to watch the second half of the AC Milan game?

"Researching a wine book," I began.

This made them all laugh. What a scam! Some people have it easy! How did you get such a cushy job? Dario here—everyone pointed to the plump owner in his mussel-stained vest—could do that. He could do that all right, and he would do it for *free*.

"So they *pay* you to drink wine?"

They laughed so hard I thought the platform would collapse. Dario went inside and brought out an ice-cold bottle of white wine in a pewter bucket. It was beautifully arranged, too, with fresh ice, a laundered white towel, a pair of tongs, and a spotless glass.

"Here," he whispered in my ear, "why don't you take this down to the beach and have a moment by yourself?"

One can rarely say enough about the kindness of Italians. One is always treated as a human being who needs unpredictable things—

like a moment by oneself with a bottle on the beach. They have a true gift for what can only be called spontaneous delicacy.

So I went down among the rows of folded umbrellas and stacked beach toys, a great paraphernalia of mindless leisure awaiting resurrection the following day. I planted the ice bucket in the sand and poured myself a glass of this ice-cold straw yellow wine from nowhere in particular—a small vineyard, I later found out, from near Gallipoli—and thought to myself that nothing I had drunk at Château Lafite was half as good as this. So peace to all men and women, I thought, remembering the tail end of a phrase from *The Colossus of Maroussi* which I consider the loveliest phrase in the English language and which could well be an epitaph for wine if it ever disappears from the world: peace to all men and life more abundant.

ACKNOWLEDGMENTS

Many people selflessly helped me in the writing of this book.

First and foremost, Jonathan Nossiter, who introduced me to wine and who, through two decades of friendship, has shared his insights and passion, not to mention the contents of his cellar—many a fireside heart-to-heart is invisibly inscribed in this manuscript, which could not have been written without him.

In New York, Chris Cross and Daniel Lerner—wine musketeers both.

In Paris, Juliette.

In and near Rome, Allston Mitchell, Nicole Franchini, Johnny Madge, Maureen and Roberto Scheda—*grazie a tutti*!

In Sirolo, Giorgio Tridenti; in Bibbona, Luisa and Sergio Chiesa; in Castellabate, Francisco Favilla. Italian kindness incarnate.